FORECASTING PRESIDENTIAL ELECTIONS

FORECASTING PRESIDENTIAL ELECTIONS

STEVEN J. ROSENSTONE

Yale University Press
New Haven and London

For my teachers:

L.M.D
E.F.B.
W.D.B.
J.S.
R.E.W.
C.H.A.

Designed by Nancy Ovedovitz and set in Times Roman type by Huron Valley Graphics. Printed in the United States of America by Edwards Brothers Inc., Ann Arbor, Mich.

Library of Congress Cataloging in Publication Data

Rosenstone, Steven J.
  Forecasting presidential elections.
  Bibliography: p.
  Includes index.
  1. Election forecasting—United States.
2. Presidents—United States—Election. 3. United States—Politics and government—1945–
I. Title.
JK2007.R67 1983   324.973   83-42877
ISBN 0-300-02691-9

10   9   8   7   6   5   4   3   2   1

CONTENTS

TABLES AND FIGURES

TABLES

FIGURES

ACKNOWLEDGMENTS

I am most indebted to Chris Achen, whose ideas, criticism, tenacity, and encouragement guided the formative stages of this work. I appreciate the close reading of the manuscript and detailed comments I received from John Kessel, Donald Kinder, David Mayhew, and Edward Tufte. Raymond Wolfinger, Thomas Rothenberg, Richard Bagozzi, Jon Bendor, Sue Bhakdi, Tom Hammond, and John Zaller also provided helpful suggestions.

Marian Neal Ash, Maura D. Shaw Tantillo, and Sally Serafim provided generous editorial advice and guided the book's production with patience and skill. Margo Carter and Jack Harriett carefully prepared the figures.

Caroline's encouragement and understanding have been a constant source of support.

My study of politics has been heavily influenced by the six teachers to whom I have dedicated this book.

It may be said that an explanation . . . is not complete unless it might as well have functioned as a prediction: If the final event can be derived from the initial conditions and universal hypotheses stated in the explanation, then it might as well have been predicted, before it actually happened, on the basis of knowledge of the initial conditions and the general laws.

—Carl G. Hempel

Only by trying and trying over again to make political forecasts will we finally learn to understand what really explains political behavior of people.

—Paul F. Lazarsfeld

1
FORECASTING PRESIDENTIAL ELECTIONS

Who will win the next election? How would you make a prediction? These questions, undoubtedly as old as elections themselves, are the subject of this book. My purpose is to explain how American presidential elections are currently forecasted and to formulate a theory that accurately predicts their outcome.

Every four years politicians, political strategists, pollsters, journalists, and ordinary citizens try to predict who will win the presidency. The president, after all, is the most prominent figure in the United States, and the race for the White House is the nation's most conspicuous political event. It commands virtually everyone's attention: citizens follow the campaign, watch the candidates debate, and discuss the contest with co-workers, neighbors, family, and friends. For many, voting for president is their sole act of political participation. It stands to reason that the public is curious about who will win.

Many people both at home and abroad have more than a spectator's curiosity in the outcome. A federal agency's fate, or a legislative program's, may hinge on whether the White House changes hands. A number of government workers lose their jobs when the incumbent is voted out. If interest groups or congressional leaders anticipate that a new president will be elected, they put bills that will have a higher chance of passage under the current administration on their legislative agendas and defer proposals that will fare better when the other party takes over. Democratic congressional leaders withheld confirmation of Ford nominees in 1976 because the legislators anticipated the president's November defeat. Foreign leaders monitor American elections so they can negotiate with the administration most receptive to their nation's interests (Kissinger 1979, chap. 31; Lewis 1980). Potential candidates base their decisions to run on their prognoses of their chances of victory; campaign contributors withhold financial support from candidates whose chances look bleak (Jacobson and Kernell 1981).

No one is more concerned about who will win the presidency than the nominees themselves, and their campaign staffs. The stakes are high, the desire to win intense. To maximize the probability of victory, strategists make forecasts to guide their allocation of scarce resources. Campaign managers try to anticipate which states will be easily won, which will most likely be lost, and which will be closely contested. It is common practice for candidates to write off states they think they have little chance of carrying and to concentrate their resources on the hotly contested ones.[1] Campaign schedules are set, media time is purchased, choices are made about which issues to stress and which groups of voters to attract—all on the basis of predictions. As Kelley notes, "The initial strategy of a political campaign may be usefully regarded as an investment plan in which the level of investment in the several undertakings is set in accordance with estimates of the likely return of each" (1966, p. 66).

The media, of course, also predict what will happen. Television networks, leading newspapers, and newsmagazines spend huge sums to forecast who will carry each state, who will be the popular and electoral vote winner, and how groups of voters will behave on election day.

Thus, for a variety of reasons—to anticipate changes in personal well-being, to promote political interests or political causes,

1. Every presidential campaign seems to follow this strategy: In 1932 see Farley (1938, pp. 172; 184–85); in 1948 Ross (1968, pp. 29–34) and Yarnell (1974, p. 30); in 1960 Kelley (1961, pp. 70–72) and Sorenson (1965, p. 187); in 1964 Kelley (1966, pp. 50–52; 64–65; 72–73) and Kessel (1968, p. 191); in 1968 Chester, Hodgson, and Page (1969, p. 621) and Napolitan (1972, p. 62); in 1972 Napolitan (1972, pp. 273–77) and White (1973, p. 312); in 1976 Caddell (1976, p. 8), Apple (1976a, p. 1), Moore and Fraser (1977, pp. 123–24), Witcover (1977, p. 536), and Schram (1977, pp. 239–49); in 1980 Smith (1980a, p. D14), Wirthlin (1980, p. 357), Caddell (1981), and Moore (1981, pp. 188; 198; 213–15; 221–23; 240).

to advance a candidate's standing, to sell newspapers, or simply to satisfy curiosity—people forecast elections. In some years, such as 1952, 1956, 1964, and 1972, the outcome seems to be known by August or September with relative certainty. In others—1948, 1968, 1976—this apparent certainty evaporates by election day. Sometimes, as in 1980, the winner's margin of victory is unanticipated.

Despite widespread interest in who will win, political scientists still cannot provide accurate forecasts. We have very little advantage over the rest of the public.[2] Like everyone else, we follow public opinion polls, journalists' accounts, and political gossip in the weeks preceding the balloting in order to gauge who will win. At best our expertise helps us to select and weigh information more carefully than others might, but it has not provided us with a set of rules with which to forecast the outcome.

We cannot forecast elections, because we do not have a theory of elections. Most political scientists have focused exclusively on voters; they have had little to say about elections[3] (Key 1960, pp. 54–55). We know why, in a particular year, some people vote for the Democratic candidate and others for the Republican (Campbell et al. 1960; Goldberg 1966; Popkin et al. 1976; Kinder and Kiewiet 1979; Fiorina 1981a; Kinder and Abelson 1981). But we cannot explain why Democrats win some *elections* but lose others. The difference between these questions is important. The interesting problem is not why some people voted for Ford and others for Carter; but why the Republicans won in 1972, lost in 1976, and won again in 1980.

To explain why a party wins one year but loses the next, one must identify factors that have changed between the two contests and are responsible for changing the result. Differences among

2. Few scholars engage in political forecasting of any kind. Only 18 (2 percent) of the more than 950 references Armstrong (1978) cites in *Long-Range Forecasting* are political forecasts. Political scientist William Ascher makes no mention of political forecasts in his book, *Forecasting: An Appraisal for Policy-Makers and Planners* (1978).

3. Although Pomper (1967) and Barber (1980) have proposed election typologies, and Burnham (1970) and others have investigated electoral cycles, a general theory that explains election outcomes over time has not been formulated.

election outcomes are explained by differences in the political and economic conditions that prevail at the time of the election. If the candidates change, if the voters' political predispositions or issue positions change, if the important issues change, or if the incumbent party's management of the economy or foreign affairs changes, the election outcome will be different.

For the most part, scholars are insensitive to the ways in which changes in the electoral context affect outcomes.[4] They rely on cross-sectional data (from a single slice in time), which of course cannot explain differences *among election outcomes*. All the conditions that describe the electoral setting—the salient issues, the candidates, whether there is an incumbent, peace or war, prosperity or recession—are held constant when voters in a single election are examined. There is no hint of the impact the setting itself has either on how people vote or on the election result. One cannot ascertain the effect of factors that vary across elections. If these conditions help determine whether a party will win or lose, cross-sectional analyses will be hopelessly misleading (Kramer 1981). There is a difference between estimating how much more likely people are to vote against the incumbent party in a bad economic year than in a good year and estimating whether, in a bad economic year, the people who are worse off financially are more likely to vote against the incumbent than those less adversely affected by a recession. To estimate the effect of economic adversity on election outcomes, one must figure out how much the incumbent party's vote would increase were the *election year* economy to improve (Kramer 1981).

In short, to forecast elections one needs a theory that *explains differences among election outcomes*, not differences among voters at a single point in time. I have formulated such a theory and use it in this book to forecast the 1976 and 1980 presidential elections.

It is important to construct theories that both explain the past and predict the future. A good predictive model, of course, is a

---

4. A partial exception is congressional election scholarship, which has examined some changes in electoral context such as incumbency and campaign spending (Jacobson 1979). I will discuss some other exceptions in chap. 2.

general explanatory model; it not only gives order to elections that have already occurred but also anticipates the future.[5] A theory that can both predict and explain is more powerful and complete than a theory that can do one but not the other.

"Who will be the next president?" is an important question, then, not only because it is interesting in its own right, but because of what the question requires of us when we try to answer it. The question demands a response that we are currently ill equipped to provide. To wrestle with it we are forced to formulate theories that generalize beyond a single election and are sufficiently complete to explain as well as predict. The answer is not nearly as important as what the answering process leads us to think about. To a large degree, forecasting presidential contests is merely a convenient vehicle for the more important question: What determines election outcomes?

We tend to forget how much we rely on predictions in everyday life. Whenever we must anticipate what the future will hold, we hazard a forecast. We buy a house in a particular neighborhood because we predict that it will appreciate faster than one in another part of town. We order veal because we think the restaurant will prepare it better than chicken. We wait in the grocery checkout line on the left because we believe it will move faster than the one on the right.[6] On the basis of the title, the jacket blurb, or a quick thumbing through, you made a prediction about this book's contents.

Most of our forecasts are ad hoc—and probably should be. Little is at stake. We would rather endure tough veal than formulate an elaborate method for forecasting what to order in restaurants. When the cost of a misforecast rises, however, we give greater care to our method of prediction: we think more about

---

5. As Hempel points out, the logical structure of a prediction is the same as that of an explanation. "The customary distinction between explanation and prediction rests mainly on a pragmatic difference between the two: while in the case of an explanation, the final event is known to have happened, and its determining conditions have to be sought, the situation is reversed in the case of prediction: here the initial conditions are given, and their 'effect'—which, in the typical case, has not yet taken place—is to be determined" (Hempel 1965, p. 234).

6. This prediction is always wrong.

the problem, develop better theories, or search for more reliable data.

Decision makers frequently make high-risk choices that depend upon a prediction of what the future will hold. An investor purchases a stock because he anticipates that its future value will be greater than its cost; an automobile manufacturer builds small cars because he expects a greater demand for fuel-efficient autos than for gas guzzlers. Weapons systems are designed to meet defense needs five or ten years in the future. Decisions about electrical power plants, health care facilities, or mass transit systems prompt policy makers to consider the future demand for these services (Ascher 1978; Armstrong 1978).

Regardless of the amount of care that goes into the forecast or the sophistication of the method employed, about the same procedure is followed. The forecaster must make a choice predicated on his prognosis of the future. He examines the conditions that prevail at that moment. He makes the prediction by applying to these data a rule or theory (about restaurants, grocery-store lines, or whatever) established through prior experience. The rules may be an explicit set of equations or they may be implicit guides: "Italians cook veal better than they do chicken." But the procedure is the same. The only difference is the explicitness of the forecasting rules. My predictions rely on explicit rules rather than hunches or intuition.

I begin in chapter 2 by surveying how elections are currently forecasted. My focus is on the techniques political strategists, journalists, pollsters, and social scientists use to predict how people will vote. I discuss the implicit assumptions underlying each method, the accuracy of its forecasts and the errors commonly made. I pay particularly close attention to how well these methods performed in 1976 and 1980. This review of the "state of the art" provides a baseline against which my own efforts can be compared.

To forecast elections, I must first develop a theory that explains how people vote in different settings. This is done in chapter 3. People do not come to each election with a clean slate—some vote for the same party each year. There are also secular trends that cause citizens, gradually over time, to drift from their traditional party. My theory is sensitive to these changes as well as to shifts in the political context: the issues that are important, the electorate's positions on these issues, the state of the economy, whether there is peace or war. It also takes into account characteristics of the candidates—their positions, their home states and regions—and whether an incumbent is running.

I use state-level aggregate data from the 1948 to 1972 presidential elections to estimate the effect that each component of the theory has on elections during this period. How much of an electoral advantage does an incumbent enjoy? Do vice-presidential nominees really run better on their home turf as politicians think? How much do issues affect election outcomes? Has their impact changed? What effect does the incumbent party's management of the economy or foreign affairs have on the result? I use these findings both to evaluate the theory and to assess the relative merits of the different approaches taken in the past to the study of voters and elections. No one factor alone—issues, the economy, or secular political trends—explains elections. These are not alternative perspectives among which one should choose; each makes a unique contribution to our ability to account for outcomes.

In chapter 5 I evaluate the extent to which my theory explains the 1948 to 1972 elections. That is, how well does the theory fit the data? I examine how accurately it predicts (within the sample) each state's vote for president as well as the national popular and electoral vote. I compare my errors, which are small, to the errors others have made.

The 1976 and 1980 election forecasts are reported in chapter 6. I forecast both each state's popular vote and the national popular and electoral vote. How well the model predicts these elections—cases not in the original analysis—is a test of its completeness. I also try out the model as a forecasting tool by generating predictions that rely solely on information available prior to the election. In both years I correctly predict the winner, although I underestimate Reagan's 1980 margin of victory. I also compare these forecasts to the election predictions made in these years by journalists, pollsters, candidate strategists, and social scientists.

As a final step, in chapter 7 I simulate a variety of election scenarios. How would election results be different if the candidates, the economy, the salient issues, or the nominee's position were to change? What would the outcome have been had different political or economic conditions prevailed in 1980? What would have happened if Kennedy had been nominated? Would Rockefeller have done appreciably better than Goldwater in 1964? How different would the 1976 and 1980 election results have been had New Deal social welfare issues been more important in those years than they actually were? Would the 1960, 1976, or 1980 election outcomes have been different if the economy had been a bit better in each of those years? Consideration of conditions that did not exist but might have helps to clarify further the forces that determine who will occupy the White House.

In the last chapter, I suggest ways of expanding the basic theory and outline several paths that future analysis might take. I also speculate on the implications of election forecasting for the conduct of elections and for representative government.

2

HOW ELECTIONS ARE FORECASTED

Elections do not always turn out as expected. The 1976 and 1980 returns certainly surprised most observers. When Carter locked up the 1976 nomination, a Democratic landslide seemed assured. Carter stood 33 points ahead of Ford in the July polls; Gallup described it as "one of the largest leads in polling history" *(Gallup Opinion Index,* December 1976, p. 2). By the end of August, although his lead had been cut almost in half, Carter was still a whopping 18 points in front of Ford. The Carter staff began to plan their transition to office.

Journalists also anticipated a clean Carter sweep in 1976. As Roscoe Drummond (1976, p. 27) noted in late August, "No, Virginia, the election is not over! It only looks that way because the opposition is a dozen laps ahead before the President is off the starting line." The press predicted an electoral college runaway for Carter. *U.S. News and World Report* concluded in mid-September: "Jimmy Carter now appears to hold a lead over President Gerald Ford so large that if the election were held right now, he could very well pull off an electoral-vote landslide" (20 September 1976, p. 12). Their projections, like those in the *Christian Science Monitor,* showed Carter winning by an electoral vote plurality of 200.

As it turned out, all the early forecasts—opinion polls, politicians' prognoses, and journalists' assessments—were way off the mark. By election eve, Jimmy Carter's predicted landslide had turned into one of the closest elections of the century. None of the last minute polls—Gallup, Roper, Harris, CBS/*New York*

Times, or NBC—could say with certainty who was ahead. "Analysts across the country," R. W. Apple, Jr., reported the weekend before the election, "were unwilling to hazard predictions" (1976b, p. 1).

"Volatile" was the word journalists used most frequently to describe the 1980 contest. The opinion polls seesawed back and forth. Carter led Reagan by 10 points in early May. A month later, it was Reagan by 3; by early August Reagan's margin jumped to 16 points. Carter was back out front by mid-August and held the lead, which peaked at 8 points, through late October (*Gallup Opinion Index,* December 1980).

Throughout the campaign most tallies showed Carter trailing Reagan in the electoral college. Hendrick Smith (1980b) reported in October that "with only a month left until Election Day, Ronald Reagan appears to lead in enough states to win an electoral majority." He made a slightly more cautious prognosis two days before the election: "Ronald Reagan, aided by a surge of support after his debate with President Carter, has taken a substantial lead in the battle for electoral votes but is not yet far enough ahead to be assured an electoral majority" (1980c).

Although most of the final pre-election public opinion polls showed that Reagan had inched ahead by a few points, most journalists characterized the election as a "virtual dead heat." *Time* reported in its final pre-election wrapup, "Seldom has an American election headed into such a wildly unpredictable windup" (Church 1980, p. 18). No one anticipated Reagan's runaway popular vote victory or his electoral college landslide.

How are elections forecasted? How accurate are the methods and what kinds of errors do they commonly make? What assumptions underlie each approach? Why did these methods fail to anticipate the narrowness of Carter's 1976 victory and the decisiveness of Reagan's win in 1980?

POLITICIANS AND POLITICAL STRATEGISTS

Politicians and political strategists have no doubt always tried to forecast elections. Their earliest forecasts were collections of predictions made by local party workers who were "closer to the people," had knowledge of the particulars of the locale, and who presumably were thus better able to predict how a candidate would do on election day. (See Robinson 1932.) To some extent, strategists still rely on political intelligence to project how well candidates will run in particular precincts, counties, or states.

Several problems are likely to undermine forecasts based on political intelligence. It is not obvious that state and local politicians can reliably assess how voters will behave on election day. Not only are political elites' opinions unrepresentative of the electorate's (McCloskey, Hoffman, and O'Hara 1960; Kirkpatrick 1976, chap. 10; Fenno 1978), but politicians, after all, have their own goals to promote, and hence have an incentive to misrepresent their candidate's standing. To attract additional national campaign resources, local politicians may *underestimate* the closeness of the contest. This is most likely to occur when state and local elections are held concurrently with presidential balloting.

Even though the sources of political intelligence have shifted in recent years from party leaders to political consultants and the candidate's personal staff, perceptual errors are still likely to be made. Campaign workers tend to make overly optimistic assessments of their candidate's standing. "Information reported by party workers, who are emotionally involved in the campaign, is often unreliable because of their wish to please the candidate by giving him news he wants to hear" (Levin 1962, p. 186). This occurs because supporters both selectively perceive and selectively report data to campaign decision makers. Not surprisingly, candidates are "often victims of the 'echo effect.' A closed circuit of information develops which feeds on itself and continuously reinforces the original views of the candidates. The 'information,' however, is often unrelated to reality" (Levin 1962, p. 187).

The lack of set rules to guide the weighing of the many different, sometimes contradictory, bits of political intelligence creates further problems. Two types of errors are frequently made. Overoptimism frequently prevents strategists from giving sufficient weight to signs that a candidate is doing poorly or that current strategies are ineffective (Steinberg 1976, p. 179). As a result, predictions are likely to be biased in the candidate's direction. Like campaign workers, strategists also suffer from the "elation complex," as Claude E. Robinson calls it. "The game of politics, of course, demands that the candidates of lost causes be hood-winked into believing they will win; otherwise their spirit would be sapped and their morale broken." The result is a "sort of self-hypnosis leading to a feeling of elation with regard to their election prospects" (1932, pp. 10–11).

Perceptual errors made when political intelligence is gathered are compounded by judgmental errors in its evaluation. Decision makers tend to take information at their disposal at face value. The data's reliability is rarely questioned; information that is not predictive is rarely discounted; a prediction's accuracy is likely to be overestimated (Tversky and Kahneman 1974).[1]

Given these problems, it is no wonder that political strategists make errors—sometimes large ones. State campaign chairmen in 1928 incorrectly predicted 30 percent of the state outcomes; their forecasts were off an average of 5.5 percentage points (table 2.1). Democrats consistently forecasted a vote more favorable to Al Smith; Republicans forecasted outcomes more favorable to Herbert Hoover. The average Democratic error was 9.0 percentage points; the winner was incorrectly predicted in half the states. Although Republicans correctly predicted a Hoover victory in each state, their average state forecast error was 3.7 percentage points.

Even though campaign strategists have relied less on grapevine political intelligence and more on campaign consultants' "scientific" methods during the past half-century, their forecasts have not substantially improved. Ford, Carter, and Reagan strategists in 1976 and 1980 did not outperform their 1928 counterparts. Carter adviser Hamilton Jordan's forecast in June 1976 projected that Carter would win 199 electoral votes from 17 states and the District of Columbia. He regarded the 8 large industrial states (comprising two-fifths of the electoral votes) as tossups, and predicted that Ford would carry the remaining 25 (Schram 1977, pp. 240-41). Jordan's more detailed August projections included a plan for the allocation of campaign resources among the states.

1. For example, 4 of the 10 states Democratic strategists regarded as *strong* Carter states in 1980 were won by Reagan; 4 more Carter won by less than 53 percent of the vote (fig. 2.3, below).

Table 2.1 An Evaluation of Campaign Strategists' Forecasts of the 1928 Presidential Election

State	Democratic Strategists		Republican Strategists	
	Forecast	Error*	Forecast	Error*
Illinois	43.6	13.7	57.2	0.1
Indiana	-	-	54.6	3.4
Iowa	-	-	55.0	7.1
Kentucky	47.9	11.5	52.7	6.7
Maryland	49.1	8.3	53.5	3.9
Minnesota	-	-	54.8	3.7
Missouri	48.0	7.7	53.2	2.5
Nebraska	55.7	7.8	55.7	7.8
Nevada	-	-	55.9	0.6
New York	50.2	1.0	51.7	-0.5
Ohio	53.0	12.2	58.0	7.2
Oregon	-	-	70.0	-5.0
Pennsylvania	55.6	10.1	61.9	3.8
South Dakota	-	-	57.6	2.9
Texas	-	-	52.6	-0.8
Wyoming	-	-	60.9	3.3
				Combined
Average Error		9.0		3.7 5.5
Percentage of States Correct		50.0		100.0 83.3

Source: Claude E. Robinson, *Straw Votes: A Study in Political Prediction* (New York: Columbia, 1932), p. 9, table 1.
* The error is the actual Hoover vote minus the forecasted Hoover vote.

He estimated the likelihood of each state's voting Democratic if worked effectively and assigned a number (9.0, 6.7, 4.5, or 2.2) to represent the size of its "Democratic potential" (Schram 1977, p. 248).

Comparing these projections to the actual vote (figure 2.1), we see that Jordan missed 5 states in addition to the 8 tossup states for which he did not make forecasts. If these 8 states were assumed to be equally likely to go for Carter as for Ford, then Jordan correctly predicted 82 percent of the state outcomes. However, his electoral college total was 117 votes too optimistic.[2] Although his August forecasts were closer to the actual electoral college result—off by only 22 votes—Jordan was suffering from the elation complex when he claimed, "Ford lacks a base of support—there is not a region of the country nor a political

2. The District of Columbia has been removed from this and all state-level forecasts evaluated in this chapter.

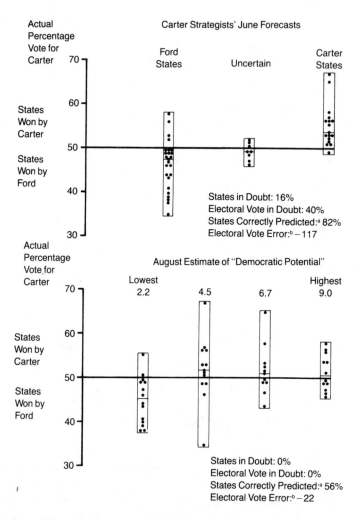

Source: Martin Schram, *Running for President, 1976* (New York: Stein and Day, 1977), pp. 240–41; 386–88; *Congressional Quarterly, Guide to 1976 Elections* (Washington, D.C.: Congressional Quarterly, Inc., 1977).

a. States in doubt are assumed to have a .5 probability of going for Carter. The District of Columbia has been deleted from all calculations in this figure.

b. The error is the actual national electoral vote for Carter minus the forecasted national electoral vote for Carter. The electoral vote for states in doubt was divided evenly between the two candidates.

Figure 2.1 Evaluation of Carter Strategists' 1976 Presidential Election Forecasts

grouping of states that he can count on in November" (Schram 1977, p. 247). Six of the 12 states Jordan identified as having the highest Democratic potential (scored 9.0) actually went for Ford in November, as did 5 of the 11 states scored 6.7. States in the 9.0 category actually had a *lower* median Carter vote in November than the 4.5 or 6.7 states. If states scored 2.2 and 4.5 are counted as Ford states and those scored 6.7 and 9.0 as Carter states, Jordan's August forecasts correctly predicted only 56 percent of the states—a remarkably poor result, not much better than chance.

The Ford camp also made state predictions in 1976. Chief strategist, Richard Cheney, identified states as either part of the "Ford base," the "Carter base," or "swing states." These predictions were not noticeably better than those made by the Carter camp (figure 2.2). Although Cheney was less inclined than Jordan to overestimate his candidate's strength, this tendency was still evident. Of the 15 states Cheney identified in Ford's base, 4 (27 percent) were actually won by less than 1 percent and 7 states (nearly half) by less than 4 points. Similarly, Carter won 4 (16 percent) of the states classified as "swing states" by more than 54 percent of the vote. Furthermore, uncertainty abounded: Cheney classified half the states, comprising 368 electoral votes (two-thirds of the total), as swing states. If one assumes a fifty-fifty chance of a Ford victory in the swing states, then Republican strategists correctly predicted 75 percent of the states and over-predicted their candidate's strength by only 26 electoral votes.

Both Carter and Reagan strategists underpredicted the size of the Republican electoral vote sweep in 1980. Pollster Pat Caddell, who prepared the June 1980 Carter forecasts, projected that the president would carry 13 states (comprising 115 electoral votes); 27 states (277 electoral votes) were conceded to Reagan; the remaining 10 states (143 electoral votes) were classified as "swing states" (figure 2.3). Again, if the swing states are divided equally between the major party candidates, 76 percent of Caddell's state predictions were correct, but he was 141 electoral votes too optimistic. The October 1980 forecasts were even worse. Although the level of uncertainty remained about the same (10 states, comprising 30 percent of the electoral college,

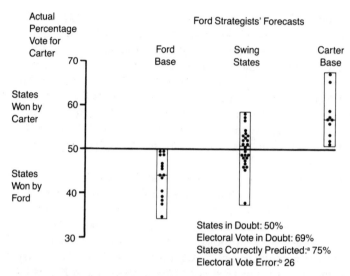

Source: Martin Schram, *Running for President, 1976* (New York: Stein and Day, 1977, p. 262; *Congressional Quarterly, Guide to 1976 Elections* (Washington, D.C.: Congressional Quarterly, Inc., 1977).

a. States in doubt are assumed to have a .5 probability of going for Carter. The District of Columbia has been deleted from all calculations in this figure.

b. The error is the actual national electoral vote for Carter minus the forecasted national electoral vote for Carter. The electoral vote for states in doubt was divided evenly between the two candidates.

Figure 2.2 Evaluation of Ford Strategists' 1976 Presidential Election Forecasts

were regarded too close to call), only 64 percent of the states were correctly forecasted. The electoral vote projection was now off by 241 votes.

Reagan strategist Richard Wirthlin's March 1980 assessment was barely better than a shot in the dark. He could not assign half the states (comprising 72 percent of the electoral college) to either Reagan or Carter (figure 2.4). He graded these "battle-ground states" from C− to B+ to reflect the likelihood of a Reagan victory, but his scoring bore little resemblance to how these states actually voted on election day. Reagan captured all of them; his vote in the B+ states was not significantly higher than his vote in the C− ones. If the battleground states are

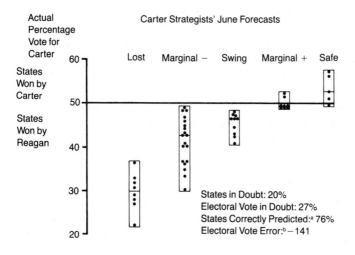

Carter Strategists' June Forecasts

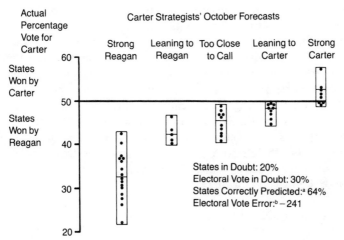

Carter Strategists' October Forecasts

Source: Patrick H. Caddell, "General Election Strategy," 25 June 1980, in Elizabeth Drew, *Portrait of an Election* (New York: Simon and Schuster, 1981), p. 393; *Time,* 27 October 1980, p. 16; *Congressional Quarterly Weekly Report,* 17 January 1981.

a. States in doubt are assumed to have a .5 probability of going for Carter. The District of Columbia has been deleted from all calculations in this figure.

b. The error is the actual national electoral vote for Carter minus the forecasted national electoral vote for Carter. The electoral vote for states in doubt was divided evenly between the two candidates.

Figure 2.3 Evaluation of Carter Strategists' 1980 Presidential Election Forecasts

divided evenly between Reagan and Carter, Wirthlin correctly forecasted 69 percent of the state outcomes and underpredicted Reagan's electoral college total by 223 votes. The October 1980 Republican forecasts, naturally, were an improvement. Only 10 states, representing a quarter of the electoral college, were seen as too close to call; 80 percent of the state outcomes were correctly forecasted. Nevertheless, the Reagan electoral vote margin was still underpredicted by 142 votes.

In sum, presidential campaign strategists' forecasts are filled with uncertainty. On average, one-fifth of the states, comprising a third of the electoral college, could not be forecasted in 1976 and 1980. Strategists' forecasts are imprecise. They predict who will win the state, but they do not forecast the state popular vote, nor can they assess how certain they are of the outcome. For instance, some states assigned by Ford strategists to the Carter base in 1976 were won by as little as 1 percentage point, others by as many as 17 points. States in the Ford base were won by between .5 and 15 points. Swing states were won by margins as large as 12 points. Even greater imprecision prevailed in 1980. This is most clearly seen in figures 2.1 to 2.4, by the vertical spread of points within each forecast category. The greater the variance within each category, the less precise the forecast. Beyond uncertainty and imprecision, there are, of course, sizable errors both in the state-by-state forecasts and the electoral vote projections. The strategists' average forecast correctly predicted 75 percent of the states and had an electoral college error of 141 votes.

POLITICAL CANVASS

Candidates and parties sometimes rely on a canvass—a tally of the voting intentions of people living in a particular political unit, such as a precinct or state—to predict how their candidate will run. It is common practice for canvassers also to solicit support for their candidate, so on election day, these supporters can be encouraged, by a call or personal visit, to vote. To make state-level forecasts, the precinct-level canvasses are often "adjusted" to reflect county or state politicians' "insight or feel for the situation" (Robinson 1932, p. 3).

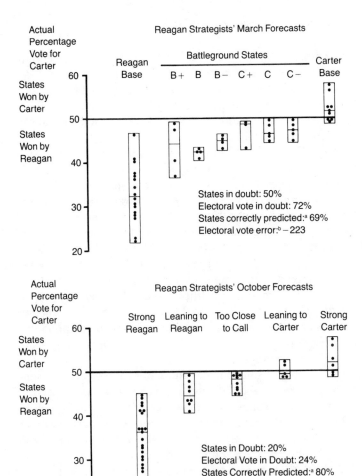

Actual Percentage Vote for Carter

Reagan Strategists' March Forecasts

Battleground States

Reagan Base | B+ | B | B- | C+ | C | C- | Carter Base

States Won by Carter

States Won by Reagan

States in doubt: 50%
Electoral vote in doubt: 72%
States correctly predicted:[a] 69%
Electoral vote error:[b] -223

Actual Percentage Vote for Carter

Reagan Strategists' October Forecasts

Strong Reagan | Leaning to Reagan | Too Close to Call | Leaning to Carter | Strong Carter

States Won by Carter

States Won by Reagan

States in Doubt: 20%
Electoral Vote in Doubt: 24%
States Correctly Predicted:[a] 80%
Electoral Vote Error:[b] -142

Source: Richard Wirthlin, "Some Initial Strategic and Tactical Considerations," 28 March 1980, in Elizabeth Drew, *Portrait of an Election* (New York: Simon and Schuster, 1981), pp. 360–91; *Time,* 27 October 1980, p. 17; *Congressional Quarterly Weekly Report,* 17 January 1981.

a. States in doubt are assumed to have a .5 probability of going for Carter. The District of Columbia has been deleted from all calculations in this figure.

b. The error is the actual national electoral vote for Carter minus the forecasted national electoral vote for Carter. The electoral vote for states in doubt was divided evenly between the two candidates.

Figure 2.4 Evaluation of Reagan Strategists' 1980 Presidential Election Forecasts

As one might expect, canvass forecasts are quite inaccurate. For example, a county-by-county canvass conducted in one "east north central" state a month prior to the 1928 election was off, on average, by 6.5 percentage points.[3] The forecast made by aggregating the county estimates missed the state popular vote by 3 points (Robinson 1932, p. 8).[4]

The 1964 Goldwater campaign canvassed nearly 3.4 million voters in 39 states, and predicted that their candidate would only lose 6 of the states (Kessel 1968, p. 169); in fact, he lost 33. Rather than assume, as they did, that Goldwater would win half the undecided votes, John Kessel, a political scientist and then member of the Republican National Committee staff, suggested that "a more realistic assumption would be that those intending to vote for Goldwater would tell this to Republican workers, while those intending to vote for Johnson would either report a Democratic preference or say they were undecided" (1968, p. 169). Although this assumption reduced the error, the prediction was still wide of the mark: the outcome was incorrectly predicted in 9 states (nearly a quarter of those canvassed); the average state error was 7.5 percentage points.[5]

Several problems contribute to the large canvass errors. Supporters most likely failed to contact a random sample of the state's voters. In 22 states the Goldwater effort covered no more than 10 counties. Because campaign workers were probably more willing to canvass neighborhoods sympathetic to their cause, the tally was slanted in the Republican direction. Further bias was introduced by workers identifying themselves as Goldwater supporters. As noted, most likely people were reluctant to admit to a Republican, even in 1964, that they were unwilling to vote for Goldwater. Errors were introduced in counting the responses: How were undecided voters scored? How was each person's likelihood of voting estimated?

3. The errors ranged between .2 and 17.5 percentage points.
4. Robinson cites the "percent plurality error," which is the plurality error divided by the total votes cast. One-half this number is the percentage point error I report.
5. These data are derived from Kessel (1968, fig. 4, p. 270). The publisher reversed the axis labels in that figure.

The predictive reliability of canvass responses are suspect. For a forecast to be of value to a political strategist, it must be made early in the campaign—a month or so before the election. Yet in many years, as will be seen later, citizens' preferences in August and September are unreliable guides to their behavior in November.

For good reasons, presidential campaigns have abandoned this method of forecasting. The few hard data available indicate that the average state error is over 7 percentage points and that the estimates are likely to be biased toward the candidate who conducts the canvass.

BELLWETHER DISTRICTS

Election forecasters sometimes look to "bellwether" districts. A bellwether is a political unit (usually a state or county) whose vote in previous elections has closely paralleled the national vote, and therefore, it is thought, will predict how the rest of the country will go on election day. Three types of bellwethers have been suggested: *all-or-nothing districts,* which vote for the national winner; *barometric districts,* which predict the "national share of votes received by the winner"; and *swingometric districts,* which follow "the shifts, or swings in the national share of the vote from election to election" (Tufte and Sun 1975, pp. 2–3).

The media pay the most attention to bellwether districts. They frequently send journalists to these counties to size up the election outlook. Sometimes they even conduct polls in bellwether districts to help forecast the outcome (Stroud 1977, p. 392).[6] As Steven V. Roberts reported in the *New York Times* a few days before the 1980 election:

County That Votes with Winners Seems a Tossup

Emmetsburg, Iowa, Oct. 30—Only two counties have voted with the winner in every Presidential election in this century. One is Crook County in Oregon, and the other is Palo Alto County here in north central Iowa, a flat stretch of rich black farmland marked by small,

---

6. Bolton East, regarded as a bellwether constituency in the 1979 British general election, was surveyed and frequently visited by party leaders (Apple 1979, p. 3).

prosperous towns, towering grain elevators and a passion for high school football.

President Carter won handily here four years ago with 54 percent of the vote, but this year Palo Alto and its 1,300 residents were just as confused as the rest of the country. Mike Flannegan, publisher of the Palo Alto County Gazette, calls it a "very close, very close race." Dutch Hendinger, proprietor of Dutch's Diner, the town's favorite gathering spot, adds, "I wouldn't bet a nickel either way right now, and I love to bet."

A straw poll conducted by Mr. Flannegan's paper among Mr. Hendinger's patrons gives the President a small lead. But a mail poll conducted by the Emmetsburg Reporter and Democrat shows Mr. Reagan ahead. Unscientific interviews by The New York Times turned up 10 votes for Mr. Carter, 10 for Mr. Reagan, and 5 undecided. [Roberts 1980, p. 36]

Similar pre-election guides on "What to Watch for on Election Night" appear in newsmagazines. *Time* advised its readers in 1976 to pay particular attention to the vote in Illinois, New Mexico, and Palo Alto County, Iowa. *U.S. News and World Report* urged its readers to watch three counties—Laramie, Wyoming, Crook, Oregon, and Palo Alto, Iowa—all of which had voted for the winner in every election in this century.

Some political writers and scholars tout the bellwether approach to forecasting. Louis H. Bean, a persistent bellwether advocate, argues that "since 1948, four states (California, Indiana, Iowa, and New York) illustrate the adage 'as your state goes so goes the nation' " (1969, p. 99). C. Anthony Broh (1980) ranks states according to the percentage of times each voted for the winning presidential candidate. The five best all-or-nothing bellwethers (which went with the winner at least 83 percent of the time) are New Mexico, Illinois, California, Minnesota, and New York. Stanley D. Brunn (1974, p. 16) identifies 16 barometric counties whose votes in 1964 through 1972 were each within 2 percent of the winner's vote. Some election night forecasters project state winners from bellwether county and precinct returns (Shaffer 1975).[7]

Bellwethers were an unreliable guide in 1976: only 2 of the 7

7. This method of projecting results from bellwether precinct returns was first employed in 1883 by Charles H. Taylor, editor of the *Boston Globe* (Gallup 1972a, p. 221).

Table 2.2 Evaluation of Bellwether Presidential Election Forecasts in 1976 and 1980

	Vote in 1976		Vote in 1980	
	Carter (Correct)	Ford (Wrong)	Reagan (Correct)	Carter (Wrong)
Bellwether States				
California		X	X	
Illinois		X	X	
Indiana		X	X	
Iowa		X	X	
Minnesota	X			X
New Mexico		X	X	
New York	X		X	
Bellwether Counties				
Napa, California		X	X	
New Castle, Delaware	X		X	
Fulton, Illinois		X	X	
Harrison, Indiana	X		X	
Pike, Indiana	X			X
St. Joseph, Indiana		X	X	
Virgo, Indiana	X		X	
Palo Alto, Iowa	X		X	
Greenup, Kentucky	X			X
Powell, Kentucky	X			X
Glacier, Montana		X	X	
Clark, Nevada	X		X	
Lake, Ohio	X		X	
Crook, Oregon	X		X	
Harris, Texas		X	X	
Tarrant, Texas		X	X	
Okanogan, Washington	X		X	
Putnam, West Virginia	X		X	
Laramie, Wyoming		X	X	
Percentage Correct	*1976*		*1980*	
Bellwether States	29		86	
Nonbellwether States	51		88	
Bellwether Counties	63		84	
Nonbellwether Counties	55		71	

bellwether states and 12 of the 19 bellwether counties went for Carter (table 2.2). Half the barometer counties identified by Brunn were off by more than 2 percentage points (the average error was 3.1 percent). Bellwether states in 1976 actually were worse predictors of the outcome than nonbellwether states: bellwethers were 29 percent correct, while the rest of the states were 50 percent correct. The bellwether counties only slightly outperformed the remaining 3000-plus counties (63 versus 55 percent correct). Bellwether forecasts in 1976 worked about as well as an uneducated guess.

Bellwethers were of little help in 1980 either. Although 6 of the 7 bellwether states went with the winner, these states still did not forecast the election more accurately than the remaining 43. Bellwether counties were 86 percent correct, nonbellwether counties 71 percent correct.

The 12 best swingometric counties identified by Tufte and Sun missed the national shift to the Democrats in 1976 by an average of 4.3 percent and erred on the national swing to the Republicans in 1980 by 5.0 percent. Some swingometric districts were off by as much as 8 points. In short, bellwethers chosen prior to the election because their vote would allegedly foreshadow the winner, the national vote, or the national swing were unreliable guides in 1976 and 1980.

Even if reliable bellwethers could be found, the forecasting problem would not be solved. Chance alone naturally will produce some electoral units that mirror the national vote over a series of elections. Is a state or county a bellwether because it is a microcosm of the entire country, or is it chance that explains its movement with the national vote? If it is chance, a randomly chosen district (or for an all-or-nothing bellwether a coin flip!) would work just as well in the next election. Even if chance is not the explanation, the bellwether district vote would still have to be forecasted before the national outcome could be projected. The forecasting problem would be simply changed, not solved.

PUBLIC OPINION POLLS

The use of public opinion surveys to predict elections is as old as mass suffrage. The Harrisburg *Pennsylvanian* conducted the first "straw vote taken without discrimination of parties" in 1824. That same year the *Raleigh Star* canvassed sentiment at political meetings in North Carolina to assess "the sense of the people" (Fenton 1960, pp. 3; 7). Although newspaper-sponsored straw polls were commonplace throughout the nineteenth century, it was not until 1892, when the *New York Herald* gathered pre-election straw polls from editors across the nation, that the first forecast based on a national poll was made. In collaboration with three other newspapers, the *Herald* conducted a nationwide straw poll of 37 states in 1912. Other polls soon appeared. The *Literary Digest* began its nationwide presidential straw poll in 1924, as did the Hearst newspaper chain; in 1928 the *Farm Journal, Pathfinder* magazine, and others joined the pack of forecasters.

The press relied on a variety of methods to distribute straw ballots and record citizens' preferences. *Pathfinder* and some Hearst newspapers printed ballots for readers to cut out, mark, and mail or carry to the sponsor (Robinson 1932, p. 52). A more common technique, employed by the New York *Daily News* and the *Chicago Tribune,* among others, was to send canvassers equipped with straw ballots and ballot boxes to collect votes in offices, factories, clubs, hotels, and homes, on trolley cars and street corners, or wherever people could be found (Robinson 1932, p. 53). The mails were also used, most notably by the *Literary Digest.* Names were gathered from voter registration rolls, tax lists, telephone directories, and automobile registration files. In the months preceding the election, straw ballots were mailed to prospective voters (10 million in 1936, for example), who marked them and mailed them back to the magazine.

Straw-poll election forecasts, of course, were unreliable. Although they usually correctly foretold the winner, their popular vote errors were huge. The 1912 and 1916 *New York Herald* and 1924 to 1936 *Literary Digest* straw polls had an average state error of 10 percentage points. Nevertheless, they correctly forecasted 87 percent of the state winners; their national popular vote forecast error averaged only 3.3 points. The 1924 *Literary Digest* forecasts, typical of the period, correctly predicted the winner in all but 3 states, and missed the national popular vote by only 2.7 percent. However, the state popular vote error averaged 12 points and one-quarter of the state forecasts were off by more than *20* percentage points. As is well known, the *Literary Digest*'s 1936 forecast of a 3-to-2 victory for Republican Alf Landon over incumbent Franklin Roosevelt sounded the death knell to straw polls, when Roosevelt won by 62.5 percent of the vote and carried all but two states.

Sampling bias and *response* bias were the chief culprits in the *Literary Digest* debacle. The straw poll did not select a random sample of voters to interview. This problem became particularly acute in 1936, when the Depression caused magazine and telephone subscribers and automobile owners to become an even less representative sample of the population. As the relationship between social class and the vote grew stronger, so did the Republican sample bias. Response bias, however, probably contributed the lion's share of the error (Bryson 1976). Only 2.4 million ballots—less than one-quarter of those mailed out—were returned and tallied. In all likelihood, the well off, those in white-collar occupations and with intense interest in the campaign—all more likely to vote Republican—were the ones who cast straw votes.

The 1936 presidential election marked not only the end to straw polls, but the birth of "scientific" polling, which attempted to interview a representative sample of voters.[8] The sampling and response biases that plagued straw polls were reduced. In contrast to the *Literary Digest*'s whopping 22-point error, the 1936 predictions made by Gallup, Crossley, and Roper were off by a *mere* 6.8, 8.7, and .8 percentage points respectively (Roll and Cantril 1972, p. 10). But more important, the new pollsters, unlike the *Literary Digest,* correctly forecasted a Roosevelt victory.

Over the years, polls have become the principal method politicians, the press, and the public rely upon for presidential election forecasts. Since 1960, presidential campaign strategists have leaned heavily upon surveys to examine the electorate's perception of the candidates and to identify candidate constituencies (White 1961, p. 111; Napolitan 1972, chap. 4). Parties and candidates also use poll data to estimate their standing in each state to guide their allocation of scarce resources (Stroud 1977, p. 391; Witcover 1977, pp. 527–28; Kayden 1978, p. 111). The Carter and Ford teams each devoted about $500,000 to polling.[9] Carter and Reagan each spent about twice that amount in the 1980

8. An exception is the New York *Daily News,* which continued to conduct straw polls well into the 1960s. Their presidential, gubernatorial, and mayoral predictions between 1930 and 1966 had an average error of 5.9 percentage points; 1 forecast in 5 was off by over 10 points (Roll 1966, p. 253).

9. Carter spent 1.9 percent of his budget or $438,952 on polling in 1976 ($591,660 in 1980 dollars); Ford spent 2.3 percent or $521,537 ($702,975 in 1980 dollars) (Alexander 1979, pp. 372, 418).

general election. Candidates perceive polling as essential for a successful campaign.

The media also view polls as a key ingredient in their coverage of campaigns. Television networks, weekly newsmagazines, and leading daily newspapers all conduct and widely report polls. By one count, nearly 150 newspapers and broadcasters conducted surveys in 1980 (Dionne 1980, p. 10). Although the media ostensibly use polls to better understand a candidate's source of support, nearly every story mentions the "horse race"; six out of ten focus primarily on which candidate is ahead (Carmody 1976, p. 21). As Pat Caddell puts it: "Everyone follows polls because everything in American life is geared to the question of who's going to win—whether it's sports or politics or whatever. There's a natural curiosity" (May and Fraser 1973, p. 246).

In light of this widespread reliance on polls, how accurately do they forecast presidential elections? The 1936 to 1956 Gallup polls were off by an average of 3.9 percentage points. By improving their sampling procedure and conducting the final survey a few days (instead of weeks) before the election, Gallup reduced his average error to 1.6 percentage points in the 1960 to 1980 elections.[10]

Of course, it is not surprising that estimates made the weekend before the election are usually close to the outcome. The campaign is over. Most voters have already made up their minds. Given the science of survey sampling, accurate estimates should be expected. This is hardly proof that a poll is a reliable method for *forecasting* elections, if by forecasting one means predicting an electoral outcome before it is actually about to be registered.

A poll merely measures respondents' preferences *at the time the survey is administered.* It cannot forecast *future* preferences. The 1948 poll predictions that Dewey would beat Truman are probably the most notorious reminder that surveys cannot anticipate future behavior. A major reason for the 1948 error was that 14 percent of the electorate decided how to vote *after* the final poll

10. The average error in poll estimates of Labour and Conservative votes in postwar British elections is about the same: 1.8 percentage points (Teer and Spence 1973; *Gallup Political Index,* various issues; *Economist,* various issues).

was conducted, and 75 percent of these late deciders cast ballots for Truman (Mosteller et al. 1949, pp. 251–53).

A similar problem occurred in 1980. The leading national polls, conducted a few days before the election, underpredicted Reagan's strength by an average of 3.9 percentage points.[11] State surveys were no more reliable: their average error was 4.6 points.[12] The winner was incorrectly predicted in one-fifth of the states.[13] The *New York Times* post mortem revealed that "one registered voter in five changed his or her mind about whom to vote for, or whether to vote at all, in the last few days of the Presidential campaign and about three-fifths of that group made a change that hurt President Carter" (Clymer 1980, p. 1).

Final decisions made at the last gasp of the campaign are not peculiar to 1948 or 1980. Since 1952, an average of 36 percent of the voters have decided how to cast their presidential ballots in the period following the party conventions; half this group have decided in the final two weeks (table 2.3). Over 40 percent of the electorate in 1968, 1976, and 1980 waited until after the conven-

11. The final 1980 national pre-election poll errors are as follows:

Pollster	Error
CBS News/*New York Times*	−4.7%
Gallup	−3.6%
ABC News/Harris	−2.4%
NBC News/Associated Press	−1.5%
Washington Post	−7.2%

The error is the actual vote for Carter minus the poll estimate. Undecided respondents and those who preferred minor parties are deleted (*Opinion Outlook*, 17 November 1980, p. 1).

12. This is the mean error for the 21 state polls conducted within four weeks of the election.

13. State poll forecasts of gubernatorial and senatorial races in 1978 performed just as poorly: 35 newspaper poll predictions were off an average of 3.4 points; the polls incorrectly predicted the winner in 8 races (Plissner 1979). Private pollsters also made huge errors in their midterm forecasts. Robert Teeter's last poll showed Senator Edward W. Brooke of Massachusetts 8 points ahead; Brooke lost by 10 percentage points. Peter D. Hart claimed that Senator Dick Clark had a big lead in Iowa; Clark lost by 4 points (Clymer 1978, p. E4). McIntyre lost to Humphrey in New Hampshire despite McIntyre's 30-point lead in Caddell's mid-October poll. Primary polls are even more unreliable. The standing of the top two candidates in ten primary polls conducted in 1968 and 1972 were off by an average of 7.2 percentage points (Felson and Sudman 1975).

Table 2.3 Time When Voters Reach Final Presidential Vote Decision, 1952–80 (Percentages)

| | Time of Decision | | | |
Year	After Convention	Within Two Weeks of Election	Day of Election	Total Post-convention
1952	21	9	2	32
1956	12	8	2	22
1960	26	9	3	38
1964	21	9	4	34
1968	19	15	7	41
1972	22	8	5	35
1976	22	17	7	46
1980	15	17	9	41
Average 1952–80	20	12	5	36

Source: Center for Political Studies, American National Election Studies 1952-80.

tions to make their choices. Even in 1956, a virtual rerun of the 1952 election, 1 voter in 10 did not make up his or her mind until the final two weeks. A full 24 percent of the electorate in 1976 made their decision within two weeks of the election, while 7 percent reported making their decision on election day itself. *Nearly 10 percent of the voters in 1980 made up their minds on election day.*

The implication is clear: because polls at best measure citizens' current preferences, and because a large proportion of the electorate do not reach their decision until a few weeks (and in some years, hours) before the balloting, polls conducted before these final choices are made are likely to be unreliable predictors of the vote cast on election day. As Mosteller and associates concluded over thirty years ago (1949, p. 54), the possibility that voters will decide how to vote after the poll is conducted "limits the ultimate accuracy of election forecasts based on public opinion polling."

The inability of polls to forecast can be seen by comparing estimates from Gallup polls conducted immediately after the nominating conventions with the actual presidential popular vote cast a few months later. As table 2.4 shows, these post-nomination polls are extremely poor predictors of the vote. On average, the post-convention poll misses the eventual outcome by 5.8 percentage points. Although in 1952 and 1956 the survey was only

Table 2.4 Evaluation of Popular Vote Forecasts from Post-Convention Gallup Poll, 1936–80

Year	Gallup Estimates		Actual Outcome	
	Date of Survey	Percentage Democratic*	Percentage Democratic*	Error**
1936	7/20-25	52.4	62.5	10.1
1940	7/21-26	51.0	55.0	4.0
1944	9/22-27	51.0	53.8	2.8
1948	8/13-18	43.5	52.4	8.9
1952	7/25-30	46.6	44.6	- 2.0
1956	9/9-14	44.1	42.2	- 1.9
1960	7/30-8/4	46.8	50.1	3.3
1964	8/27-9/2	69.1	61.3	- 7.8
1968	9/1-6	33.3	42.9	9.6
1972	8/25-28	31.9	38.2	6.3
1976	8/20-23	57.5	51.1	- 6.4
1980	8/15-18	50.6	44.7	- 5.9
1936-80	Average absolute error			5.8
1960-80	Average absolute error			6.6

Source: The Gallup Poll: 1935-71; Gallup Opinion Index, various issues. Preferences for nonmajor party candidates and undecided responses were deleted, except in 1968, when Wallace voters were included.
* Percentage of two-party vote except in 1968, when it is percentage of three-party vote.
** Actual vote minus the estimated vote.

off by about 2 points, it performs more poorly in most years. Both the 1976 and 1980 post-convention polls overestimated Carter's eventual winning margin by about 6 percentage points.[14]

14. Early pre-election polls work slightly better in Great Britain, but the margin of error is still substantial. Since 1945 the average Labour and Conservative error in polls conducted a month before the general election has been 2.5 percentage points. The September 1974 polls missed the October vote by an average of 3.1 points; the April 1979 polls missed the May vote by 6.1 points (Teer and Spence 1973; *Gallup Political Index*, various issues; *Economist*, various issues).

Whiteley (1979) tries to improve these forecasts by modeling pre-election trends in Gallup poll support for the Labour Party. Whiteley does not forecast the Labour Party's general election vote, but rather its standing in the final pre-election poll. Although the average error in his forecast of the final *poll* is 2.3 percentage points, his average Labour party *election* forecast error is 2.7 points. Moreover, he overstates the precision of his estimates. The election forecast variance is the variance of his forecast of the final Gallup poll plus the variance of the poll's forecast of the election (assuming the two are uncorrelated). Whiteley only takes the former into account.

Given the track record of the first post-convention poll, to be 95 percent certain of popular vote forecast from this survey, one would have to allow a margin of error of plus or minus *14.1* percentage points![15]

State polls, of course, are no better. The 26 state surveys conducted in September of 1976 had an average forecast error of 3.6 percentage points. On election day 8 states (30 percent) went for the candidate who was trailing in these early polls. The 23 state polls conducted between late August and mid-September of 1980 had an average error of 3.5 points; in 5 surveys (22 percent) the leader failed to carry the state on election day.

The inability of polls to anticipate the formation of, or changes in, voter preferences is the most serious barrier to their successful use in election forecasting, but other problems also undermine their accuracy. While everyone is familiar with the widely reported *random sampling error* that results from making population estimates from a sample, this is the least troublesome source of additional error. *Nonresponse error* is introduced in selecting respondents: some pollsters (like Gallup, ABC/Harris, and NBC/AP) do not attempt to reach households where no one was home on the first contact *(Public Opinion* December/January 1981, p. 18). Instead, adjustments are made to correct for people who cannot be reached, refuse to reply, or do not have telephones (if phone interviewing is used). *Response error* also occurs. Sometimes (as in 1956, 1964, and 1972) citizens are reluctant to give seemingly unpopular answers to interviewers (Perry 1979, p. 316). Furthermore, respondents who are only leaning to a candidate are weighted the same as people whose preferences are firmer. Those who are undecided, even after additional prodding by the interviewer, are deleted from the estimate, which is equivalent to assuming they have a fifty-fifty chance of going for either candidate. Because barely more than half the citizens actually turn out to vote, pollsters also must estimate which respondents should be included (or how they should be weighted) in the

---

15. This is the standard error of the residuals (6.4) times the .975 fractile of the T-distribution with 11 degrees of freedom (2.2).

tally.[16] Several pollsters in 1980 blamed errors in their turnout estimates for their underprediction of Reagan's vote (Reich 1980, p. 24).[17] Although pollsters have devised sensible solutions that in all likelihood do not introduce systematic bias in their totals, nonresponse, response, and turnout errors all increase the variance of a poll estimate. Thus, even as an assessment of voter preferences at the time the poll is administered, the margin of error is greater than the commonly reported plus or minus 3 points.[18]

Although many pollsters and political strategists recognize that polls are inherently incapable of forecasting elections (Perry 1972, p. xxi; Napolitan 1972; Gallup 1972a, p. 127; Steinberg 1976, p. 183; Crossley and Crossley 1979, p. 5; Sears 1980, p. A19), politicians, the media, and the public still look to polls, more than anything else, for a prediction of who will win the presidency. This happens despite pollster Charles Roll's warning (1966, p. 259): "To expect a poll to predict the winner of an election—even next week's election—can be like photographing a horse race in the back stretch and expecting the developed picture to show how the horses will cross the finish line."

JOURNALISTS

Newspapers, magazines, and the rest of the media not only report the results of public opinion polls, they also predict which states each candidate will carry and what the electoral college result will be. To make these projections journalists rely heavily on public and private state polls, but their calculations also rest

16. Because 4 states in 1980 either did not require voter registration or allowed citizens to register on election day, and an additional 8 permitted citizens to register as late as two weeks prior to the election, estimating voter turnout from a respondent's report that he is registered may be hazardous.

17. Similarly, British pollsters blamed the 1970 decline in turnout on election eve polls incorrectly forecasting a Labour victory (*Economist*, 17 June 1970, p. 23).

18. For example, if the variance of these other estimates is roughly equal to the sampling variance, a reported margin of error of plus or minus 3 points should be increased to plus or minus 4.2 points (assuming these other errors are uncorrelated with the sampling error).

on political intelligence gathered by reporters, conversations with candidate strategists, and the judgments of editors and in-house political experts.

While at the beginning of this century some newspapers conducted straw polls, others canvassed editors' projections of the state-by-state presidential vote.[19] Although large errors were made, these early forecasts were slightly closer to the mark than the straw polls of the day. The average state popular vote error of the New York *World*'s 1912 canvass of newspapermen from all 48 states was 4.5 percentage points. Their 1920 poll of 300 editors of leading dailies was off, on average, by 11.0 points. A similar effort by *Editor and Publisher* in 1928 had a state forecast error that averaged 6.5 points (Robinson 1932, p. 17).[20] Not only did journalists make sizable errors—off about 7 points per state—but their forecasts were usually (80 percent of the time) biased in favor of the loser. In all likelihood they forecasted close elections both because they preferred a newsworthy contest and because they wanted to minimize the likelihood of miscalling a state.

Without making a specific popular vote prediction, journalists also forecast which way a state will go. The 331 journalists' forecasts, made within a week of the 1904 to 1928 elections, correctly predicted 84 percent of the state outcomes. However, when states won by pluralities of more than 10 percent are deleted (the then solid South and Republican states like Vermont and Pennsylvania), reporters fared less well: they correctly predicted only 61 percent of the remaining states,[21] and one-third of the time they did not hazard a forecast because they were uncertain of the outcome (Robinson 1932, pp. 19–22).

Even with their increased reliance on public opinion polls, journalists' forecasts have not improved much since 1928. Their 1976 and 1980 forecasts, evaluated in tables 2.5 and 2.6, are

19. As one might expect, newspapers have been making presidential election forecasts since the advent of universal mass suffrage. See, for example, "Who Is to Be Next President" (*sic*), *New York Herald,* 26 October 1836, p. 2.

20. Robinson reports the plurality error, which is twice the percentage point error I cite.

21. States that were not forecasted because of journalists' uncertainty I assign a .5 probability of being correctly predicted.

Table 2.5 Evaluation of Journalists' 1976 Presidential Election Forecasts*

Forecaster	Date**	States in Doubt (%)	Electoral Vote in Doubt (%)	States Correctly Predicted§ (%)	Electoral Vote Error§§
"*Early*"					
U.S. News and World Report	9/13	26	20	73	-102
Christian Science Monitor	9/16	8	8	74	-141
New York Times	10/3	20	25	80	- 77
"*Election-Eve*"					
Newsweek	10/25	22	27	77	- 82
U.S. News and World Report	10/25	34	38	79	- 49
Christian Science Monitor	10/29	32	40	78	- 25
Associated Press	10/31	28	29	80	- 75
Washington Post	10/31	16	24	81	17
New York Times	11/1	18	22	85	16
Time	11/1	30	33	83	- 57
NBC News	11/1	40	45	80	10

* The District of Columbia has been deleted from all calculations in this table.
** Magazine dates are the day they first appeared on the newsstand: one week before the cover date.
§ States in doubt are assumed to have a .5 probability of voting for Carter.
§§ The error is the actual national electoral vote for Carter minus the forecasted national electoral vote for Carter. The electoral votes for states in doubt were divided evenly between the two candidates.

divided into two groups: "early" forecasts were made at least one month before the election; "election eve" forecasts were made within a week of the election and represent the medium's final election prediction.

Uncertainty and error characterize the early forecasts. The 1976 prognoses correctly predict about 3 out of 4 states, but grossly overestimate Carter's electoral college standing by between 77 and 141 votes. The forecasters at *U.S. News and World Report,* for instance, were uncertain of the outcome in 26 percent of the states, which contained 20 percent of the national electoral vote.

Although the level of certainty did not increase in the ensuing weeks, the accuracy of the forecasts did. Forecasters were still unsure about who would win 16 to 40 percent of the states, which would cast 22 to 45 percent of the total electoral vote. The election eve forecasts made fewer state errors and the miss in the forecasted electoral college vote was substantially reduced. The *New York Times* and the *Washington Post* made the best election eve forecasts in 1976. Their state predictions were over 80 percent correct; the *Times* underpredicted Carter's margin by only 16 electoral votes, the *Post* by 17. But even the *Times* was uncertain of the outcome in 9 states and was wrong in 3 others. Although NBC News correctly forecasted the outcome in 30 states, they did not make predictions for the other 20, which comprised 45 percent of the electoral college.

Like the pollsters, journalists underestimated Reagan's strength in 1980. Although their early forecasts correctly predicted three-quarters of the states, they undershot Reagan's electoral college total by an average of 151 votes. The election eve forecasts were even worse. Journalists were in doubt about the outcome in 1 out of 4 states, comprising a third of the electoral college; they correctly predicted only 74 percent of the states; they underpredicted Reagan's electoral college standing by an average of 174 votes. NBC's November 1 projections were slightly better than the rest of the pack: they generated forecasts for all but 11 states, correctly predicted the outcome in nearly 4 states out of 5, and underestimated Reagan's electoral college total by *only* 128 votes.

In conclusion, there is uncertainty in journalists' forecasts. Predictions for one-quarter of the states, comprising a third of the electoral college, were in doubt in 1976 and 1980. Forecasts made more than a month before the 1976 election grossly overstated Carter's electoral vote margin and were wrong in their predictions for one-quarter of the states. Only in the final weeks before the 1976 election did a few organizations make fairly accurate forecasts, and of course by then they could use late pre-election surveys as a guide. However, in 1980 these election eve polls were of little help and journalists like everyone else underpredicted the size of Reagan's win. Finally, like political strategists' forecasts, journalists' projections are crude. States *Newsweek* viewed as leaning to Ford in 1976, for example, were won by anywhere from 50.4 to 60.6 percent of the popular vote; states *Time* reported as leaning to Reagan in 1980 were won by 50.7 to 59.9 points.

Table 2.6 Evaluation of Journalists' 1980 Presidential Election Forecasts*

Forecaster	Date**	States in Doubt (%)	Electoral Vote in Doubt (%)	States Correctly Predicted§ (%)	Electoral Vote Error§§
"*Early*"					
Newsweek	9/1	16	24	77	-106
Christian Science Monitor	9/18	11	32	71	-170
NBC News	9/26	26	40	71	-192
New York Times	10/5	18	16	79	-131
Washington Post	10/5	14	19	76	-157
"*Election-Eve*"					
U.S. News and World Report	10/27	18	26	74	-187
Time	10/27	18	25	75	-177
Newsweek	10/27	30	35	75	-177
Christian Science Monitor	10/28	22	27	73	-177
NBC News	11/1	22	30	79	-128
New York Times	11/2	26	30	71	-175
Washington Post	11/2	26	31	69	-198
Associated Press	11/3	32	47	74	-172

*   The District of Columbia has been deleted from all calculations in this table.
** Magazine dates are the day they first appeared on the newsstand: one week before the cover date.
§   States in doubt are assumed to have a .5 probability of voting for Carter.
§§ The error is the actual national electoral vote for Carter minus the forecasted national electoral vote for Carter. The electoral votes for states in doubt were divided evenly between the two candidates.

SOCIAL SCIENTISTS

Each forecasting method discussed so far relies on an *indicator* of candidate standing to predict what will happen on election day. Polls, political canvasses, and journalists' assessments point out who is ahead; the predicted outcome is extrapolated from this sounding. Implicit assumptions underlie each method. Polls or political canvasses assume that voters have reached their final decision, their preferences are stable, and their responses accurately reflect how they will cast their ballots. If political intelligence or journalists' forecasts are relied upon, trust is placed in the ability of these political observers to foretell what the outcome will be.

Social scientists take a different approach. While they naturally watch the polls, follow journalists' state tallies, and comb articles for clues to the winner, they do not focus solely on these indicators of candidate standing. Social scientists consider the *causes* of how well candidates will do on election day. *Theories about how voters make decisions guide their prognoses.*

There are several obvious problems with this approach: How much credence should be given to the alternative theories? Which theories have the greatest predictive validity? How much weight should be given to the many variables one might consider? For example, how much should the candidates' positions count in the forecast relative to the economy or other factors?

A common solution is to formulate a mathematical representation of the theory and statistically to estimate, with earlier election data, each variable's effect. The estimated coefficients can be used to forecast the next election. Although theories and empirical studies about how voters make decisions are in abundance, few can be used to forecast elections.

The Simulmatics Project

The "Simulmatics Project," established in 1959 by Ithiel de Sola Pool, Robert A. Abelson, and Samuel Popkin, was one of social science's earliest attempts to forecast an election. Although its chief purpose was to foretell, through simulation, the effect of issues (Catholicism, civil rights, and foreign policy) on Kennedy's 1960 popular and electoral vote, Pool and associates did generate postdictive predictions of the 1960 and 1964 presidential vote (1965, tables 3.1 and 6.1).[22] Before I evaluate their forecasts, let me describe briefly how the forecasts were made.

The Pool team drew data from 65 national surveys conducted between 1952 and 1960. Based on the respondent's region, sex, religion, ethnicity, partisanship, socioeconomic status, and city size, he was classified into one of 480 "voter-types." For example, a Republican, Protestant, white-collar male who lives in an urban area of the Midwest was one voter-type; a Democratic, Catholic female with a blue-collar occupation who lives in a rural

22. There is some inconsistency between the Simulmatics' account of their contribution to the campaign and Sorenson's (1965, p. 184) assessment of their impact.

area of the East another. Next, each voter-type's responses to 52 survey questions were tabulated to yield 52 480-cell tables (one for each issue). To simulate the state electorate's opinions on these issues, the responses for each voter-type were counted in proportion to their share of the state population. (This proportion is estimated from aggregate data.)[23]

The next step was to predict the outcome itself. "Common sense, social science theory and similar guides . . . [and their] best judgment of how different types of voters would respond to a campaign focused on the . . . issue" determined how much weight they gave to each of the model's components (1965, pp. 54–56). For the religious issue, Pool, Abelson, and Popkin assumed that Protestant Republicans would vote exactly as they did last time, Protestant Democrats and independents, because of competing pressures, would be twice as likely as usual not to vote, and one-third of Catholic Democrats and independents "which the Democrats normally lost in Congressional contests would come back to them in a Kennedy campaign where the religious issue was at the top of attention" (1965, pp. 47, 50, 51).

This approach obviously warrants appraisal. First, Pool and his colleagues do not indicate how accurately this handful of demographic variables predict issue preferences. (Other evidence suggests that on most issues, demographic variables alone are poor predictors of political opinions [Dawson 1973].) A more fundamental problem, however, stems from their use of voter-types to simulate state electorates. The surveys were not representative samples of citizens in each state. They assume that "a voter of a given voter-type would be identical regardless of the state from which he came" (1965, p. 40). Thus, beyond region, the Pool team assumes that no other contextual variables influence voters' issue positions or candidate preferences. In other words, the entire difference between the political preferences that citizens of Mississippi and Massachusetts hold can be attributed solely to the number of each voter-type that reside

23. It must have been difficult to make these aggregate demographic estimates, since the 1960 census data were not yet available. In addition, it is not clear how the individual-level concept of partisanship was measured at the aggregate level, or the extent to which the individual and aggregate measures were compatible.

in the state (Seidman 1975, p. 331). Their decision on how much to weight each variable, although sensible, certainly is arbitrary. It is not clear how much faith should be put in predictions generated from these assumptions.

Despite these problems, their simulations closely fit the actual 1960 and 1964 election results. Pool, Abelson, and Popkin retrospectively chose variable weights that would best fit the state presidential vote in each election.[24] Because the model coefficients were chosen with knowledge of the actual election results, it is not strictly a forecast, or even an out-of-sample postdiction. Although their "best fit simulation" only overestimated Kennedy's electoral college standing by 8 votes, the outcome was incorrectly predicted in 25 percent of the states (12 out of 48). The average state vote was off by 3.6 percentage points.[25] The 1964 electoral college result was overpredicted by only 7 votes, and the correct winner was missed in 13 percent of the states; the state popular vote error in 1964 jumped to 4.4 percentage points.[26]

Budge and Farlie

Ian Budge and Dennis Farlie (1977, chap. 7) generated 1976 election forecasts for several different candidate scenarios. One was a Ford-Carter contest. Their model holds that a citizen bases his choice upon his previous voting behavior, "reactions to candidates," and the candidates' stands on salient issues. The Center for Political Studies 1974 National Election Study is their primary data base. They assume that "the political watershed of 1973–4, with its revelations of Watergate, and the deterioration in the economy, renders insignificant any subsequent differences between early 1975 [when the last interviews in this study were conducted] and late 1976" (1977, p. 473). Questions about Jimmy Carter did not appear on the 1974 survey, so they created a surrogate measure of voters' reactions to him. On the basis of aggregate poll data reported by the press in the early months of 1976, Budge and Farlie "conceived of Carter's public appeal as a

24. It is not clear whether a maximum likelihood procedure, such as regression, was employed.
25. This is the mean miss. The median error is 3.0 percent.
26. The median error rose to 4.0 percent.

combination of those of Humphrey and Wallace. Electors who liked both Humphrey and Wallace could be typed as pro-Carter, electors who disliked both as anti-Carter, and the remainder fell . . . into mixed categories" (1977, p. 474). Budge and Farlie then generated regional estimates for the 1972–76 Democratic swing, which they added to the 1972 presidential vote for each state in the region to forecast its 1976 vote.

Budge and Farlie summarize their 1976 presidential election forecast as follows: "Under all conceivable conditions this predicts a Democratic sweep of the electoral college paralleling 1964. Only the Mountain states (comprising 35 votes) and Indiana are attributed to the Republicans" (p. 479). Their forecast overpredicts Carter's national popular vote by 14.2 percentage points. The average state popular vote error is 14.4 points and the correct winner is predicted in only 62 percent of the states. As a result, their electoral college forecast is off by 192 electoral votes. Even the June 1976 Gallup poll trial heat between Ford and Carter produced a more accurate forecast than the Budge-Farlie model.[27]

Forecasts from Changes in the Economy

A third approach relies on changes in the economy to estimate the division of the national popular vote. Taking their lead from Gerald Kramer's (1971) seminal work, Lepper (1974), Niskanen (1975), Tufte (1978), Fair (1978), and Rabinowitz and Zechman (1978) have estimated equations that could be used to forecast the national presidential popular vote. These efforts share several features. They all use national aggregate data from twentieth-century elections. The dependent variable is the proportion of the popular vote for the Democratic party (or some variation, such as the proportion for the incumbent party). Although the underlying voter calculus in each model is somewhat different, all are motivated by the belief that fluctuations in economic conditions are largely responsible for changes in presidential election outcomes. One or two variables that measure aggregate changes in the economy are at the core of each equation. Tufte relies on

27. Further efforts to forecast elections in twenty-three nations are reported in Farlie and Budge (1981).

election year change in real disposable personal income per capita, while Fair uses change in real gross national product per capita. Niskanen includes changes in the net national product, unemployment, and prices.

Very few political factors enter these equations, and usually only as control variables. Tufte includes a measure of "net presidential candidate advantage" to capture the public's evaluation of the two candidates. Two "political" variables appear in Fair's equations: a linear time trend (to control for changes in partisanship); and whether an incumbent president is running. Niskanen also controls for incumbency, as well as for wars and for changes in federal revenue and expenditures. These are narrow representations of the voter's decision rule. Little can be learned from these models about how changes in the political environment affect election outcomes.

One reason for the dearth of political variables is that the national level analysis rests on very few data points: the number of observations range from 8 elections in Tufte's work to 20 in Fair's. And, as Fair wryly observes, only 5 more observations will be available by the year 2000. The small data set limits the number of variables that can be included in a model. Furthermore, some variables are difficult to measure at the national level; others are so interrelated that it is hard to isolate their effect.

Two further consequences of making national-level estimates would trouble a forecaster. Because only a few data points are used to estimate the equations, the standard error of the forecast, other things being equal, is quite large.[28] This would be particularly troublesome in close contests. Moreover, although these equations can be used to forecast the division of the national popular vote, they can predict neither how states will vote nor which candidate will win an electoral college majority.[29]

28. This is because the standard error of the forecast decreases with the square root of the number of cases.

29. Electoral vote predictions can be made from the following equation: ELVote = a + b(POPVote); where ELVote is the log-odds of the Democratic proportion of the electoral vote and POPVote is the Democratic proportion of the popular vote. If the 1980 popular vote were known with certainty, based on the 1948–76 data, the 1980 forecast is that the Democrats would receive 100 electoral votes (that's 51 off the mark). (The 95 percent confidence interval on this forecast is 47 to 192 electoral votes.)

The 1976 and 1980 national presidential popular vote can be forecasted from the Tufte, Niskanen, and Fair equations.[30] All three models predict a Ford victory in 1976, although by different margins. Tufte makes the smallest error: 2.4 percentage points (he predicts 48.7 percent for Carter instead of the 51.1 percent he received). Niskanen underpredicts the Democratic vote by 9.0 points; Fair predicts 44.0 percent of the vote going to Carter—an error of 7.1 points. Tufte's model predicts Reagan receiving 48.1 percent of the 1980 popular vote (a 3.4 point error). Fair made two 1980 pre-election forecasts. The first, which assumed that voters respond to election year economic fluctuations, predicted that Reagan would receive 49 percent of the two-party vote (a 6.3 point error). The second, which assumed that voters have shorter memories and react only to changes in real growth in the previous six months, predicted 52 percent for Reagan (an error of 3.3 points).

CONCLUSION

There are, of course, many other ad hoc methods for forecasting presidential elections (Bean 1948, 1969, 1972; Lichtman and Keilis-Borok 1981). The taller candidate wins, it is said. This guide fails in 1976 (five-foot-ten-inch Carter defeated six-foot-one-inch Ford), but works in 1980 for six-foot-two-inch Reagan. A higher Dow Jones industrial average on the Monday before the election signals a victory for the incumbent party (works in 1976 but not in 1980). The World Series is another surefire guide: Democrats win when the National League team takes the series; the Republicans win with the American League. (Works in 1976, not in 1980.) Although these unorthodox approaches are widely re-

30. The 1976 Niskanen forecast is reported in Niskanen (1975). The 1976 Fair forecast is not strictly a forecast but the within-sample predicted vote. Given the size of this residual, the forecast error would be even larger than the one reported here. About a year before the election, Fair predicted that the Republican would win the 1976 election with about 56 percent of the vote—7 points off the mark (Fair 1978). The 1980 forecasts were provided by Fair. The Tufte forecasts are made by using the data reported in Tufte (1978) for the years prior to the election to reestimate his equation. The actual election year data are used with these coefficients to generate the predicted vote.

Table 2.7 Accuracy of Presidential Election Forecasts

| | Forecasts | | | |
| | State | | National | |
Forecaster	Popular Vote (% Point Error)	Winner (Percent Correct)	Popular Vote (% Point Error)	Electoral Vote (Error)
1. Political Strategists				
Both parties, 1928	5.5	70		
Carter, June 1976		82		10
Carter, August 1976		56		22
Ford, August 1976		75		26
Carter, June 1980		76		141
Carter, October 1980		64		241
Reagan, March 1980		69		223
Reagan, October 1980		80		142
2. Political Canvass				
Goldwater, 1964	7.5	78		
3. Polls				
Straw polls, 1912-36	10.0	87	3.3	
Post-convention poll, 1936-80			5.8	
Early state polls, 1976	3.6	69		
Final state polls, 1976	1.9	81		
Early state polls, 1980	3.5	78		
Final state polls, 1980	4.6	76		
Final national polls, 1976			.9	
Final national polls, 1980			3.9	
4. Journalists				
1912, 1920, and 1928	7.5			
1904-28		75		
Early 1976		76		107
Early 1980		75		151
Election eve, 1976		80		41
Election eve, 1980		74		174
5. Social Scientists				
Simulmatics, 1960	3.6	75		8
Simulmatics, 1964	4.4	87		7
Budge and Farlie, 1976	14.4	62	14.2	192
Niskanen, 1976			9.0	
Fair, 1976			7.1	
Fair, 1980 (1-year memory)			6.3	
Fair, 1980 (6-month memory)			3.3	
Tufte, 1976			2.4	
Tufte, 1980			3.4	

ported in the popular press—not always with tongue in cheek—for obvious reasons they warrant the proverbial grain of salt (the most obvious reason—they don't work.)

How well, then, do current methods forecast presidential elections? It depends, in part, on what is being forecasted. State-level popular vote predictions are off, on average, by about 6 percentage points. The best forecasts err by about 1.9 points; the worst miss by more than 14 points. State winner predictions would be 50 percent correct if one simply flipped coins. A rudimentary understanding of American politics should allow one to predict an additional 6 or 7 states, so it should be no surprise when 60 to 65 percent of state outcomes are predicted. Current methods do slightly better; on average they are correct 75 percent of the time. Still, except when there are landslide elections, rarely are more than 80 percent of the state outcomes correctly forecasted.

Social scientists and most pollsters forecast the national popular vote. Polls are poor predictors of the eventual vote: the first post-convention poll has an average error of 5.8 percentage points. Some social scientists do better than this, some worse. The Budge-Farlie 1976 national popular vote forecast was off by 14.2 percentage points. The Tufte, Fair, and Niskanen economic models had errors of 2.4, 7.1, and 9.0 percentage points in 1976; there was a slight improvement in 1980. A national popular vote forecast error that is less than 2.4 points in 1976 and less than 3.3 points in 1980 would improve upon the best of these models.

Social scientists generally have ignored the most relevant political quantity—the electoral vote. (The Simulmatics group and Budge and Farlie are exceptions.) To gauge who is ahead in the electoral college we currently must rely on forecasts generated by journalists and candidate strategists. Although both Carter and Ford politicos made fairly accurate electoral college predictions in 1976 (off by no more than 26 electoral votes), their 1980 forecasts went wide of the mark. Journalists made an even poorer showing, especially in forecasts made a month or more before the election. Journalists' early forecasts were off, on average, by more than 100 electoral votes in 1976 and by more than 150 votes in 1980. Of the four types considered, electoral college forecasts are the easiest to make, because even though there may be large state errors, if the misses are random, they will cancel out. Though Carter strategists, for instance, correctly predicted the outcome in just 56 percent of the states in August of 1976, their electoral college forecast was off by only 22 votes.

We now have a baseline against which to evaluate new methods for forecasting presidential elections.

3
A THEORY OF ELECTIONS

To explain elections requires a theory that accounts for changes over time in the electorate's behavior. To figure out why the Democrats win one year but lose another, one must identify what changes could have produced the different outcomes. The voters themselves can change. Although many people vote for the same party year after year, political trends may prevent others from continuing to support that party. Which issues are important may also change, as well as the electorate's positions on those issues. The candidates, of course, also differ from one election to the next. Sometimes extreme liberals or conservatives run; at other times moderates are nominated. An incumbent president or vice-president is a candidate in some years; in others neither major party candidate has held these posts. The candidates' home states and regions also vary, which also may affect who wins. Other characteristics of the electoral environment vary across elections. Some contests are held in the midst of war; most are held in peacetime. Sometimes there is recession, sometimes prosperity.

A theory of elections must consider the effects that such changes in the electoral context have on election outcomes. The electoral setting cannot be held constant—it may be one of the most important determinants of the vote. What distinguishes the theory developed in this chapter from most others is not so much the factors I consider as the recognition that the effect of each is understood by how much it moves voters from one election to the next.

USUAL PRESIDENTIAL VOTE

Voters are creatures of habit. They do not flip coins at an election to decide how to cast their ballots. Rather, some forces that influenced their choice in previous elections—social and ethnic political traditions and attachment to the parties—are likely to affect their current decision. Citizens who usually vote Democratic are likely to continue to do so (other things being equal); so are citizens who usually vote Republican (Campbell et al. 1960; Converse 1966a). If one had no other information about voters or elections, it would be reasonable to predict that in the next election a citizen who had always voted Democratic would do the same again (probability close to 1.0); if he had always voted Republican, he would be equally certain (probability close to 0.0) *not* to vote Democratic; a person who voted half the time for the Democrats and half for the Republicans would have a .5 probability of voting Democratic; and so on. A sensible, although certainly imprecise, election forecast would be one that simply tallied up these usual votes.

I will represent this notion as follows:

$$V_{it} = \alpha_i + U_{it} \tag{3.1}$$

where V_{it} is citizen$_i$'s probability of voting Democratic in election$_t$;

α_i is citizen$_i$'s usual Democratic vote; and

U_{it} are all the other causes of citizen$_i$s' votes in election$_t$.

Equation 3.1 says that the probability a citizen will vote Democratic in a given election (V_{it}) is equal to his usual presidential vote (α_i) plus an error (U_{it}). Contained in U_{it} are all the other causes of a citizen's behavior. Although I expect U_{it} on average to be zero, in any given election other factors—specific to that election—naturally cause citizens to deviate from their usual choice (Converse 1966a). Thus, this very simple model must be expanded.

ISSUES, ISSUE IMPORTANCE, AND CANDIDATE POSITIONS

Dozens of issues arise in every election. Some have a significant impact on the outcome because they affect how large segments of the electorate vote. Most, however, are salient only to a small subset of people. Even though they may affect how those few citizens vote, in the aggregate they have little, if any, effect on the outcome.

A fully specified model would consider every issue in every election, and would allow for the fluctuations in impact of each issue across individuals and time. In practice, this fully saturated model could be neither identified nor estimated. So some assumptions must be made that limit the number of issues considered and/or constrain some issues to have the same effect across sets of people.

One way I reduce the number of issues is to focus only on those which, to some degree, persist from one election to the next. This restriction discourages idiosyncratic explanations in favor of ones that explain variation in behavior across several elections. It also helps the forecaster, since he or she will not have information on the impact of an issue when it arises for the first time.[1] To further reduce the number of issues considered, I examine clusters of issues that together comprise a dimension, rather than examine each one separately. (Later I discuss additional restrictions on the effect of an issue across voters.)

New Deal social welfare issues have divided the political parties for more than five decades. The dispute over the federal government's role as economic manager and solver of social problems originated in the divergent Democratic and Republican responses to the Great Depression. Republicans under Hoover maintained their traditional post-Reconstruction position that "the federal government should not intervene in the affairs of business, states, local communities or private charities" (Sundquist 1973, p. 189). Even as the economy worsened, Hoover stood firm in his commitment to limited government and refused to use the federal government's resources to soften the Depres-

1. This, of course, may be dangerous if election-specific issues are responsible for changes in election outcomes. Consistent and unbiased estimates, and thus consistent and unbiased forecasts, will result only if a voter's preference for a candidate on other issues (that remain in the error term $[U_{it}]$ of the model) are uncorrelated with the voter's preferences on the issue dimensions included in the model.

sion's impact. As is well known, the Democrats, under Roosevelt, took a different position. Roosevelt's philosophy was: "Take a method and try it; if it fails, admit it frankly, and try another. But above all try something" (quoted in Sundquist 1973, p. 194). Roosevelt used the federal government's resources to try to meet social and economic problems that had hitherto gone unaddressed by the government in Washington. He was an activist.

Thus, a fundamental political cleavage developed over the extent to which the national government should actively manage the economy, police business, solve social problems, and provide for human needs. Liberals held that the federal government had a responsibility in each of these areas (Ladd 1970, pp. 182, 203). (Also see Hofstadter 1948, pp. 330–31; Leuchtenberg 1963, p. 165; Polsby and Wildavsky 1976, p. 171; King 1978, pp. 371–72; Kirkpatrick 1978, p. 251.) Conservatives, on the other hand, doubted the federal government's ability to manage the economy, opposed regulation of business, and believed that economic and social problems should be solved not in Washington but by state and local governments, or by the private sector. Over time, of course, Republicans have become less steadfast in their opposition, but they still advocate less government involvement. As Ronald Reagan puts it, "Get government off the backs of the people." Although the differences between the parties on these issues has narrowed since the 1930s, the New Deal social welfare dimension persists as the predominant issue dividing the two parties.

In the decades since the Second World War, racial issues have also been important. President Truman's ten-point civil rights program, which included voting rights for blacks, establishment of a Fair Employment Practices Commission (FEPC), and federal protection against lynching, generated considerable opposition, particularly in the South. The upshot was that four southern states deserted to Dixiecrat Strom Thurmond in 1948. Four years later, Adlai Stevenson's more moderate civil rights position allowed racial issues to cool and the Dixiecrats to return to the Democratic fold.

With the 1954 Supreme Court decision in *Brown* v. *Board of Education* voter concern over racial issues again grew. Sit-ins, marches, demonstrations, freedom rides, civil disruptions, the Civil Rights bills of 1957, 1960, and 1964, the Voting Rights Act of 1965, and George Wallace's third-party candidacy all kept racial issues in the public eye. Throughout most of the 1960s the public regarded racial matters as the most important domestic problem facing the country.

Over time, the specific issues changed: the FEPC, equal educational opportunities, school integration, elimination of separate public services, equal employment opportunities, voting rights, open housing, busing, and affirmative action. But the underlying dimension has remained more or less constant: Should the federal government actively strive to ensure equality of opportunity for blacks? Liberals have supported the passage of federal laws and programs designed to guarantee racial equality and blacks' rights. Conservatives have resisted such legislation.

The New Deal social welfare and racial dimensions encompass two sets of issues which, to a large extent, have dominated American presidential politics for half a century. Foreign policy issues—with the obvious exception of wars—"do not generate the depth of personal concern that is generated by issues closer to the daily lives of the citizenry" (Nie, Verba, and Petrocik 1976, p. 104); hence they generally have less effect on how people vote (Popkin et al. 1976; Kagay and Caldeira 1975). Accordingly, I shall not consider foreign policy issues, other than wars.[2] I have more to say about the effect of wars later in this chapter.

The next step is to incorporate the New Deal social welfare and racial issues into the voters' decision rule. The more a citizen prefers the other party candidate's issue positions to his own candidate's, the higher the probability that he will defect from his usual vote (Downs 1957, chap. 3). Conversely, the more a voter prefers his own party candidate's positions, the more likely he is to stick to his usual choice. If a voter likes the two candidates' issue positions equally, then that issue will not affect his vote. How much a particular issue affects a voter's decision depends on how strongly he prefers one candidate's positions over the

2. Kessel (1980, chap. 8) dissents from this position. I relax this assumption in chap. 6.

other's, and how important the dimension is to him. The greater his preference and the more important the issue, the greater the impact on the vote.

The specific calculus that voters use to estimate their preference between candidates on New Deal social welfare and racial issues rests on several assumptions:

1. Each issue dimension$_j$ is continuous. For convenience I shall represent each dimension by a scale that ranges between 0.0 and 1.0. The 0.0 endpoint will be the most liberal position, 1.0 the most conservative.

2. Every voter has a position on each dimension at each election. X_{ijt} will represent the position of voter$_i$ on dimension$_j$ at election$_t$. The triple subscript means that each voter's positions can vary across the two dimensions and over time.

3. Both candidates have positions on each dimension at each election. D_{jt} will denote the Democratic's position on dimension$_j$ at election$_t$; R_{jt} the Republican's position. Like the voter's, candidates' positions can vary across dimensions and across elections.

4. Voters accurately perceive the positions of the candidates on the issues. I assume that all voters make an identical estimate of the candidates' positions and that their estimates are equivalent to the candidates' true stands. Thus, I boldly assume that citizens have perfect information and do not distort candidates' positions.[3]

I believe voters employ a simple rule to calculate their preference for one candidate's position over the other's. If the Democrat is closer to (less distant from) the voter's position than is the Republican, then the voter prefers the Democrat's position to the Republican's. This is a common-sense assumption: voters prefer the closer candidate. Voter$_i$'s preference for the Democratic candidate over the Republican on dimension$_j$ at election$_t$ is written as follows:

$$(P_{D>R})_{ijt} = |X_{ijt} - R_{jt}| - |X_{ijt} - D_{jt}| \qquad (3.2)$$

where $(P_{D>R})_{ijt}$ is the amount of voter$_i$'s preference for the Demo-

---

3. I discuss ways that this assumption can be relaxed in chap. 8.

cratic candidate over the Republican on dimension$_j$ at election$_t$;

X_{ijt} is voter$_i$'s position on dimension$_j$ at election$_t$;

R_{jt} is the Republican candidate's position on dimension$_j$ at election$_t$; and

D_{jt} is the Democratic candidate's position on dimension$_j$ at election$_t$.

If $(P_{D>R})_{ijt}$ is greater than zero, then at election$_t$ voter$_i$ prefers the Democrat's position to the Republican's; if the expression is less than zero, then the voter prefers the Republican's position. If $(P_{D>R})_{ijt}$ is equal to zero, then either the candidates have the exact same position on the dimension or the voter's position is exactly midway between the two candidates'. In either case, the voter is indifferent—he does not prefer one candidate's position over the other's.

The calculus described by equation 3.2 is sometimes referred to as a "city-block" model (Coombs, Daves, and Tversky 1970, pp. 61–62; Rae and Taylor 1973). Of course, it is only one of a number of rules that could be used to represent how voters calculate their preferences for candidates. A commonly used alternative is the Euclidean model in which a voter compares the *squared* distance between his position and the candidates':

$$(P_{D>R})_{ijt}' = (X_{ijt} - R_{jt})^2 - (X_{ijt} - D_{jt})^2 \qquad (3.2')$$

(See, for example, Davis, Hinich, and Ordeshook 1970; Riker and Ordeshook 1973, chap. 11.)

Several features of the city-block model (equation 3.2) make it a more plausible representation than the Euclidean model (equation 3.2'), of how voters calculate their preference for candidates. The city-block model is a more parsimonious decision rule: voters look at simple distances, not squared ones. It seems reasonable to believe that voters would choose a simple rule over a more complicated one.[4]

4. Experiments suggest that people do employ the more parsimonious city-block model (Attneave 1950; Shepard 1964). Slovic, Fischhoff, and Lichtenstein (1977, p. 8) similarly conclude, "In general, people appear to prefer strategies that are easy to justify and do not involve reliance on relative weights, tradeoff functions, or other numerical computations."

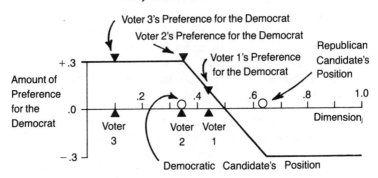

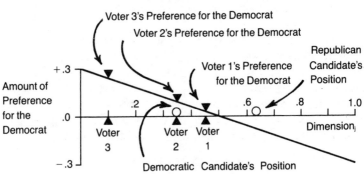

Figure 3.1 A Comparison of City-Block and Euclidean Preference Functions Using Hypothetical Data

An equally compelling reason for relying on the city-block calculus is that its substantive implications seem more plausible than those derived from the Euclidean model. To see this, it helps to use hypothetical data to compare the voter's preferences under the two rules. This comparison, which appears in figure 3.1, assumes that the Democrat has a position of .35 on the dimension and that the more conservative Republican candidate stands at .65. I graph the voter's preference as calculated by the city-block model in panel A and that generated by the Euclidean model in panel B. Each point on the curve represents the amount of preference a voter with a given position (read off the horizontal axis) has for the Democrat over the Republican candidate. For example, in each panel I show a hypothetical voter—Voter 1—who has a position of .45 on the dimension. With the city-block model, his amount of preference for the Democrat over the Republican is .1 ($|.45 - .65| - |.45 - .35|$). With the Euclidean model, the same voter's preference for the Democrat over the Republican is .03 ($[.45 - .65]^2 - [.45 - .35]^2$).

A serious drawback of the Euclidean model is that even as a voter moves to the left, out past the Democrat's position, his preference for the Democrat continues to grow. Voter 3, for instance, has a position of .1, far to the left of both candidates, but by the Euclidean calculus his preference for the Democrat is about three times greater than Voter 2's, even though Voter 2 and the Democratic candidate share the exact same position! This isn't plausible. The anomaly disappears with the city-block calculus. Here the maximum preference for a candidate is reached when his position and the voter's coincide. Voters with positions to the left or right of a given candidate show no greater preference than voters who share his position.[5]

While the city-block model shows how voters might calculate their preferences for candidates on a particular dimension, I still must specify why these preferences affect their vote. Some voters enjoy tangible benefits if their preferred candidate is elected. If a New Deal social welfare liberal wins, for instance, voters might receive an increase in social security or veteran's benefits, job training programs, health insurance, or the like. The psychic benefits derived from supporting a candidate whose positions are similar to their own also motivate voters, who conversely wish to avoid the conflict they would experience from voting for the less preferred candidate.

To incorporate issue preferences into the voter's decision rule, I must bear in mind a point broached earlier. The probability that a voter will cast a ballot for the candidate he prefers on a given

5. As I mentioned, many other models are possible. It is reasonable that the preference for a candidate declines as the voter moves to the left or right of *both* candidates. A voter on the fringes might have less preference for a candidate than a voter whose position is equivalent to that of one of the candidates.

issue depends not only on the strength of his preference, but also on how important the issue is to him in that year. Other things being equal, the greater the importance of an issue to the voter, the higher the probability that he will vote for the candidate whose position on that dimension he prefers. Each year preferences for candidates on the New Deal social welfare and racial issues must be weighted by the importance of the dimension to the voter. I amend the model to include the effect of these issues:

$$V_{it} = \alpha_i + \beta_{i1t}(P_{D>R})_{i1t} + \beta_{i2t}(P_{D>R})_{i2t} + U_{it} \qquad (3.3)$$

where β_{ijt} is the importance of dimension$_j$ to voter$_i$ in election$_t$;

$(P_{D>R})_{ijt}$ is the amount of voter$_i$'s preference for the Democratic candidate (D) over the Republican (R) on dimension$_j$ in election$_t$ as defined in equation 3.2;

j is 1 for the New Deal social welfare dimension and 2 for the racial dimension.

If $(P_{D>R})_{ijt}$ equals zero for both dimensions, then voter$_i$ has probability α_i of voting Democratic. That is, if there is no difference between the positions of the candidates on both dimensions, if the voter's position lies exactly halfway between the candidates' positions on both dimensions, or if both issues are unimportant to the voter, then issues will not affect his vote that year.[6]

MANAGEMENT OF THE ECONOMY

As I have already noted in chapter 2, the incumbent party's management of the economy appears to be an important factor affecting election outcomes. If the economy is in bad shape, or is thought to be, the party in control of the White House suffers at the polls.

Economic concerns affect the vote differently from New Deal social welfare and racial issues. On those issues, it is the degree of the voter's preference for the candidate's positions that affects his decision. When it comes to economic issues, however, this rule is not very helpful because presidential candidates rarely stake out well-articulated alternative economic policies, focusing instead on how well the incumbent administration has managed

6. In chap. 4 I further constrain β_{ijt} to be constant across sets of voters.

the economy. Rather than propose any specific alternative policy, the challenger claims that he, not the incumbent, will control inflation, lower unemployment, increase personal income—in short, bring prosperity. Candidates debate how well the incumbent party has managed the economy, ignoring the mechanisms for achieving good times.

Because citizens cannot compare alternative policy positions (in a spatial sense), the city-block model is of little help here. An alternative decision rule is this:

> If the performance of the incumbent party is "satisfactory" according to some simple standard, the voter votes to retain the incumbent governing party in office to enable it to continue its present policies; while if the incumbent's performance is not "satisfactory" the voter votes against the incumbent, to give the opposition party a chance to govern. [Kramer 1971, p. 134]

This formulation argues that a voter views an election as a "referendum on the *performance* of the governing party" (Niskanen 1975, p. 5)—he punishes the incumbent party for a poor performance, rewards it for a good one. The distinction between this "satisficing" rule and the preference "maximizing" rule used earlier for the New Deal social welfare and racial dimensions should be clear: "Throwing the rascals out is very different from choosing between two or more parties on the basis of their advocacy of alternatives of government action" (Stokes 1966, p. 170). (See Fiorina 1981a.)

Kramer also reasonably hypothesizes that this year's economic expectations are formed relative to last year's economic performance. A voter is satisfied if there is an improvement, unsatisfied if there is a decline. So, the greater the boost in this year's economy over last year's, the greater the likelihood a citizen will vote for the incumbent party; the greater the decline, the greater the likelihood he will vote against the incumbent party.[7] The

---

7. Scholarship subsequent to Kramer's has supported this general formulation. Suggestions that voters base their evaluations on the performance of the incumbent party since the last election, two years before (Stigler 1973), or since the last presidential election four years before (Niskanen 1975), have not fit the data as well as models using as the voters' baseline the previous calendar year (Tufte 1978; Fair 1978). As Fair puts it: "Voters do not look back very far. . . . Voters

incumbent party's management of the economy can be incorporated into the voter's decision rule as follows:

$$V_{it} = \alpha_i + \beta_{i1t}(P_{D>R})_{i1t} + \beta_{i2t}(P_{D>R})_{i2t} + \beta_3(I_t\Delta Y_{it}) + U_{it} \qquad (3.4)$$

where I_t is 1 when the Democrats are the incumbent party, -1
      when the Republicans are; and
      ΔY_{it} is the election year change in the economy.

WAR

The conflicts in Korea and Vietnam were the most prominent issues in 1952 and 1968. Since the electorate turned out the incumbent party in both years, it seems reasonable to think that Truman's and Johnson's handling of the wars had something to do with the outcome of these elections.[8]

Neither Adlai Stevenson nor Dwight Eisenhower presented voters with a clear set of policy alternatives that they would follow if elected in 1952. "Both in Republican propaganda and popular understanding, the issue was simply a matter of the Democrats having gotten the country into a war from which Eisenhower would extract us—whether by bombing Manchuria or evacuating South Korea was not made clear" (Stokes 1966, p. 172). The Democrats were hurt not because voters preferred the superior policy alternatives the Republicans offered, but because of voters' "lack of confidence in the capacity of the Democratic Party to deal with the problem" (Campbell et al. 1960, p. 546; Miller 1967, p. 216).

The candidates treated Vietnam in a similar fashion in 1968. Again, they did not present alternative policies; meaningful differences between Nixon's and Humphrey's positions could not be detected.

Both candidates agreed closely about how many troops should be maintained in Vietnam: they favored a gradual reduction contingent on their

---

do not consider the past performance of the non-incumbent party with respect to the incumbent party, they consider only the events within the year of the election" (1978, p. 171). I test this assumption in chap. 4.

   8. Vietnam was relatively unimportant in 1972; only one citizen in four viewed the war as the most important problem that year, compared to 42 percent in 1968.

replacement of South Vietnamese. . . . Neither candidate specified when withdrawals should begin, what pace they should follow or whether a residual force should remain. . . . Taken as a whole, the Vietnam positions of both candidates amounted to advocacy of war as usual, with a rather gradual de-escalation of American effort if and when certain conditions were met. [Page and Brody 1972, pp. 984–85]

Whatever effect the Korean and Vietnamese wars had on the 1952 and 1968 elections, it certainly could not have resulted from citizens choosing one set of war policies over another. Indeed, if this approach were used to model the voter's choice between candidates, the war's impact would be missed. If Korea and Vietnam affected the election outcome it was because voters viewed the incumbent party's performance as poor. As with the economy, voters punished the party in office for its mismanagement. The greater the dissatisfaction with the administration's conduct of the war, the higher the probability that citizens will cast their ballots for the opposition party. When the nation is at peace, of course, war is not an issue; incumbents are not rewarded for avoiding wars.

It is not entirely clear why some questions become management issues and others policy issues. How candidates, particularly challengers, treat the issue appears to be a crucial factor. Candidates could, of course, formulate a detailed set of economic or military policies that would distinguish them from their opponents. But this hasn't happened. (If Eugene McCarthy or Robert Kennedy had been nominated in 1968, for instance, the Vietnam issue might have easily turned into a debate over distinct courses of action.) The more complex the issue, the greater the uncertainty over what are actually "good policies," the greater the uncertainty over the electorate's position on the issue, and the more the issue cuts across the predominant political cleavage, the more likely candidates are to criticize the incumbent's management of the problem rather than debate alternative solutions. When faced with uncertainty, challengers take the safe course of action: they run against the incumbent's record.

I amend the model to take into account citizens' evaluations of the incumbent party's management of wars:

$$V_{it} = \alpha_i + \beta_{i1t}(P_{D>R})_{i1t} + \beta_{i2t}(P_{D>R})_{i2t} + \beta_3(I_t\Delta Y_{it}) +$$
$$\beta_4(I_tW_{it}) + U_{it} \qquad (3.5)$$

where I_t is 1 when the Democrats are the incumbent party, -1
when the Republicans are; and

W_{it} is citizen$_i$'s assessment of the incumbent party's management of the war at time$_t$. When the United States is
not at war, W_{it} is 0.

INCUMBENCY

It is widely believed that incumbent presidents enjoy enormous
electoral advantages over their opponents. Election results seem
to bear this out: during this century incumbents have won 11 of
the 15 elections in which they have run. Only the most unusual
circumstances have brought defeats. William Taft lost the three-
way 1912 contest against Theodore Roosevelt and Woodrow Wil-
son; Herbert Hoover was denied a second term in the depths of
the Depression; Ford, an appointed president, was defeated in
his first national election in 1976; Carter failed to be reelected in
the worst election year economy since the 1930s. Barring the
extraordinary, incumbents win.[9]

The incumbency advantage may, in part, originate from the
symbolic importance that the president has in citizens' political
perceptions. Americans' respect for the presidency is an out-
growth of childhood perceptions that the president is benevolent
and personifies the government (Greenstein 1960, 1969; Easton
and Dennis 1969; Dennis and Webster 1975). If these early out-
looks shape adult attitudes, they may explain why incumbents
attract so many votes.

9. The incumbency advantage has been estimated to be worth between 3 and
10 percentage points. Political consultant V. Lance Tarrance, for instance, ap-
praises the value of incumbency at about 6 percentage points (Cook 1979, p. 327).
Niskanen (1975) estimates the advantage to be between 3 and 6 points; Fair
(1978) finds it is worth about 3.5 points; Meltzer and Vellrath (1975) estimate that
Johnson was advantaged by between 3.3 and 8.3 points in 1964, while Nixon's
1972 vote was boosted by between 5.0 and 9.8 points. Incumbent members of
Congress are advantaged as well (Kostroski 1973; Mayhew 1974b; Erickson 1972;
Cover 1977; Mann and Wolfinger 1980; Cover and Mayhew 1981; Johannes and
McAdams 1981; and Fiorina 1981b).

Because citizens do not clearly distinguish between the *president* and the *presidency,* the incumbent also benefits from the electorate's attachment to the symbols of office. Voters are impressed by the accouterments of the presidency: Air Force One, the presidential limousine, Secret Service agents, scurrying aides, and of course, the White House (Drew 1977, pp. 28–29; Stroud 1977, p. 392). The president can act "presidential." Incumbents behave as though they are nonpartisan national leaders, hard at work running the government. This Rose Garden strategy allows a president to portray himself not as a politician out campaigning for votes, but as the nation's diligent leader, above the fray—signing bills, meeting with aides and foreign dignitaries, touring military bases (Burke 1971, p. 2940; Friedman 1971, p. 3028; Martin 1971, pp. 2590–91; Pomper 1981, p. 22).

The president, of course, also controls the instrumental resources of office. He has staff, is privy to intelligence data, can shape the political agenda to his benefit, and can make political appointments to attract social and ethnic groups to his coalition (Leuchtenberg 1971, p. 2830; Caddell 1980, p. 66; Polsby 1981, p. 40).

Incumbents design policies with elections in mind. As Pat Caddell advised Carter shortly after the 1976 victory: "We cannot separate politics and government" (1976, p. 2). Economic policy is a particularly important weapon in the incumbent's arsenal. For instance, Carter's 1981 budget, more than his previous ones, was sensitive to the demands made by traditional Democratic, labor, urban, and minority supporters (Tolchin 1980, p. 1). Presidents attempt to make election year economies better than they otherwise would be; they time boosts in transfer payments like social security and veterans' benefits to arrive close to election day (Tufte 1978, chaps. 1 and 2).

Many activities are scheduled to maximize their political impact. Carter's "Economic Revival Plan," which included $27.6 billion in tax cuts, was introduced Labor Day weekend—the opening of the 1980 campaign. The Sunday before the Iowa caucuses Carter formally proposed a boycott of the Summer Olympic games to be held in Moscow; two days before the Illinois primary he further emphasized his strong opposition to the Soviet invasion of Afghanistan by hinting that he would reverse the strategic arms treaty; on the morning of the Wisconsin primary, the president announced an apparent breakthrough in negotiations with Iran for release of U.S. hostages held since November (Pomper 1981, p. 21).

To shore up political support in specific cities or states, the president can strategically distribute "particularized benefits" (Mayhew 1974b, p. 53). The Carter administration, for instance, timed federal grant announcements to maximize their political impact during the primary season:

> Maine received $75.2 million in Federal grants during January, up from $15 million in November and $23 million in December. New Hampshire benefited from $45.2 million in grants during January, again more than twice the amount committed in the two previous months.
>
> Four days before the New York primary, Mr. Carter told interviewers from five New York City television stations that he would soften the effects of his budget cuts with $500 million in new urban assistance. When he announced on March 31, the day before the Wisconsin primary, that he would save $1.5 billion a year by changing the schedule of cost-of-living increases for various programs, he exempted dairy subsidies. [Clark 1980, p. A19]

Carter also punished Kennedy supporters.[10]

The federal bounty is funneled into critical states during the general election campaign as well. To attract Florida's 17 electoral votes in 1976, Ford announced a $33 million missile contract for Martin-Marietta of Orlando and an $18 million mass-transit program for Miami. He agreed to speed up the naturalization of Cubans living in the state and promised to finish Interstate 75 to Fort Meyers (Drew 1977, p. 400). To appease farm states, during the 1980 campaign the Carter administration announced that it would boost price supports by $1 billion (Hudson 1980). It also scrapped Department of Agriculture efforts to head off the pre-election increase in federal milk price supports (Pine 1980, p. 1) and committed $300 million to farmers suffering from drought.

---

10. Shortly after Representative Paul Simon of Illinois endorsed Kennedy, for instance, the city of Carbondale, in Simon's district, was denied a $150,000 urban-development grant that it had expected to receive (Clark 1980, p. A19).

Michigan's 21 electoral votes were wooed by $50 million in hous-
ing and transit grants and $1 million for laid-off automobile and
chemical workers. Vice-president Mondale sailed into a Philadel-
phia navy yard aboard the U.S.S. *Saratoga,* where the aircraft
carrier began a $526 million overhaul that brought thousands of
jobs and millions of dollars in contracts to Pennsylvania (27 electoral votes), Delaware (3), and New Jersey (17). (At the time,
Carter was running neck-and-neck with Reagan in Pennsylvania;
Virginia, which lost the contract, seemed safely in Reagan's column.) The administration delayed school desegregation decisions
that would have alienated some voters in Illinois (26 electoral
votes) and Texas (also 26) (Rosenbaum 1980, p. 32).

The tremendous amount of media coverage that presidents receive certainly must also contribute to their incumbency advantage. As Herbert Gans (1979, p. 9) unsurprisingly concludes:

The single individual who appears in the news most often, year after
year, is the president; and normally, he appears without fail in every
issue of the newsmagazine and on virtually all television news
programs. . . . Unlike other people who get into the news only when
they are involved in unusual, innovative, or dramatic activities, he is the
only individual whose routine activities are deemed newsworthy.

Grossman and Kumar (1981, p. 28) reach a similar conclusion:
"The combined efforts of the White House and the networks
have made the President the single biggest continuing story on
television news."[11]

More important than the sheer volume of stories are the positive images they convey. For every unfavorable story about the
White House, there are two favorable ones. Pictures too, are
overwhelmingly positive. Even negative news items are likely to
be accompanied by a favorable photograph of the president in
the Rose Garden, hard at work in the Oval Office, or leaving
church (Grossman and Kuman 1981, pp. 256–69). This favorable

11. Between 1953 and 1978 the *New York Times* ran on average 9 White House
articles in each issue (including 2 on every front page); *Time* magazine ran 4
stories in each issue. CBS news devoted 4 stories each night to the White House,
one of which appeared before the first commercial break (Grossman and Kumar
1981, p. 264).

coverage is due, in part, to White House control over the media's access to the president. To a large extent, White House staff filter the media's information; they determine when the press will meet with the president; they pick the locality and lay the ground rules (Grossman and Kumar 1981, chaps. 4 and 5).

During the campaign presidents are better covered than their opponents. Nixon received nearly *three times* more air time on the network news than McGovern did in 1972: 112.3 hours for Nixon versus 39.6 hours for McGovern (Patterson and McClure 1976, pp. 34–39). Nixon was advantaged on all three networks: 2.2 times more coverage on CBS; 2.9 times more on NBC; and 3.9 times more on ABC. A similar incumbency advantage prevailed in 1980: between January and September, the CBS evening news devoted six hours and ten minutes to its coverage of Carter, nearly twice the time it spent on Reagan, and four times the air time given to Anderson (Leiser 1980).

The president is, of course, the best-known figure in American politics; 98 percent of the electorate can identify him (Greenstein 1974, p. 124).[12] Voters know more about an incumbent president than they do about his opponent[13] and view him more positively than his challenger.[14]

Finally, presidents may be advantaged because they are able to scare off strong challengers. Franklin Roosevelt faced relatively weak opponents in 1936 and 1944 (Alf Landon and Wendell Willkie); Dwight Eisenhower faced Adlai Stevenson for the second time in 1956; Lyndon Johnson ran against Barry Goldwater in 1964; Richard Nixon faced George McGovern in 1972. Only

12. In contrast, only 57 percent of the public can identify one of their U.S. senators (Greenstein 1974, p. 125).

13. For instance, only 14 percent of the electorate said they knew very little or nothing about Lyndon Johnson in October 1964; more than twice as many—33 percent—knew very little or nothing about Barry Goldwater (Benhan 1965, p. 186). Citizens made more comments in response to open-ended questions about incumbent presidents in 1956, 1964, 1972, and 1980 than they did to similar questions about the challengers. (Data are from Miller, Miller, and Schneider 1980, pp. 128–30, and Center for Political Studies 1980 National Election Study.)

14. This has held in 5 of the last 6 elections when an incumbent has run. Voters more positively evaluated incumbents than their opponents in 1948, 1956, 1964, 1972, and 1980. (Data are from Tufte 1978, p. 121, and Kagay 1981.)

when modern incumbents have looked exceedingly vulnerable, as in 1932, 1948, 1976, and 1980, have strong challengers emerged. Thus, there may be an incumbency advantage because politicians think there is one and act accordingly (Jacobson and Kernell 1981, chap. 3).[15]

In sum, there is good reason to believe that incumbency affects election outcomes because citizens are more likely to vote for incumbent presidents than for other candidates. The electoral advantage stems from the incumbent's control of the symbols and resources of office, and his ability to influence political events, take popular positions, distribute particularized benefits, dominate the media, and discourage strong challengers from running.

This logic also suggests that when an incumbent *vice*-president seeks the presidency, he too may enjoy advantages of incumbency, but this boost certainly should be less than an incumbent president's. Although a vice-president is widely recognized by the electorate, has had national campaign experience, and enjoys some prestige of office, he cannot structure events, command attention, or manipulate the symbols of office as effectively as the president.

Vice-presidential incumbency may even be a liability:

[A vice-president] suffers from the disadvantages both of having to defend an existing record and of being a new man. He cannot attack the administration in office without alienating the President and selling his own party short, and he cannot claim he has experience in office. It may be difficult for him to defend a record he did not make and may not wholly care for. His is the most difficult strategic problem of all the candidates. [Polsby and Wildavsky 1976, p. 75]

These constraints might erode whatever advantage that recognition and prestige would bring. Nixon's fate in 1960 and Humphrey's in 1968 lend credence to Polsby and Wildavsky's assessment and make one doubt that vice-presidents are advantaged.

---

15. Incumbents not only scare away good challengers but, by virtue of already having reached the presidency, are also probably better candidates than the average contender.

In equation 3.6 I incorporate these incumbency effects into the model:

$$V_{it} = \alpha_i + \beta_{i1t}(P_{D>R})_{i1t} + \beta_{i2t}(P_{D>R})_{i2t} + \beta_3(I_t\Delta Y_{it}) +$$
$$\beta_4(I_tW_{it}) + \beta_5(I_tPI_t) + \beta_6(I_tVPI_t) + U_{it} \qquad (3.6)$$

where I_t is 1 when the Democrats are the incumbent party, -1 when the Republicans are;

PI_t is 1 when an incumbent president is running, 0 otherwise;

VPI_t is 1 when an incumbent vice-president is running for president, 0 otherwise.

I expect that β_5 and β_6 will be positive and that β_5 will be greater than β_6—the presidential incumbency effect should be greater than the vice-presidential incumbency effect.

HOME-STATE AND REGIONAL EFFECTS

It is common wisdom that candidates run well in their own home state and region. This expectation is most clearly evident in the selection of vice-presidential nominees. Running mates are ordinarily chosen to "balance" the ticket (Key 1964, p. 429; Pomper 1966, pp. 159–63; Polsby and Wildavsky 1976, pp. 145–50; Sindler 1976, p. 31). Politicians balance tickets to unify their party and to boost their vote in November. Ticket balancing can take a number of forms: a presidential nominee selects a running mate to appeal to specific racial or ethnic groups or to politicians who lost the nomination (Johnson's selection in 1960); to emphasize specific issues in the campaign (Nixon's selection in 1952 to exploit the issue of alleged Communist infiltration in the federal civil service); or to balance the ticket ideologically (Mondale's selection by Carter in 1976).

A balanced ticket usually also means that the presidential and vice-presidential candidates come from different regions. Seventeen of the eighteen major party tickets since 1948 have been regionally balanced. Needless to say, this is not accidental—regional balance is an explicit calculation in the vice-presidential selection process (Witcover 1977, p. 316). Only northerners ap-

peared on Carter's 1976 vice-presidential short list.[16] Ford selected Dole of Kansas to shore up farm belt support in the Midwest (Witcover 1977, pp. 109; 501–10; Schram 1977, p. 236).

The premise underlying this balancing strategy is that citizens
are more likely to vote for candidates from their own home state
and region than for candidates from other sections of the country. (See, for example, Sorenson 1965, pp. 187–88; 215.) Voters
may be more familiar with a home-state candidate, may have
even voted for him in the past, and thus may be more likely to
vote for him in a presidential contest.[17] Moreover, they may reason that they are helping to elect a person who will understand
and promote their interests.

V. O. Key, Jr. (1949) found a similar "friends-and-neighbors"
politics at work at midcentury in the South, particularly Alabama. A southern candidate wins support "not primarily for what
he stands for or because of his capacities, but because of where
he lives." Voters are more likely to "back the home town boy"
(p. 41) than candidates from other parts of the state. This same
process may operate on a regional level as well. Regional pride
and the belief that Carter would promote southern interests, observers suggest, increased support in his native South. Citizens
may vote for a candidate from their home area because his policy
positions are likely to coincide with their own. Because voters'
preferences for the candidates on the New Deal social welfare
and racial dimensions are already taken into account, for presidential candidates, at least, I will be able to distinguish the
friends-and-neighbors effect from issue voting.

While politicians seem to be convinced of the significance of
state and regional effects, most political scientists disagree
(Polsby and Wildavsky 1976, p. 150). Key, writing nearly thirty
years ago, doubted whether regional loyalties accounted for
much in presidential elections:

16. They were Muskie (Maine), Church (Idaho), Glenn (Ohio), Stevenson
(Illinois), Jackson (Washington), Rodino (New Jersey), and Mondale (Minnesota).

17. The congressional incumbency advantage results, in part, from name recognition alone (Nelson 1978).

In recent decades the issues and forces of national politics have tended to wear down sectional groupings. The new issues push people, wherever they live, towards divisions different from the traditional sectional cleavages and the states gradually have become more alike in the manner of their presidential voting. . . . Sectionalism in national politics may very well be undergoing a decline. [Key 1956, pp. 26–27]

Others have also found an increased nationalization of politics (Stokes 1967, pp. 182–202).

If state and regional friends-and-neighbors effects do exist, I suspect that their impact will be small—a few percentage points at most—and that the home state and regional presidential candidate effects will be greater than those for vice-presidential candidates. Moreover, home-state effects should be greater than regional effects. These candidate characteristics are incorporated into the model as follows:

$$V_{it} = \alpha_i + \beta_{i1t}(P_{D>R})_{i1t} + \beta_{i2t}(P_{D>R})_{i2t} + \beta_3(I_t\Delta Y_{it}) +$$
$$\beta_4(I_tW_{it}) + \beta_5(I_tPI_t) + \beta_6(I_tVPI_t) + \beta_7(SDP_{it} - SRP_{it}) +$$
$$\beta_8(SDVP_{it} - SRVP_{it}) + \beta_9(RDP_{it} - RRP_{it}) +$$
$$\beta_{10}(RDVP_{it} - RRVP_{it}) + U_{it} \qquad (3.7)$$

where SDP_{it} is 1 when the Democratic presidential nominee is from voter$_i$'s state, 0 otherwise;

SRP_{it} is 1 when the Republican presidential nominee is from voter$_i$'s state, 0 otherwise;

$SDVP_{it}$ is 1 when the Democratic vice-presidential nominee is from voter$_i$'s state, 0 otherwise;

$SRVP_{it}$ is 1 when the Republican vice-presidential nominee is from voter$_i$'s state, 0 otherwise;

RDP_{it} is 1 when the Democratic presidential nominee is from voter$_i$'s region, 0 otherwise;

RRP_{it} is 1 when the Republican presidential nominee is from voter$_i$'s region, 0 otherwise;

$RDVP_{it}$ is 1 when the Democratic vice-presidential nominee is from voter$_i$'s region, 0 otherwise; and

$RRVP_{it}$ is 1 if the Republican vice-presidential nominee is from voter$_i$'s home region, 0 otherwise.

I expect that β_7 will be greater than β_8, β_9 will be greater than β_{10}, β_7 will be greater than β_9, and β_8 will be greater than β_{10}.

SECULAR POLITICAL TRENDS

Over a series of presidential elections, there may well be a gradual secular shift in a citizen's probability of voting for one party
over the other (Key 1959, p. 199). This trend may be independent of the other factors that affect the vote in any particular
election. Some voters, over time, may grow more likely to vote
Democratic, others to vote Republican. Over the past forty years
southerners' attachment to the Democratic party has gradually
eroded, while northeasterners' allegiance has grown. These secular trends are reflected in the midterm congressional vote. If a
person usually votes Democratic for president but Republican for
Congress, there is a decreasing likelihood that he will vote
Democratic in the next presidential election.

Needless to say, the midterm vote not only measures secular
political trends; it also is sensitive to other short-term changes in
the political environment. Midterm elections are referendums on
the president's performance (Arseneau and Wolfinger 1973;
Tufte 1978, chap. 5). Watergate, the poor economy, and dissatisfaction with Ford's pardon of Nixon all contributed to a higher-
than-usual Democratic vote in the 1974 congressional elections,
for example. While short-term forces and secular political trends
are theoretically distinct constructs, I will not empirically distinguish between their effects. The midterm vote reflects both, and
both probably affects how people vote in the subsequent presidential election.

The effect of secular political trends on presidential elections
may not be a simple one. Three possibilities suggest themselves
(fig. 3.2). First, both parties may be able to convert secular political trends into presidential votes at about the same rate (case 1).
Here, if a citizen's probability of voting Democratic in the midterm election were to increase 30 percent, for example, the magnitude of the effect on his probability of voting Democratic for
president would be the same as a comparable shift in the Republican direction.

The conversion rate may not be symmetrical. If a voter's probability of voting Democratic in the midterm election increases,
the marginal increase in his probability of voting Democratic for

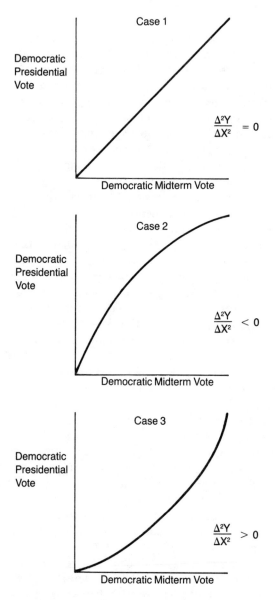

Figure 3.2 Alternative Effects of Secular Trends on Presidential Elections

president may be *less* than the marginal boost to the Republicans from a comparable shift in their direction. In this second case, Democratic secular political trends are less efficiently converted to Democratic presidential votes than Republican trends are converted to Republican presidential votes. To put it differently, a Democratic presidential candidate enjoys a smaller payoff from pro-Democratic political changes than a Republican presidential candidate receives from pro-Republican trends.

The final case is the opposite of this second one. Although an unequal conversion rate still prevails, here Democratic trends are more efficiently converted to Democratic votes than Republican trends are converted to Republican presidential votes. The next chapter shows which of these three cases has prevailed in recent elections.

As a measure of secular political trends, the midterm congressional vote is obviously contaminated by two factors. Some congressional seats (mostly held by Democrats) are uncontested. This means that in some districts a Democratic midterm vote may only reflect the lack of an opportunity to vote Republican. Congressional incumbency also contaminates the midterm vote. Incumbency itself affects how people vote for Congress (Erickson 1972; Cover 1977; Mann and Wolfinger 1980; Cover and Mayhew 1981), so the midterm vote must be purged of this factor as well. Moreover, since the impact of congressional incumbency has probably grown (Erickson 1972; Cover and Mayhew 1981), the correction must vary with time. I will purge the midterm vote of the influence of uncontested congressional seats and incumbent congressional candidates, leaving an uncontaminated measure of secular political trends.

The effect of secular political trends, as well as the corrections for uncontested congressional seats and incumbency, are added to the model as follows:

$$\begin{aligned}
V_{it} = & \ \alpha_i + \beta_{i1t}(P_{D>R})_{i1t} + \beta_{i2t}(P_{D>R})_{i2t} + \beta_3(I_t\Delta Y_{it}) + \\
& \beta_4(I_tW_{it}) + \beta_5(I_tPI_t) + \beta_6(I_tVPI_t) + \beta_7(SDP_{it} - SRP_{it}) + \\
& \beta_8(SDVP_{it} - SRVP_{it}) + \beta_9(RDP_{it} - RRP_{it}) + \\
& \beta_{10}(RDVP_{it} - RRVP_{it}) + \beta_{11}(CONG_{it-2}) + \\
& \beta_{12}(CONG_{it-2})^2 + \beta_{13}(CUNC_{it-2}) + \beta_{14}(CINC_{it-2}) + \\
& \beta_{15}(CINC_{it-2} \times Time) + U_{it}
\end{aligned} \tag{3.8}$$

where CONG_{it-2} is the probability of citizen$_i$ voting Democratic in the previous midterm congressional election;

CUNC_{it-2} is 1 when a Democrat ran unopposed for the House in the previous midterm election in citizen$_i$'s district, -1 when a Republican ran unopposed, and 0 otherwise;

CINC_{it-2} is 1 when an incumbent Democrat ran for Congress in the previous midterm election in citizen$_i$'s district, -1 when an incumbent Republican ran for Congress, and 0 otherwise.

β_{11} should be greater than zero. If β_{12} is greater than zero, then Democratic secular political trends are more efficiently converted into Democratic presidential votes than Republican trends into Republican presidential votes. If β_{12} is less than zero, then the opposite asymmetry holds. And if β_{12} equals zero, then Democratic and Republican secular trends convert into presidential votes with equal efficiency. Since CUNC_{it-2} corrects the midterm congressional vote for uncontested races, β_{13} should be negative. β_{14} likewise should be negative, since CINC_{it-2} purges the midterm vote of the effect of congressional incumbency. β_{15} should be negative if the congressional incumbency effect has grown over time.

Equation 3.8 summarizes the forces that I believe explain presidential elections and changes in their outcome. There is an underlying stability—the usual vote—that gets modified by the conditions that prevail in a given election. Changes in either citizens' preferences on the issues, the candidates' stands, or the importance of the issues change the electoral outcome. When the economy or wars are mismanaged, the incumbent party suffers at the polls. Outcomes are also affected by whether an incumbent president or vice-president is running. The home state and region of the candidates may also matter. Other secular political trends that erode people's allegiance to their parties probably affect who wins the presidency. Why the Democrats win one year but lose another can be understood by examining these changes in the voters, the candidates, and the electoral setting.

4

DETERMINANTS OF ELECTION OUTCOMES: 1948–72

So far, I have identified a set of factors that might explain changes in election outcomes. Forecasts cannot be made until it is known how much weight should be assigned to each variable. How much impact does the economy have compared, say, to presidential incumbency or racial issues? The effect of each variable will be estimated from 1948 to 1972 election data. Before examining the results, I will briefly describe the data and how the estimates are made.

Ideally, since the theory concerns how electoral settings affect individual behavior, individual-level data should be used. Appropriate survey data are not available, however. For many variables in the model there are no data; for some questions the wording has changed over time; others have been asked only in a few elections; some items are extremely unreliable.[1] Moreover, since there are few state-by-state surveys, state popular vote results or the electoral college outcomes cannot be forecasted. National surveys do not typically interview people from all fifty states and include only a few respondents from any single state.[2]

1. For instance, there are no data on how respondents usually vote, and questions that ask voters to recall their vote in previous elections are notoriously unreliable (Keith et al. 1977, p. 35; Brody 1977, p. 23n). Survey measures of fluctuations in economic well-being only exist for elections since 1956, and are unreliable indicators of an individual's true change in economic welfare.

2. For example, the Center for Political Studies 1972 National Election Survey did not interview people in 13 states; it surveyed 45 or fewer respondents in 16 other states who were not a representative sample of the state's population.

A different set of problems is encountered with national aggregate data. There are few data points (only 9 since 1948); many variables are difficult to measure at the national level, others are nearly collinear. State popular vote outcomes and the national electoral vote still cannot be forecasted.[3]

I will use state-level aggregate data from the 1948 to 1972 presidential elections to estimate the model's coefficients. The unit of analysis is an election within a state; the seven years are pooled to yield 343 cases.[4] To be compatible with the state data, the model discussed in the last chapter must be aggregated across voters in the state at each election. Thus, V_{it} can be thought of as no longer representing the probability that $individual_i$ will vote Democratic at $election_t$, but the sum of these individual probabilities: the Democratic percent of the presidential vote in the $state_i$ at $election_t$. Among the advantages that arise from using state data is that variables that could not be measured with survey data can be estimated at the state level (e.g., average presidential vote, midterm congressional vote, and change in economic well-being). Not only can state popular vote projections be made, but national electoral college and national popular vote forecasts can also be generated.[5]

Even state-level data, however, have a drawback: biased and inconsistent estimates will result unless the individual-level parameters are the same for all citizens (Theil 1954; Theil 1971, pp. 556–63).[6] (This bias, however, should be smaller than the bias that would occur if national-level data were used.)

3. The electoral vote might be estimated by an equation similar to the one reported early in chap. 2, n. 27.

4. Alabama is deleted in 1964 because the Democrats' votes were not tallied.

5. Disaggregation of the national popular vote forecast into individual state forecasts that are later reaggregated has the added advantage of reducing the variance of the national forecast if the state errors are independent (Armstrong 1978, pp. 455–58).

6. This assumption is tested by including in the equation interaction terms that allow the effect of variables to vary across types of states. But, as Achen (1979a, p. 3) warns, a variable's impact can still vary across cases at the micro level even though an interaction term is insignificant at the macro level. Although only a few interaction terms appear (they are reported in table 4.1), this does not guarantee that the micro-level model is properly specified.

I discuss in appendix A the method used to measure preferences for candidates on New Deal social welfare and racial issues. In appendix B I provide the details of the dummy variable generalized least squares (GLS) procedure used to estimate the model's coefficients and describe the coding procedures and sources of the data in appendix C. The estimated coefficients are reported in table 4.1. The remainder of the chapter discusses each variable's effect on the 1948 to 1972 elections.

USUAL PRESIDENTIAL VOTE

Some states usually vote Democratic, others Republican. Nebraska, Idaho, Kansas, Vermont, Utah, Arizona, Wyoming, New Hampshire, Indiana, and Nevada were about 25 percent more Republican over the 1948–72 period than the least Republican states (fig. 4.1). The former Confederacy, plus Massachusetts, Rhode Island, West Virginia, Hawaii, Delaware, and Minnesota, were Democratic strongholds.[7] While the usual presidential vote differentiates Democratic states from Republican ones, it alone is a poor predictor of how states will vote in any particular election.[8] Other, election-specific variables, discussed in this chapter, cause citizens to deviate from their usual presidential vote.

ISSUES, ISSUE IMPORTANCE, AND CANDIDATE POSITIONS

There is considerable controversy over the extent to which issues affect voting in presidential elections. Although issues are thought to have had very little influence in the 1950s (Campbell et al. 1960), some scholars believe that they now play a much greater role. Citizens' positions on racial issues, social welfare issues, and the war in Vietnam are thought to have had a substantial effect on the 1968 vote (Boyd 1972). Ideology and issues

7. The South's Democraticness, in part, is due to my counting Thurmond's 1948 votes as Democratic votes.
8. A model with only the usual presidential vote as a right-hand-side variable has an average state error of 8.6 percentage points; the standard error of the regression is 12.4 percent. This compares to an average miss of 2.9 percent and a standard error of 4.5 percent for the model reported in table 4.1.

Table 4.1 Causes of Presidential Election Outcomes, 1948–72

Variable	Coefficient	Standard Error
New Deal social welfare issues		
North '48, '60, '64, '72	.099	.037
North '68	.181	.061
South '60, '64, '68, '72	.209	.085
Racial issues		
North '48, '64, '72	.081	.047
North '68	.171	.068
South '52, '68, '72	.974	.154
South '56, '60	.694	.211
South '64	1.566	.126
South '48, '68 (3rd party)	.440	.093
Change in real disposable income per capita	.701	.143
Change in real disposable income per capita squared	-2.442	1.062
Incumbent president	.041	.032
Incumbent president × the congressional vote(t-2) for the opposition party	.096	.034
Incumbent vice-president	.039	.018
Home-state presidential candidate	.039	.013
Home-state vice-presidential candidate	.025	.014
Home-state third-party presidential candidate	- .091	.037
Southern presidential candidate	.027	.019
Catholic population (1960 only)	.109	.056
Mismanagement of war	- .156	.079
Congressional vote(t-2)	.507	.176
Congressional vote(t-2) squared	- .209	.143
Uncontested congressional seats(t-2)	- .036	.029
Incumbent congressional seats(t-2)	.031	.011
Incumbent congressional seats(t-2) × time	- .009	.002
State Intercepts		
Nebraska	- .096	.019
Idaho	- .088	.018
Kansas	- .088	.019
Vermont	- .088	.020
Oklahoma	- .068	.019
Utah	- .064	.018
Arizona	- .055	.019
Wyoming	- .055	.019
New Hampshire	- .051	.019
Colorado	- .050	.019
Nevada	- .050	.019

Variable	Coefficient	Standard Error
Indiana	- .050	.019
Maine	- .044	.019
Illinois	- .041	.019
Iowa	- .038	.019
New Mexico	- .038	.019
New Jersey	- .036	.019
Montana	- .033	.019
North Dakota	- .033	.019
Wisconsin	- .032	.019
South Dakota	- .030	.020
Washington	- .024	.018
Ohio	- .024	.018
Alaska	- .023	.025
Oregon	- .023	.019
Connecticut	- .021	.019
Maryland	- .020	.018
Kentucky	- .014	.019
New York	- .014	.019
Pennsylvania	- .011	.018
Michigan	- .010	.018
Missouri	- .001	.019
Minnesota	.006	.019
Delaware	.007	.018
Hawaii	.008	.025
West Virginia	.022	.019
Rhode Island	.034	.020
Massachusetts	.042	.020
Virginia	.063	.024
Tennessee	.071	.023
Florida	.076	.026
Texas	.104	.027
Louisiana	.126	.033
North Carolina	.133	.024
Mississippi	.135	.034
Arkansas	.149	.029
Alabama	.154	.031
South Carolina	.158	.032
Georgia	.177	.030
(Constant)	.311	.062

Rho (1956, 1972)	.22
R^2	.93
Standard error	.045
Number of cases	343

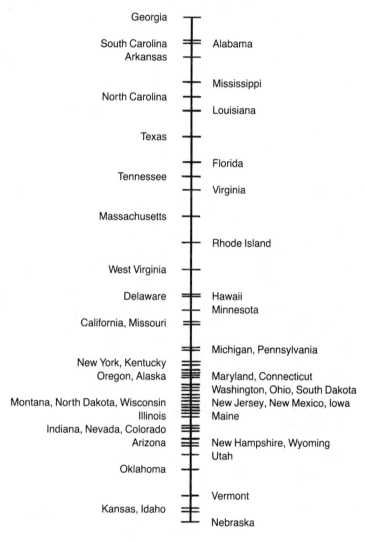

Most Democratic States

Georgia

South Carolina — Alabama
Arkansas

— Mississippi

North Carolina
— Louisiana

Texas

— Florida
Tennessee
— Virginia

Massachusetts

— Rhode Island

West Virginia

Delaware — Hawaii
— Minnesota
California, Missouri

— Michigan, Pennsylvania
New York, Kentucky
Oregon, Alaska — Maryland, Connecticut
Washington, Ohio, South Dakota
Montana, North Dakota, Wisconsin — New Jersey, New Mexico, Iowa
Illinois — Maine
Indiana, Nevada, Colorado
Arizona — New Hampshire, Wyoming
— Utah
Oklahoma

— Vermont
Kansas, Idaho
— Nebraska

Most Republican States

Source: Table 4.1.

Figure 4.1 Usual Presidential Vote, 1948–72

are seen as important determinants of the outcome in 1972 (Miller et al. 1976). Nie, Verba, and Petrocik (1976, chap. 10) argue that since the relationship between political attitudes and the vote has increased and citizens are now more likely to refer to issues when they evaluate candidates and parties, issue voting has risen. Not everyone agrees. Popkin and associates (1976, pp. 782–84) claim that while issues were important in 1972, they had no greater impact than two decades earlier.[9]

9. Several problems plague these individual level estimates. They are all cross-sectional analyses subject to the problems I raised in chap. 1. In addition, some assessments are based on standardized regression coefficients ("betas") or correlation coefficients (e.g., Pomper 1972; Nie, Verba, and Petrocik 1976). These coefficients, unlike unstandardized slopes, or percentages in a table, are sensitive not only to an issue's effect but to the variance of the variables as well. An issue may have the same impact in two elections, but if either the variance of the vote changes (a close election instead of a landslide) or the variance of voters' issues positions changes (consensus instead of polarization), the correlation coefficient or standardized regression coefficient also will change (Cain and Watts 1970; Achen 1977). Thus, conclusions about the effect of issues, or the change over time in their effect, based either on correlation coefficients or standardized regression coefficients, are suspect. The "normal vote" procedure employed by Miller et al. (1976), Boyd (1972), and others, leads to misleading results, but for different reasons (Achen 1979b).

It is also inappropriate to assume that the effect of issue preferences on the vote explains the entire relationship between the two variables. For some citizens (the policy voters), causality runs from opinion to behavior. For others, causality may run from behavior to opinion (Page and Brody 1972, p. 452). What is thought to be issue voting might actually be citizens rationalizing their positions to be consistent with their candidate choice, learning their candidate's position after the vote decision has been made, or projecting their own positions onto the candidate they favor. If these other processes are at work, recursive models will yield biased and inconsistent estimates of the effect of issues. Although simultaneous equation methods have been employed to take into account these other processes (Page and Jones 1979; Markus and Converse 1979), the estimates are so inefficient that it is extremely difficult to make reliable comparisons of the impact of issues over time.

Some of these problems go away at the aggregate level. Exogenous measures of voter preferences for candidates on the issues—measures not contaminated by rationalization, persuasion, learning, or candidate choice—are used (appendix A). Pooled data from the 1948 to 1972 presidential elections allow for consistent and efficient estimates of the effect of issues as well as reliable tests of whether their effect has changed over time. However, the gains are not without cost: there are measurement problems, I am restricted to two issue dimensions, and some assumptions about voters, outlined in chap. 3, must be made.

New Deal Social Welfare Issues

Two factors contribute to the effect that an issue has on the vote: the amount of preference voters have for one candidate over the other and the importance of the dimension to the electorate. When an issue is unimportant, voters' preferences for a candidate on that issue have very little impact on their vote. The more important the dimension, the larger the effect voter preferences will have on the outcome. The coefficients reported in table 4.1 are estimates of the aggregate electoral importance of the New Deal social welfare and racial dimensions in each election. The larger the coefficient, the more important the set of issues is to voters in that election. Each dimension's importance varies by region: different parameters are estimated for southern states than for the rest of the country. When coefficients within a region appeared (in preliminary analysis) to be the same in two or more years, only one parameter was estimated for that set of elections.

How much New Deal social welfare issues contribute to a state's presidential vote is learned by multiplying the amount of the state's preference for the Democrat over the Republican by the importance of the dimension in that year. To gauge how much New Deal social welfare issues affect the vote each year, the marginal impact of the dimension in the most liberal state must be compared to the marginal effect in the most conservative state. That is, in that year how much more likely is the most liberal state to vote Democratic compared to the most conservative state, once other features of the electoral context have been taken into account? I report these estimates in figure 4.2.[10]

The electoral impact of New Deal social welfare issues has increased over time. The fifties were indeed "issueless"—at least, these issues had no detectable effect on election outcomes.[11] But these years do not characterize the entire 1948–72 period. The

10. Variables to estimate the effect of preference for third-party candidates in 1948 and 1968 are included in the model. The 1948 variables are preference for Thurmond over Dewey; in 1968 they are preference for Wallace over Humphrey. The calculated effect of issues in these years (as reported in figs. 4.2 and 4.3) takes into account both preference for the Democrat over the Republican as well as preference for the minor party candidates.

11. $Pr = .52$.

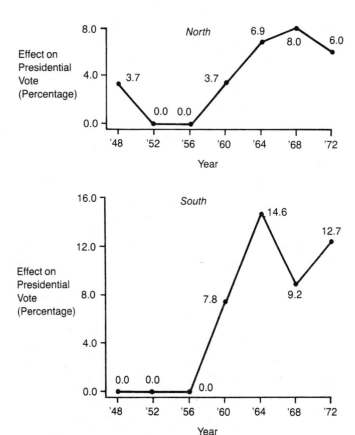

Source: Table 4.1.

Figure 4.2 Effect of New Deal Social Welfare Issues on Presidential Elections, 1948–72, by Region

most liberal northern state in 1960 was 3.7 percentage points more Democratic than the most conservative one. The effect in 1964 was 6.9 points; 8.0 points in 1968; and 6.0 points in 1972. The 3.7 percent effect of New Deal social welfare issues in 1948 further highlights the uniqueness of the 1952 and 1956 elections. Election outcomes changed, in part, because the effect of New Deal social welfare issues changed.

A similar picture emerges in the South. As in the rest of the country, these issues had no discernible impact on the vote during the 1950s.[12] Like the North, their impact increased in 1960 to 7.8 percentage points, and rose further in 1964 to 14.6 points. The effect decreased to 9.2 points in 1968 and 12.7 points in 1972. With the exception of 1968, between 1960 and 1972 New Deal social welfare issues had about twice as much impact on election outcomes in the South as in the rest of the country.

Racial Issues

Racial issues had about the same effect in the North as New Deal social welfare issues did (fig. 4.3). The most racially liberal northern state was 2.2 percentage points more Democratic in 1948 than the most conservative state. Race had a 4.6 percentage point effect in 1964, 8.0 point effect in 1968, and a 4.2 percentage point effect in 1972. The "issueless fifties" again stand out; racial issues had an inconsequential impact between 1952 and 1960.[13]

In contrast, racial issues had a huge effect on how southern states voted throughout the 1948–72 period. Compared to the most racially liberal state in the union, the most conservative southern state was less Democratic by 21.4 percentage points in 1948; 23.8 points in 1952; 16.9 points in 1956; and 16.8 points in 1960. As civil rights activities increased and federal legislation and court decisions aimed at the South took hold, the impact of racial issues on the southern vote grew. If the most conservative southern state had been as liberal as the most liberal state in the union, between 1964 and 1972 nearly all its vote would have gone to the Democrats. Johnson's popular vote would have increased by about 90.2 percentage points; Humphrey's 1968 vote would have increased by about 82.4 points; McGovern's 1972 vote would have increased by about 51.4 percentage points.[14] The increased importance of racial issues explains southern defections from the Democratic party in these years. The huge impact of race in the South between 1964 and 1972 stands in contrast both

12. Pr = .40.
13. Pr = .60.
14. These estimates extrapolate beyond the range of the data and thus are somewhat unreliable.

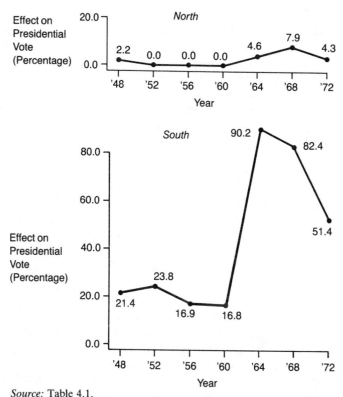

Source: Table 4.1.

Figure 4.3 Effect of Racial Issues on Presidential Elections, 1948–72, by Region

to the more modest effects in the rest of the country over the entire 1948–72 period and to the 17 to 24 percentage point effects in the South between 1948 and 1960.

In sum, at least on these two dimensions, issue voting has increased. New Deal social welfare issues had a greater impact on the 1964, 1968, and 1972 elections than in earlier years. The rise can, in part, be attributed to an increase in the importance of these issues to voters. However, most of the rise results from an increase in policy differences between the candidates. Relatively little distance separated the major party nominees between 1948 and 1960: they stood an average of 15 units apart on the 100-point racial and New Deal social welfare scales. This average difference nearly doubled, to 28 units, in the 1964, 1968, and 1972 elections. (See fig. A.5 in appendix A.) The greater the distance between the candidates' positions, the greater a voter's preference for one candidate over the other. The greater the preference, the greater the effect the issue has on the vote. These issues matter more when candidates present voters with clear choices.

MANAGEMENT OF THE ECONOMY

The election year economy has a substantial impact on election outcomes (fig. 4.4). A 5 percent change in real disposable income per capita (ΔY) produces a 2.9 percent change in the state popular vote.[15] The effect is nonlinear: the marginal effect of ΔY decreases; the next 5 percent increment in income yields only an additional 1.7 points. The marginal effect of more than a 10 percent change in real disposable income per capita is negligible.

Voters have short memories. They compare their current economic well-being to conditions that prevailed a year ago, not those in either the previous midterm year (Stigler 1973) or the previous presidential election year (Niskanen 1975).[16] In a similar vein, accelerations in income (the election year change relative to the previous year's change) do not affect the vote.[17] Neither positive nor negative accelerations in income, alone, matter either.

The effect of ΔY is symmetrical. That is, the impact (in absolute magnitude) of an increase in real disposable income is the same as the effect of a decrease. Voters reward parties just as much as they punish them. I find no support for the claim that parties are punished for bad economic times but go unrewarded

---

15. This estimate is half the size of Tufte's (1978) national-level estimate of 6.5 percent and is about twice the size of Kramer's (1971) estimate of a 1.4 percent effect.

16. The coefficient for the second year difference is .094 with a standard error of .131 (pr = .36). A distributed lag model is equally fruitless: the coefficients truncate after the first year.

17. The coefficient is .019; the standard error is .108 (pr = .57).

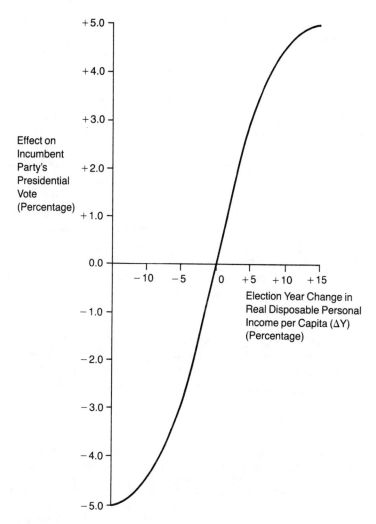

Source: Table 4.1.

Figure 4.4 Effect of Election Year Change in Real Disposable Personal Income per Capita on Presidential Elections, 1948–72

for good times (Bloom and Price 1975, p. 1244).[18] In addition, bad times hurt Republicans as much as Democrats.[19] There is no political asymmetry (Bloom and Price [1975] and Meltzer [1975] notwithstanding). The electorate is evenhanded in its treatment of the two parties.

Unemployment does not have an independent effect on the outcome of presidential elections. Whether one looks at the proportion of the electorate that is unemployed, the percentage point change in unemployment, or percent change in unemployment, the impact is negligible.[20] Moreover, voters do not systematically vote Democratic (presumably for policy reasons) when unemployment is high (Kiewiet 1982). Although unemployment clearly affects the aggregate level of personal income, it does not have an independent, direct effect on election outcomes. Recessions affect nearly everyone, but relatively few people are unemployed. Only twice between 1948 and 1972 has more than 6 percent of the labor force been out of work in an election year. And, as I have demonstrated elsewhere (Rosenstone 1982), the unemployed are less likely to vote—many potential punishers do not make it to the polls.

Inflation also does not exert an independent effect on the vote. High inflation's only impact is through its likely reduction of per capita real disposable income. If income keeps pace with inflation, then the incumbent party does not suffer at the polls.[21]

KOREA AND VIETNAM

Korea and Vietnam were responsible, in part, for Republican victories in 1952 and 1968.[22] By election day of 1952, the Korean

18. The probability that the coefficient for increases is different from the coefficient for decreases in income is only .75. The substantive difference is also small.

19. The probability that the effect of ΔY is different when Republicans occupy the White House than when Democrats do is less than .35.

20. All the coefficients are substantively tiny; none has more than a .5 probability of being different from zero.

21. This last conclusion is a bit tenuous because only national-level, not state-level, measures of inflation are available over the 1948–72 period.

22. Detailed evidence on this point is thin. Campbell et al. (1960, fig. 19-1) show only that voters' attitudes on foreign policy issues favored the Republican

war was in its third year; casualties had passed the 200,000 mark. Less than a month before, truce negotiations (which had begun only fourteen months earlier) recessed indefinitely. "Frustration and resentment over the stalemated Korean War, which had never been well understood by the American people, were widespread and intense" (Campbell et al. 1960, p. 527). A plurality of the public thought the United States' involvement in Korea was a mistake (Mueller 1973, p. 46). Lack of confidence in the Democrats' capacity to end the war was reflected in the public's belief, by a margin of 2 to 1, that the Republicans were the party of peace (*Gallup Opinion Index,* September 1976, p. 6).

A similar situation prevailed in 1968. Full-scale U.S. involvement in the fighting was in its fourth year; casualties approached 250,000. Peace negotiations had not yet begun and prospects for an early end to the war looked bleak. Americans resented the administration's handling of the war; a majority of the public thought the U.S. had made a mistake sending troops to fight in Vietnam (Mueller 1973, p. 55). Although between 1961 and 1966 the public viewed the Democrats as the party of peace, by a 2-to-1 margin, the Republican party seemed the best hope in 1968 (*Gallup Opinion Index,* September 1976, p. 6).

The estimated effect of the Korean and Vietnam wars, reported in table 4.1, can be summarized as follows: for every 10 percent of the electorate that opposed the handling of the war, the incumbent party lost approximately 1.6 percentage points at the polls. The Korean war cost the Democrats about 6 percent of the popular vote in 1952. Vietnam cost the Democrats approximately 8 percent of the popular vote in 1968.[23] Democratic mis-

party in 1952. Popkin et al. (1976, p. 784) claim that Republicans gained about 3.4 percent of the vote because of foreign policy issues in 1952. Converse et al. (1969, table 5) report that among whites, positions on Vietnam are correlated with ratings of Nixon, Humphrey, and Wallace. (All these estimates are subject to the simultaneity bias discussed in n. 9 of this chapter). Page and Brody (1972, p. 994), on the other hand, conclude that because voters could not perceive clear differences between the parties on Vietnam "policy preferences had little effect on the major-party vote."

23. This estimate is inefficient, because only a national-level measure for the variable is available. Yet I am 95 percent certain that a 10 percentage point increase in opposition will decrease the incumbent party vote total by between .06

management of these wars was an important determinant of the 1952 and 1968 election outcomes. If public confidence in the Democrats' ability to end these wars had been greater, or the wars had been concluded, the election results would have been different.

INCUMBENCY

Incumbents, as I argued in chapter 3, have advantages over their challengers—advantages that can be directly translated into votes on election day. They control political resources, enjoy the prestige and symbols of office, profit from their tremendous amount of press coverage, both before and during the campaign, and are likely to be more widely known than their opponents, to encounter weak challengers, and to structure events in their favor.

The incumbency advantage is not constant across states. It is smallest (about 6 percent) in states that voted most heavily for the incumbent party in the previous midterm election and highest (about 10 percent) in states that were least supportive of the president's party. In other words, where the president already enjoys support, the marginal effect of incumbency is less than where his party is relatively weak. When a Republican president runs for reelection, his incumbency has a greater impact on Democratic voters than on Republicans, who are likely to vote for the incumbent anyway. Incumbency, it appears, is more effective in neutralizing the opposition's vote than in increasing support within one's own party.

The incumbency effect is the same for Democratic presidents (Truman and Johnson) as for Republican ones (Eisenhower and Nixon).[24] However, even though incumbency is not intrinsically more valuable to Republicans, because of the current division of

---

and 3.6 percentage points. I am 95 percent certain that the effect of the Korean war was between .3 and 12.9 percent and that the effect of Vietnam was between .3 and 16.5 percent. These estimates are similar to Niskanen's (1975) finding that war reduced the incumbent party's vote by between 5 and 9 percentage points in 1944, 1952, and 1968.

24. There are fewer than 6 chances in 100 that the effect for a Democratic incumbent is different from that of a Republican incumbent.

partisan allegiance and incumbency's greater impact on members of the opposition party, Republican incumbents are likely to enjoy a slightly bigger boost. Finally, although at the congressional level the incumbency effect has grown, presidential incumbency is worth about the same over the entire 1948 to 1972 period.[25]

When an incumbent vice-president seeks the presidency, he enjoys a small vote advantage—about 3.9 percentage points.[26] Unlike the presidential advantage, this effect is constant across all types of citizen: vice-presidents are not more likely to woo members of the opposition party. These incumbency estimates are internally consistent: as expected, the vice-president's electoral advantage is smaller than the president's.

HOME STATE AND REGION

Politicians believe that candidates run better in their home states and regions. Modest home-state effects do exist, but regional effects generally do not. Between 1948 and 1972, 11 of the 14 major party presidential nominees carried their home states. After the usual state party vote, issue preferences for the candidates, and the other factors that affect election outcomes are taken into account, a presidential candidate attracts an additional 3.9 percent of his home state's vote.[27]

The home-state advantage for vice-presidential nominees, as might be expected, is smaller than the one for presidential candidates. Between 1948 and 1972 only 8 of the 14 vice-presidential candidates carried their home states. Voters in the vice-presidential nominee's home state are 2.5 percent more likely to vote for his ticket than they otherwise would be.[28] This means that parties

25. This holds even when 1976 is added to the analysis. The estimated incumbency advantage may be off because of selection bias. If incumbents bow out when their prospects for reelection look bleak and run when they look good (Jacobson and Kernell 1981), then the estimated incumbency effect may be biased (Achen 1983).

26. The 95 percent confidence interval is .4 to 7.3 percent.

27. The 95 percent confidence interval is 1.2 to 6.5 percent. Third-party candidates Henry Wallace, Strom Thurmond, and George Wallace enjoyed about a 9.1 percentage point home-state advantage.

28. The 95 percent confidence interval is −.3 to 5.2 percent.

should select running mates from high-stake states—ones with a large number of electoral votes. Republicans have done this: of the 9 nominations between 1948 and 1972, 3 were from California, 1 from New York, 1 from Massachusetts, 2 from Maryland, and 1 from Texas—all states that have large blocks of electoral votes. The Democrats have less frequently employed this strategy: only 3 of their last 9 vice-presidential nominees have come from big electoral vote states.

The modest vote advantage in their home state generally does not spill over to surrounding states—a regional friends-and-neighbors effect exists only when a presidential candidate is from the South.[29] Strom Thurmond and George Wallace drew an additional 2.7 percent of the southern vote in 1948 and 1968 because they were southerners. However, in no other election between 1948 and 1972 did presidential candidates run better in their home regions than would be expected on the basis of other factors in the model. Kennedy did not do better in the Northeast than otherwise would be expected;[30] Stevenson, Humphrey and McGovern ran no better in the Midwest than otherwise would be expected. That a friends-and-neighbors effect holds only in the South should not be surprising, given the region's unique historical experience. Moreover, the small effect indicates that the lion's share of Strom Thurmond's and George Wallace's support in the South resulted from their issue stances, particularly on race, rather than their southern background.

The only electoral advantage a party gains from a regionally balanced ticket is the extra 2.5 percent that the running mate pulls in his home state. Beyond this, contrary to what politicians believe, the region of the vice-presidential candidate has nothing to do with election outcomes.[31]

29. This effect did not exist in Texas and Florida, so these states were dropped from the South for estimates of regional candidate effects.

30. Other things being considered, Catholics were about 11 percent more likely to vote for Kennedy in 1960 than non-Catholics. This boosted Kennedy's 1960 national popular vote by 2 to 3 percentage points. This variable, included in the equation reported in table 4.1, only made a difference in 1960. Its effect was about half as large as the impact estimated by Converse (1966b).

31. This conclusion could be wrong for two reasons. Since nearly every ticket studied was regionally balanced, it is hard to tell what would happen if both

SECULAR POLITICAL TRENDS

Secular political trends have a large positive effect on the presidential vote. The marginal impact—after the midterm congressional vote has been purged of the contaminating effect of uncontested house seats and incumbent congressional candidates as well as the other variables in the model—is displayed in figure 4.5.[32] A state that voted 80 percent Democratic in the previous midterm election will be 18 percent more Democratic in the subsequent presidential election than a state that cast only 20 percent of its midterm vote for the Democrats. While by most standards this is a substantial effect, it indicates a very large degree of discontinuity between secular political trends, as reflected in congressional elections, and presidential voting (Ladd and Hadley 1975, chap. 5). Secular trends have not had nearly as much impact on presidential elections as one might expect. A 10 percent shift in the congressional vote would cause less than a 3 percent shift in the presidential vote.

The rate at which secular political trends are converted into presidential votes is different for the two parties. Democratic trends are not as efficiently converted into Democratic presidential votes as Republican trends are into Republican votes. Com-

---

candidates came from the same part of the country (e.g., Alabama and Georgia, or New York and Connecticut). In this situation region itself might become an issue and strong regional effects could emerge. There might also be simultaneity. If vice-presidential candidates are selected because they come from regions where the party anticipates it will run poorly, then I may have underestimated their electoral impact.

32. These two corrections perform as expected. The vote is corrected downward in states where uncontested house seats would distort the midterm vote as a measure of secular trends. For instance, if 50 percent of a state's midterm congressional races had Democrats running unopposed, the effect of the midterm congressional vote on the subsequent presidential vote in the state would be reduced 1.8 percent. Prior to 1960, congressional incumbents had a slight positive effect on the presidential vote. After 1960, as the advantages of congressional incumbency grew and split-ticket voting surged, incumbency caused the congressional vote to overstate the secular political trends present at the midterm election. The midterm vote in a state comprised entirely of Democratic incumbents, for example, overstates the effect of secular political trends by .4 percent in 1960, 1.3 percent in 1964, 2.2 percent in 1968, and 3.1 percent in 1972.

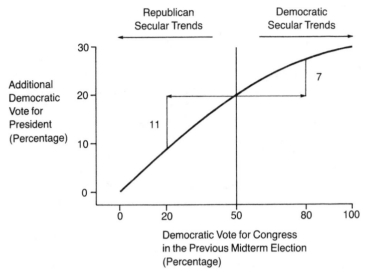

Source: Table 4.1.

Figure 4.5 Effect of Secular Political Trends on Presidential Elections, 1948–72

pared to a state that divided its vote evenly between the two parties in the previous midterm election, a 30-point Democratic gain would yield the Democrats an additional 7 points in the subsequent presidential election. Yet a move of equal magnitude in the Republican direction would produce a G.O.P. presidential vote gain of 11 points—about one and one-half times as great. Thanks to the greater disharmony within the Democratic party and the disintegration of the New Deal coalition, the Democrats are not as successful as the Republicans at translating secular political changes into presidential votes.

CONCLUSION

A variety of factors determines who will win the presidency. Although there is some continuity in the vote from one year to the next, there is abundant volatility. Changes in the electoral context explain changes in outcomes. When the incumbent administration has mismanaged the economy, or a war, voters punish that party. When a candidate is out of step with voter preferences on important issues, he suffers at the polls. Changes in the candidates' positions, the voters' preferences, and the importance of issues all produce changes in election outcomes. The more important the issues are and the greater the difference between the candidates, the greater the impact of issues on the vote. Indeed, as V. O. Key, Jr., (1966) noted, "Voters are not fools."

Other political variables also affect election outcomes. When an incumbent president or vice-president seeks the presidency, his party will do better than otherwise would be expected. Nominees run better in their home states, but only southern presidential candidates bring extra votes to their party from their home region. Secular political trends also affect election results, but the Democrats have been less successful than the Republicans at converting these shifts into presidential votes.

The explanation of election outcomes is not a simple one. No single variable alone will account for changes in the result. A voter's traditional vote; his or her preference for candidates on salient issues; the economic or foreign policy performance of the incumbent administration; candidate characteristics—none of these factors can be considered in isolation. Far from representing alternative theoretical postures among which to choose, each contributes uniquely to our understanding of election outcomes. None of these perspectives alone does a very good job of explaining who wins elections. Together, they not only explain who won but predict who will win.

5
PREDICTIONS: 1948–72

So far I have introduced a theory of elections and have discussed the substantive effect that each variable has on outcomes. But how well does the theory fit the data? This chapter evaluates how well the model explains the 1948 to 1972 elections. I examine the model's within-sample state presidential vote predictions as well as its forecasts of the national popular vote and electoral college results, comparing my errors to those other scholars have made, when available.

The theory does indeed fit very closely. The model explains 93 percent of the variance in the state vote for president; the moderately low standard error of the estimate—.045—indicates that about two-thirds of the within-sample state election forecasts are off by no more than 4.5 percentage points.[1] While these summary statistics give a general sense of the model's explanatory power, a clearer picture emerges if the misses themselves are examined directly.

STATE LEVEL WITHIN-SAMPLE PREDICTIONS

Tables 5.A.1 to 5.A.7, which appear at the end of this chapter, report each state's actual popular vote, its predicted vote, and its error for the 1948 to 1972 elections. Rather than recount, election by election, every state's miss, I have prepared a few charts that summarize these tables.

---

1. The forecast error is slightly smaller in 1956 and 1972 because of the correction for serial correlation in these years.

Table 5.1 Summary of State Errors by Year, 1948–72 (Percentages)

Year	Average State Error	Average State Residual*
1948	2.9	-0.1
1952	2.5	0.1
1956	3.5	0.4
1960	1.9	0.0
1964	3.7	0.1
1968	2.6	-0.1
1972	3.3	-0.4
Total	2.9	0.0

Source: Table 4.1.
* A positive residual indicates that the equation overpredicts the Democratic vote; a negative residual indicates that the equation underpredicts the Democratic vote.

First, I assess the state popular vote errors by election. On average, the state presidential popular vote is missed by 2.9 percentage points (table 5.1). The largest errors occur in "landslide" elections: state vote predictions are off an average of 3.7 percentage points in 1964; 3.5 points in 1956; 3.3 points in 1972. However, the model does not systematically underestimate or overestimate these landslides as seen by the residuals. The equation underpredicts the vote for Eisenhower in 1956 and Johnson in 1964, but overestimates the Nixon victory in 1972. Generally, the state-by-state errors are much smaller in close elections. The average miss is less than 3 percentage points in 1948, 1952, and 1968. The mean state error of the closest election in the sample— 1960—is only 1.9 percentage points. Also, there is no systematic tendency for the model either to underpredict or to overpredict the state-level Democratic vote in these nonlandslide years.[2]

There is variance in the errors: some states are missed by a fraction of a percentage point, others by as much as 7 or 8 points. Half the time, the state presidential vote is predicted within 2.2 percentage points of the actual vote cast. About one-quarter of

2. This is not to suggest that the errors are heteroskedastic. The residual variance is not systematically related to the predicted state margin of victory.

the predictions are off by less than 1 point. Three out of 4 predictions are within 4 points; only 1 state in 20 is missed by more than 8 percentage points. Thus, although in a few instances the model misses the actual state presidential vote by a sizable margin, most of the time errors are relatively small.

The errors are also analyzed by state.[3] Table 5.2 lists each state, from the one with the smallest errors (Ohio) to the one with the largest errors (Mississippi). On average, most states are predicted within 3 percentage points.[4] Populous states are not more or less accurately predicted than less populous ones, though the model tends to fit the data less well in the eleven former Confederate states.[5]

The model's ability to capture the dynamics of presidential contests since 1948 can be seen by how closely its predicted vote tracks changes in the actual vote over time. Plots for a few of the best- and worst-fitted states are displayed in figure 5.1. There is extremely close correspondence between the actual and predicted vote in Ohio and Michigan—the predicted vote is never off by more than 3 points. A slightly greater discrepancy between the actual and predicted vote is seen in two of the worst-fitting states, Maine and Georgia, where the misses average over 5 points. But even in these states, the over-time trends and fluctuations in the vote are captured by the theory. Even when the model errs in its prediction of the exact vote, it picks up changes in party fortunes, such as Kentucky's and Georgia's Republican drift since 1948.

3. The average residual for every state is zero because each state has its own intercept in the vote equation.

4. There is no relationship between the number of ballots cast in the state and the variance of the residuals. (See appendix B.)

5. This amounts to a violation of the Gauss-Markov assumption that the variance of the residuals is constant across observations. The residual variance for the southern states is about one and one-half times the variance for the rest of the country. The likely consequence of this is a slight underestimate of the coefficient standard errors. I decided to ignore this problem, because if two equations were estimated (one for the South [76 cases] and one for the North [267 cases]), there would have been a tremendous reduction in the efficiency of the estimates, particularly in the South. When 1976 data are later added to the sample for the 1980 forecasts (chap. 6), the extra cases allow me to estimate separate equations for each region.

Table 5.2 Summary of Average Error by State,
1948–72

State	Average Error (Percentage)
Ohio	0.7
Michigan	1.2
New Mexico	1.2
Colorado	1.4
Missouri	1.5
Nebraska	1.6
Maryland	1.6
North Dakota	1.7
Indiana	1.8
Arizona	1.9
Washington	1.9
Pennsylvania	1.9
Connecticut	1.9
Minnesota	1.9
Montana	2.0
Wisconsin	2.1
Illinois	2.2
New York	2.2
New Jersey	2.2
New Hampshire	2.2
Kansas	2.2
Delaware	2.2
Vermont	2.2
Oregon	2.3
Kentucky	2.3
Utah	2.4
Alabama	2.7
Wyoming	2.9
California	2.9
Iowa	3.0
West Virginia	3.0
Louisiana	3.0
Nevada	3.2
North Carolina	3.3
South Dakota	3.5
Alaska	3.5
Virginia	3.6
Massachusetts	3.6
Tennessee	3.9
Arkansas	4.0
Texas	4.1
South Carolina	4.2
Florida	4.3
Idaho	4.7
Oklahoma	5.3
Rhode Island	5.3
Maine	5.5
Georgia	5.6
Hawaii	5.9
Mississippi	7.7

Source: Table 4.1.

Ninety-one percent of the time the model correctly predicts the state winner. Twelve of the 30 state prediction errors occur in 1948 alone. The abundant errors in 1948 may result from that year's four-way presidential contest (see Rosenstone, Behr, and

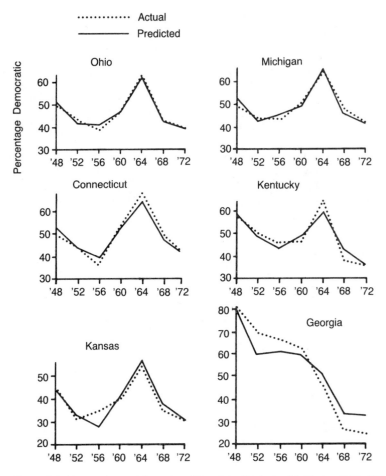

Figure 5.1 Comparison of Actual and Predicted Vote for Six States, 1948–72

Lazarus 1984) and my decision to count Wallace and Thurmond votes as Democratic votes to simplify the estimation of the vote equation. Nearly all the 1948 misses turn up in states won by margins of less than 3 percentage points, where even small errors might mean that the wrong candidate would be predicted winner.

The other outcome errors are scattered among the remaining years. Wrong winners are predicted in 3 states in both 1952 and

Table 5.3 Comparison of Within-Sample Vote Equation Predictions With Best-Fit Simulmatic Simulations of the 1960 and 1964 Elections

	1960		*1964*	
	Rosenstone	*Simulmatics*	*Rosenstone*	*Simulmatics*
Average miss (percentage)	1.9	3.6	3.7	4.4
Standard deviation of residuals (percentage)	2.4	4.8	4.9	5.5
Percentage of states with correct winner predicted	86.0	75.0	93.9	87.0
Number of states for which estimates were made	50	48	49	46

Source: Table 4.1; Pool, Abelson, and Popkin, *Candidates, Issues and Strategies*, pp. 108-09, 175.

1956. Seven mistakes are made in 1960, 3 in 1964, 2 in 1968, and none in 1972. Two-thirds of these errors occur in states won by margins of less than 3 percentage points. For example, Stevenson received 50.04 percent of the two-party vote in Kentucky in 1952; the model predicts 48.56 percent. Although off by less than 1.5 points, the state is incorrectly assigned to Eisenhower. All the 1960 errors occur in states carried by less than 1 percent of the two-party popular vote. Illinois was missed in 1960: Kennedy received 50.09 percent; the model predicts 49.97 percent.[6] Again, when states are won by narrow margins, even a tiny error can lead to an incorrect prediction of the state winner. Any model will make some mistakes in very close contests. However, even in the states won by margins of 1 point or less, the equation correctly predicts the winner nearly two-thirds of the time.

These state-level predictions are an improvement over the Simulmatics Project's 1960 and 1964 best-fit simulations (table 5.3).

6. Actually, this may not be a miss. The model's .12 percent (5,696-vote) error in Illinois is well within most observers' estimates of the number of fraudulent votes counted for Kennedy (Peirce and Longley 1981, p. 68).

Both the average miss and the standard deviation of the residuals are half the size of the errors Pool and associates made in 1960. My model predicts the winner in 11 percent more states in 1960 than did the Simulmatics group. Although there is a smaller improvement in 1964, the model's estimates of the state popular vote and its predictions of state winners are better than those made by Pool, Abelson, and Popkin.

NATIONAL-LEVEL WITHIN-SAMPLE PREDICTIONS

The model's within-sample national vote predictions can also be evaluated. Of course, the divisions of both the national popular and the electoral vote are of interest. I aggregated the model's state-level estimates to generate these national predictions. The probabilities that a candidate will enjoy a popular vote and electoral college majority are estimated as well.

National Popular Vote Predictions

The within-sample national popular vote predictions[7] for each election are extremely close to the actual division of the popular vote (fig. 5.2). In none of the seven years is the predicted national popular vote off by more than three-quarters of a percentage point. The average miss is less than half a point. The model predicts that there are more than 99 chances in 100 of a Democratic national popular vote majority in 1948 and 1964, and predicts less than 1 chance in 100 of a Democratic popular vote

---

7. The predicted proportion of the national vote cast for the Democratic candidate in a given election is:

$$\text{Democratic Proportion of the National Popular Vote} = \frac{\sum_{i=1}^{n} \hat{Y}_i \cdot (\text{Votes}_i)}{\sum_{i=1}^{n} (\text{Votes}_i)}$$

where $\hat{Y}_i$ = the predicted proportion of the votes cast for the Democratic party in state$_i$;

Votes$_i$ = the total ballots cast for president in state$_i$; and

n = the number of states in that election year.

victory in 1952, 1956, 1968, and 1972.[8] The model does not predict a clear popular vote winner in 1960, but instead shows a slight Nixon edge: it predicts only a .45 probability of a Kennedy popular vote majority. Thus, although the 1960 prediction is off by only .21 percentage points, this error, combined with the forecast standard error, does not allow the popular vote winner to be predicted with certainty.

The national popular vote errors made by this model are substantially smaller than those made by Tufte (1978) and Fair (1978). In five of the seven elections between 1948 and 1972 my model makes smaller errors than Tufte's equation. In all seven years the errors are smaller than Fair's. The model's average miss over this period is .4 percent, compared to Tufte's average miss of 1.2 percent and Fair's of 3.1 percent.

National Electoral Vote Predictions

The state predictions can also be used to project the vote in the electoral college. Since a state's predicted popular vote is just an estimate, its electoral votes should not be assigned zero-sum according to which side of the 50 percent mark the state happens to lie. Rather, the national electoral vote is computed by multiplying each state's electoral vote by the candidate's *probability* of

8. The estimated variance of the predicted national Democratic proportion of the popular vote is:

$$\hat{\sigma}^2_{NPOP} = e[X\Lambda X' + \sigma^2 I + UU']e'$$

where $\hat{\sigma}^2_{NPOP}$ = the estimated variance of the predicted national Democratic proportion of the popular vote (a scalar)

e = an n × 1 vector of weights; $e_i = \dfrac{\text{total number of votes in state}_i}{\text{total number of national votes}}$

X = an n × k data matrix of the independent variables;

$\Lambda = \sigma^2(X'X)^{-1}$ (a k × k matrix);

σ^2 = the variance of the residuals (a scalar);

I = an n × n identity matrix; and

U = an n × 1 vector of residuals.

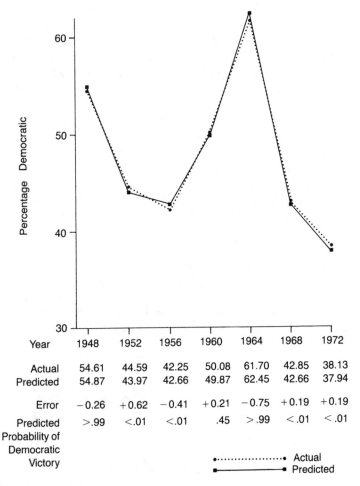

Year	1948	1952	1956	1960	1964	1968	1972
Actual	54.61	44.59	42.25	50.08	61.70	42.85	38.13
Predicted	54.87	43.97	42.66	49.87	62.45	42.66	37.94
Error	− 0.26	+ 0.62	− 0.41	+ 0.21	− 0.75	+ 0.19	+ 0.19
Predicted Probability of Democratic Victory	>.99	<.01	<.01	.45	>.99	<.01	<.01

Source: Table 4.1.

Figure 5.2 Comparison of Actual and Predicted National Popular Vote for President, 1948–72

winning the state and summing over the states.[9] This takes into account uncertainty in the forecasted state vote and should improve national electoral vote forecasts over an all-or-nothing electoral vote allocation. I also estimate the probability of a candidate receiving an electoral vote majority.[10]

The within-sample national electoral vote errors range from a low of 8 electoral votes in 1964 to a high of 49 in 1960 (table 5.4). Between 1948 and 1972 the average electoral college error is 6.2 percent.[11] The model predicts that there are better than 99 chances in 100 that the Democrats would be the electoral college

9. The predicted national electoral vote for the Democratic candidate in a given election is:

$$\text{National Democratic Electoral Vote} = \sum_{i=1}^{n} \left[\left(\Phi\left(\frac{\hat{Y}_i - .5}{\hat{\sigma}\hat{Y}_i} \right) \right) \cdot EV_i \right]$$

where $\hat{Y}_i$ = the predicted proportion of the vote cast for the Democratic party in state$_i$;

$\hat{\sigma}\hat{Y}_i$ = the standard error of the forecast for state$_i$;

EV_i = the total electoral votes in state$_i$;

Φ = the integral of the standard normal distribution at $(\hat{Y}_i - .5)/\hat{\sigma}\hat{Y}_i$; and

n = the number of states in that election year.

10. The estimated variance of the predicted Democratic national electoral vote is:

$$\hat{\sigma}^2_{NEL} = \epsilon'[X\Lambda X' + \sigma^2 I + UU']\epsilon$$

where $\hat{\sigma}^2_{NEL}$ = the estimated variance of the predicted Democratic national electoral vote (a scalar)

ϵ = an $n \times i$ vector where each element is:

$$\left[\left(\left(\phi^2\left(\frac{\hat{Y}_i - .5}{\hat{\sigma}\hat{Y}_i} \right) \right) \cdot \frac{1}{\hat{\sigma}\hat{Y}_i} \right) \cdot EV_i \right]$$

$\hat{Y}_i$ = the predicted proportion of the vote cast for the Democratic party in state$_i$;

$\hat{\sigma}\hat{Y}_i$ = the standard error of the forecast for state$_i$;

ϕ^2 = the density of the standard normal distribution evaluated at $(Y_i - .5)/\hat{Y}_i$;

EV_i = the total electoral votes in state$_i$;

X = an $n \times k$ data matrix of independent variables;

Λ = $\sigma^2(X'X)^{-1}$ (a $k \times k$ matrix);

σ^2 = the variance of the residuals (a scalar);

I = an $n \times n$ identity matrix; and

U = an $n \times 1$ vector of the residuals.

11. The percent error instead of the raw electoral vote error should be compared because the number of states in the sample, and thus the total electoral vote, is not constant across years.

Table 5.4 Comparison of Actual and Predicted Democratic National
Electoral Vote for President, 1948–72

		Electoral Votes* (Democratic)				Predicted Probability of Democratic Victory
Year	Total	Actual	Predicted	Error	Error as % of Total	
1948	531	416	397	+19	+4.5	>.99
1952	531	89	128	-39	-7.4	<.01
1956	531	74	119	-45	-8.4	<.01
1960	537	317	268	+49	+9.1	.44
1964	525	483	475	+ 8	+1.4	>.99
1968	534	79	100	-21	-3.9	<.01
1972	535	14	62	-48	-8.9	<.01

Source: Table 4.1.

* States carried by Thurmond in 1948 were counted as Democratic electoral votes. A state was assigned to the Democratic column in 1968 if Humphrey received more popular votes than Nixon and Wallace combined. Alabama was deleted from the analysis in 1964. The method for computing the predicted electoral vote is described in n. 9.

victors in 1948 and 1964 and less than 1 chance in 100 of a Democratic electoral vote majority in 1952, 1956, 1968, and 1972. An electoral college toss-up is predicted in 1960: there is only a .44 probability of a Kennedy victory.[12]

A point to keep in mind about the electoral college predictions is that although the model does not underpredict the winner's state plurality or his national popular vote, it tends to underpredict the winner's electoral vote margin. Although on average the method used to compute the electoral votes is better than a zero-sum allocation, it is a conservative method that makes the electoral college contest appear to be slightly closer than it really is.

Finally, although the state and national popular vote predictions outperform the Simulmatics Project when it comes to the

12. Given the problems of fraud, unpledged electors in Alabama and Mississippi, the bias of the electoral college system, and the closeness of the election, it is not at all clear that it is possible to predict with much certainty who the electoral college victor would have been. See Peirce 1968, pp. 141–45; Longley and Braun 1975, pp. 2–7.

national electoral vote, my model is not a clear improvement. The 1960 electoral vote error is 9.1 percent, compared to 1.5 percent for the Simulmatics effort. My 1964 error is slightly smaller than that made by Pool and associates (1.4 percent compared to 5.2 percent).

CONCLUSIONS

The theory closely fits the data. At the state level the average popular vote error is 2.9 percentage points. About 25 percent of the within-sample predictions are within 1 percentage point of the actual vote; 50 percent are within 2.2 points; only 5 percent are missed by more than 8 points. The predicted state vote closely tracks over-time political changes in states. This holds even for states with large popular vote errors. The model correctly predicts state winners 91 percent of the time.

The model performs even better at the national level. The national popular vote is never missed by more than three-quarters of a percentage point. In every year except 1960, it correctly predicts the popular and electoral college winner; a toss-up is predicted in 1960. The average electoral college error is 33 votes.

State-level errors have different consequences for national popular and electoral vote predictions. Sizable random errors in state predictions cancel out when these votes are aggregated to forecast the national popular vote. The average national level popular vote error is about one-eighth the size of the average state-level error. The standard error of the national popular vote forecast is one-fourth the state-level standard error.[13]

The state errors, however, do not cancel as neatly when aggregated to predict the national electoral vote. Here, each state is weighted not by the total votes cast, but by the electoral vote times the probability that the state will be won. Because the probability of capturing a state grows nonlinearly (since it is calculated from the standard normal distribution), the marginal electoral vote error that results from a state being slightly on the

13. This is one of the benefits of disaggregation discussed in chap. 4, n. 5.

wrong side of the 50 percent mark is greater than the marginal error that results from a larger miss. Consequently, errors are less likely to cancel. In fact, they can compound one another, since even small state errors can mean that a state will be assigned a relatively high probability of going for the wrong candidate. (Nevertheless, this method still provides better estimates than a zero-sum allocation.)

So far the model has been validated in several ways: it is well grounded in theory; the coefficients and the changes in their values over time make sense; it is a reasonably good fit to the data; and the predicted votes closely track both state and national changes in political fortunes. Why the Democrats won in 1964 but lost four years later, for example, is accounted for.

One crucial test of the theory still remains: How well will it forecast the 1976 and 1980 presidential elections—cases *outside* the original sample?

Table 5.A.1 Comparison of Actual and Predicted Democratic Vote for President, 1948 (Percentages)

State	Actual Vote	Predicted Vote	Error
Alabama	80.9	82.0	− 1.1
Arizona	56.0	54.3	1.7
Arkansas	78.9	79.8	− .9
California	52.6	53.6	− 1.0
Colorado	53.3	51.5	1.8
Connecticut	50.0	53.3	− 3.3
Delaware	49.7	55.7	− 6.0
Florida	66.4	62.9	3.5
Georgia	81.7	80.7	.9
Idaho	52.5	47.5	5.0
Illinois	50.4	52.4	− 2.0
Indiana	49.9	50.4	− .5
Iowa	52.0	50.0	2.0
Kansas	45.7	44.5	1.2
Kentucky	58.4	58.9	− .5
Louisiana	82.6	80.4	2.2
Maine	43.1	46.8	− 3.7
Maryland	50.4	54.2	− 3.9
Massachusetts	56.7	58.8	− 2.2
Michigan	50.3	53.4	− 3.1
Minnesota	59.9	56.1	3.8
Mississippi	97.4	90.6	6.8
Missouri	58.5	58.8	− .3
Montana	56.6	58.5	− 1.9
Nebraska	45.9	46.3	− .4
Nevada	52.7	47.0	5.7
New Hampshire	47.6	48.3	− .8
New Jersey	48.9	47.9	1.0
New Mexico	57.0	55.8	1.2
New York	53.7	52.4	1.3
North Carolina	67.3	75.1	− 7.8
North Dakota	47.6	51.2	− 3.6
Ohio	50.8	51.5	− .7
Oklahoma	62.8	51.3	11.5
Oregon	49.7	50.8	− 1.1
Pennsylvania	48.7	51.3	− 2.6
Rhode Island	58.5	62.3	− 3.8
South Carolina	96.2	96.5	− .3
South Dakota	48.2	54.7	− 6.6
Tennessee	63.0	63.5	− .4
Texas	75.3	68.0	7.3
Utah	55.0	53.0	2.0
Vermont	38.2	42.4	− 4.2
Virginia	58.9	64.0	− 5.2
Washington	56.8	55.6	1.2
West Virginia	57.8	61.3	− 3.5
Wisconsin	53.2	49.8	3.4
Wyoming	52.6	47.6	5.0

Table 5.A.2 Comparison of Actual and Predicted Democratic Vote for President, 1952 (Percentages)

State	Actual Vote	Predicted Vote	Error
Alabama	64.8	60.7	4.1
Arizona	41.7	45.7	- 4.0
Arkansas	56.1	57.8	- 1.7
California	43.1	43.5	- .4
Colorado	39.3	40.4	- 1.1
Connecticut	44.1	44.1	0
Delaware	48.1	42.9	5.2
Florida	45.0	49.6	- 4.6
Georgia	69.7	59.4	10.3
Idaho	34.5	38.1	- 3.5
Illinois	45.0	43.0	2.0
Indiana	41.4	39.5	1.8
Iowa	35.8	37.3	- 1.4
Kansas	30.7	32.6	- 1.9
Kentucky	50.0	48.6	1.5
Louisiana	52.9	54.5	- 1.6
Maine	33.8	39.2	- 5.4
Maryland	44.2	45.0	- .8
Massachusetts	45.6	48.6	- 3.0
Michigan	44.2	43.2	1.0
Minnesota	44.4	43.3	1.1
Mississippi	60.4	56.6	3.8
Missouri	49.2	48.7	.6
Montana	40.3	41.1	- .8
Nebraska	30.9	32.9	- 2.0
Nevada	38.6	43.3	- 4.8
New Hampshire	39.1	35.6	3.4
New Jersey	42.5	40.1	2.4
New Mexico	44.4	43.8	.6
New York	44.0	43.0	1.0
North Carolina	53.9	51.9	2.0
North Dakota	28.6	26.2	2.4
Ohio	43.2	41.6	1.6
Oklahoma	45.4	44.8	.6
Oregon	39.1	39.4	- .3
Pennsylvania	47.1	43.5	3.6
Rhode Island	49.1	52.0	- 2.9
South Carolina	50.7	58.2	- 7.5
South Dakota	30.7	33.4	- 2.7
Tennessee	49.9	43.7	6.2
Texas	46.8	51.8	- 5.0
Utah	41.1	40.2	.9
Vermont	28.3	27.9	.4
Virginia	43.5	45.8	- 2.3
Washington	45.1	42.5	2.7
West Virginia	51.9	50.6	1.3
Wisconsin	38.8	38.3	.5
Wyoming	37.2	34.7	2.5

Table 5.A.3 Comparison of Actual and Predicted Democratic Vote for President, 1956 (Percentages)

State	Actual Vote	Predicted Vote	Error
Alabama	58.8	57.2	1.6
Arizona	38.9	36.9	2.0
Arkansas	53.4	55.6	- 2.2
California	44.4	40.4	4.1
Colorado	40.1	38.7	1.4
Connecticut	36.3	39.7	- 3.4
Delaware	44.8	43.9	.9
Florida	42.7	45.1	- 2.4
Georgia	66.6	61.1	5.6
Idaho	38.8	30.5	8.3
Illinois	40.4	42.5	- 2.1
Indiana	39.9	37.3	2.5
Iowa	40.8	36.4	4.4
Kansas	34.3	27.7	6.6
Kentucky	45.4	43.1	2.3
Louisiana	42.6	51.6	- 9.0
Maine	29.1	36.3	- 7.2
Maryland	40.0	40.9	- .9
Massachusetts	40.5	47.1	- 6.6
Michigan	44.3	45.5	- 1.2
Minnesota	46.2	46.6	- .4
Mississippi	70.4	57.6	12.8
Missouri	50.1	45.2	4.9
Montana	42.9	41.9	1.0
Nebraska	34.5	30.8	3.7
Nevada	42.0	39.9	2.1
New Hampshire	33.9	38.2	- 4.3
New Jersey	34.6	39.2	- 4.6
New Mexico	42.0	40.8	1.1
New York	38.8	42.2	- 3.4
North Carolina	50.7	54.4	- 3.7
North Dakota	38.2	38.1	.1
Ohio	38.9	40.5	- 1.6
Oklahoma	44.9	38.3	6.6
Oregon	44.8	41.0	3.8
Pennsylvania	43.4	42.5	.9
Rhode Island	41.7	51.3	- 9.6
South Carolina	64.3	58.3	6.0
South Dakota	41.6	37.3	4.3
Tennessee	49.7	47.7	2.0
Texas	44.3	49.1	- 4.8
Utah	35.4	35.0	.4
Vermont	27.8	29.7	- 1.9
Virginia	40.9	44.3	- 3.4
Washington	45.7	44.1	1.6
West Virginia	45.9	45.8	.1
Wisconsin	38.1	38.8	- .7
Wyoming	39.9	37.4	2.5

Table 5.A.4 Comparison of Actual and Predicted Democratic Vote for President, 1960 (Percentages)

State	Actual Vote	Predicted Vote	Error
Alabama	57.4	55.1	2.3
Alaska	49.1	45.3	3.8
Arizona	44.4	43.6	.8
Arkansas	53.9	59.1	- 5.2
California	49.7	47.7	2.0
Colorado	45.1	47.7	- 2.6
Connecticut	53.7	53.1	.6
Delaware	50.8	50.6	.2
Florida	48.5	48.4	.1
Georgia	62.6	59.5	3.1
Hawaii	50.0	47.5	2.5
Idaho	46.2	43.2	3.0
Illinois	50.1	50.0	.1
Indiana	44.8	42.9	1.9
Iowa	43.3	46.8	- 3.5
Kansas	39.3	40.3	- 1.0
Kentucky	46.4	48.5	- 2.1
Louisiana	63.8	62.9	.9
Maine	43.0	45.9	- 2.9
Maryland	53.6	50.2	3.4
Massachusetts	60.4	61.1	- .7
Michigan	51.0	50.2	.8
Minnesota	50.7	51.1	- .4
Mississippi	59.6	55.9	3.7
Missouri	50.3	51.5	- 1.2
Montana	48.7	52.1	- 3.4
Nebraska	37.9	37.2	.7
Nevada	51.2	47.8	3.4
New Hampshire	46.6	45.8	.8
New Jersey	50.4	49.0	1.4
New Mexico	50.4	54.0	- 3.6
New York	52.6	51.0	1.6
North Carolina	52.1	51.7	.4
North Dakota	44.6	43.9	.7
Ohio	46.7	46.9	- .2
Oklahoma	41.0	45.9	- 4.9
Oregon	47.4	49.6	- 2.2
Pennsylvania	51.2	50.0	1.2
Rhode Island	63.6	62.2	1.4
South Carolina	51.2	56.0	- 4.8
South Dakota	41.8	43.2	- 1.4
Tennessee	46.4	46.9	- .5
Texas	51.0	55.5	- 4.5
Utah	45.2	41.9	3.3
Vermont	41.4	41.3	.1
Virginia	47.3	45.6	1.7
Washington	48.8	47.6	1.2
West Virginia	52.7	51.8	.9
Wisconsin	48.1	51.7	- 3.6
Wyoming	45.0	44.9	.1

Table 5.A.5 Comparison of Actual and Predicted Democratic Vote for President, 1964 (Percentages)

State	Actual Vote	Predicted Vote	Error
Alaska	65.9	62.6	3.3
Arizona	49.5	51.5	- 2.0
Arkansas	56.4	46.9	9.5
California	59.2	68.2	- 9.1
Colorado	61.6	61.0	.6
Connecticut	67.9	64.3	3.6
Delaware	61.1	62.5	- 1.4
Florida	51.2	59.1	- 8.1
Georgia	45.9	50.7	- 4.8
Hawaii	78.8	71.0	7.7
Idaho	50.9	56.2	- 5.3
Illinois	59.5	63.0	- 3.5
Indiana	56.2	59.0	- 2.7
Iowa	62.0	62.7	- .7
Kansas	54.6	56.5	- 1.9
Kentucky	64.2	60.0	4.2
Louisiana	43.2	38.4	4.8
Maine	68.8	61.7	7.1
Maryland	64.1	64.7	- .6
Massachusetts	76.5	71.9	4.6
Michigan	66.8	66.5	.3
Minnesota	63.9	69.6	- 5.7
Mississippi	12.9	29.2	-16.3
Missouri	65.5	63.2	2.3
Montana	59.2	58.3	.9
Nebraska	52.6	54.7	- 2.1
Nevada	58.6	61.4	- 2.8
New Hampshire	63.6	61.6	2.0
New Jersey	66.0	63.0	3.0
New Mexico	59.4	58.0	1.4
New York	68.7	64.7	4.0
North Carolina	56.2	50.4	5.8
North Dakota	58.1	58.6	- .5
Ohio	62.9	62.2	.7
Oklahoma	55.8	57.8	- 2.0
Oregon	63.9	66.0	- 2.1
Pennsylvania	65.2	65.1	.1
Rhode Island	80.9	72.8	8.1
South Carolina	41.1	32.5	8.6
South Dakota	55.6	57.3	- 1.7
Tennessee	55.5	62.5	- 7.0
Texas	63.4	62.9	.5
Utah	54.7	56.1	- 1.4
Vermont	66.3	59.1	7.2
Virginia	53.7	55.6	- 1.9
Washington	62.4	63.1	- .7
West Virginia	67.9	65.8	2.1
Wisconsin	62.2	65.3	- 3.1
Wyoming	56.6	58.4	- 1.8

Table 5.A.6 Comparison of Actual and Predicted Democratic Vote for President, 1968 (Percentages)

State	Actual Vote	Predicted Vote	Error
Alabama	19.0	20.5	- 1.5
Alaska	42.7	43.9	- 1.2
Arizona	35.2	35.7	- .5
Arkansas	30.3	25.8	4.5
California	45.1	46.0	.9
Colorado	41.6	42.8	- 1.2
Connecticut	49.5	47.4	2.1
Delaware	41.6	40.3	1.3
Florida	30.9	27.9	3.0
Georgia	26.8	33.5	- 6.7
Hawaii	59.8	58.3	1.5
Idaho	30.7	36.6	- 5.9
Illinois	44.3	40.8	3.5
Indiana	38.1	38.9	- .8
Iowa	41.0	45.8	- 4.8
Kansas	34.8	37.7	- 2.9
Kentucky	37.8	42.8	- 5.0
Louisiana	28.2	27.6	.6
Maine	55.3	45.1	10.2
Maryland	43.6	43.7	- .1
Massachusetts	63.2	56.6	6.6
Michigan	48.3	46.6	1.7
Minnesota	54.1	54.3	- .2
Mississippi	23.0	24.2	- 1.2
Missouri	43.7	44.0	- .3
Montana	41.8	43.0	- 1.2
Nebraska	31.8	32.9	- 1.1
Nevada	39.3	42.9	- 3.6
New Hampshire	44.0	42.7	1.3
New Jersey	44.3	45.7	- 1.4
New Mexico	40.0	40.6	- .6
New York	50.1	50.9	- .8
North Carolina	29.2	28.6	.6
North Dakota	38.3	39.9	- 1.6
Ohio	43.0	42.8	.2
Oklahoma	32.0	37.2	- 5.2
Oregon	43.9	46.1	- 2.2
Pennsylvania	47.8	46.9	.9
Rhode Island	64.1	54.7	9.4
South Carolina	29.6	30.0	- .4
South Dakota	42.0	40.5	1.5
Tennessee	28.1	33.8	- 5.7
Texas	41.1	39.4	1.7
Utah	37.1	35.4	1.7
Vermont	43.8	44.9	- 1.1
Virginia	32.7	29.0	3.7
Washington	47.2	50.7	- 3.5
West Virginia	49.6	43.7	5.9
Wisconsin	48.0	46.8	1.2
Wyoming	35.5	42.2	- 6.7

Table 5.A.7 Comparison of Actual and Predicted Democratic Vote for President, 1972 (Percentages)

State	Actual Vote	Predicted Vote	Error
Alabama	26.0	31.5	- 5.5
Alaska	37.3	43.2	- 5.9
Arizona	33.0	31.0	2.0
Arkansas	30.8	34.9	- 4.1
California	43.0	40.7	2.0
Colorado	35.6	34.4	1.2
Connecticut	40.7	40.3	.4
Delaware	39.7	40.0	- .3
Florida	27.9	19.5	8.4
Georgia	24.7	33.0	- 8.2
Hawaii	37.5	49.3	-11.8
Idaho	28.8	30.3	- 1.4
Illinois	40.7	38.7	2.0
Indiana	33.5	35.7	- 2.2
Iowa	41.3	37.1	4.1
Kansas	30.4	30.5	- .1
Kentucky	35.4	35.8	- .4
Louisiana	30.3	28.1	2.1
Maine	38.5	36.6	1.9
Maryland	37.8	36.0	1.8
Massachusetts	54.5	53.2	1.3
Michigan	42.7	42.2	.5
Minnesota	47.2	45.2	2.0
Mississippi	20.1	29.6	- 9.5
Missouri	37.7	40.1	- 2.4
Montana	39.5	34.4	5.1
Nebraska	29.5	28.2	1.3
Nevada	36.3	36.3	0
New Hampshire	35.3	37.7	- 2.6
New Jersey	37.4	39.1	- 1.7
New Mexico	37.5	37.4	.1
New York	41.3	44.8	- 3.5
North Carolina	29.4	26.7	2.7
North Dakota	36.6	33.7	2.9
Ohio	39.0	38.9	.1
Oklahoma	24.6	31.1	- 6.5
Oregon	44.7	40.6	4.1
Pennsylvania	39.8	43.8	- 4.0
Rhode Island	46.9	49.5	- 2.6
South Carolina	28.1	29.9	- 1.8
South Dakota	43.7	39.1	6.6
Tennessee	30.5	25.1	5.4
Texas	33.4	28.6	4.8
Utah	28.1	35.0	- 6.9
Vermont	36.8	37.3	.5
Virginia	30.8	23.3	7.5
Washington	40.4	43.0	- 2.6
West Virginia	36.4	43.2	- 6.8
Wisconsin	45.0	42.7	2.3
Wyoming	30.6	32.2	- 1.7

6

1976 AND 1980 FORECASTS

At the onset of the 1976 campaign it appeared that Carter would enjoy an easy victory in November: he had a comfortable 13-point lead in the polls, and journalists predicted the Democrats would carry two-thirds of the states to produce a 400-vote sweep of the electoral college. Only in the final weeks before the balloting did it become clear that the 1976 election would not end in a landslide but would be decided by a hairbreadth. The 1980 campaign began on a different note. Carter and Reagan ran neck and neck in the polls; neither had a clear claim to an electoral vote majority. Observers were stunned by the size of Reagan's margin when the votes were counted.

This chapter assesses the model's 1976 and 1980 presidential election forecasts. I have two purposes in mind. Forecasts provide an additional test of the theory. Does the model capture the essential features of presidential contests to allow elections outside the original sample to be accurately forecasted? If the predictions are grossly in error, the misses will suggest revision of the theory. Reasonably close forecasts (within the standard margin of statistical error) will boost confidence in the theory. I am also interested in how well a statistical model can forecast presidential elections. Here my concern is not so much with the theory's validity as with its utility as a forecasting device. How do the model's predictions compare with other attempts to forecast the 1976 and 1980 presidential elections?

To forecast each state's 1976 popular vote, its 1976 values on the independent variables are multiplied by their respective coefficients which were estimated from the 1948 to 1972 election data. The state popular vote forecast is the sum of these products. Following the methods discussed in chapter 5, these state forecasts are also aggregated to project the national popular and electoral vote.[1]

The 1980 forecasts are generated in the same manner, except now the 1976 election returns are included in the pool of cases and separate equations are estimated for northern and southern states. Relaxing my earlier assumption that foreign policy issues matter only in time of war, I include a measure of the electorate's assessment of the relative ability of each party to provide peace. (This is in lieu of the war variable.) A similar measure of the electorate's perception of each party's ability to keep the country prosperous is also included, as is a measure of intraparty factionalism. (These variables are described in appendix C.)[2]

The forecasts rest on several assumptions. I assume that the forces that produced the 1948 to 1972 outcomes explain the 1976 and 1980 results as well. I also assume that each variable has the same impact in 1976 and 1980 as it had in 1948 and 1972. Exceptions are the New Deal social welfare and racial issues. Their importance varies from year to year, so their effect in 1976 and 1980 must be estimated.[3] It is reasonable to assume that the importance of social welfare issues in the North in 1976 is more likely to resemble their importance in 1948, 1960, 1964, and 1972

1. The only difference is in the calculation of the forecast variance, which is larger (by the variance of the residuals) than the within-sample estimate.

2. The more voters view one party as better able to provide peace and prosperity, the higher that party's vote. If citizens believe, by a 2-to-1 margin, that a given party is better able to keep the peace, it will poll 2 to 3 points more than if voters viewed both parties as equally capable. The effect for a comparable shift in the electorate's assessment of the relative abilities of the parties to manage the economy is about 3 points. As common wisdom holds, divided parties do worse than united ones. A candidate who just barely captures the nomination (say with 50 percent of the vote) will run about 1 point behind a candidate who enjoys his party's unanimous support. (For further evidence on the effect of party factionalism on election outcomes see Behr [1982].)

3. One method would be to specify additional equations that could in turn be used to forecast the coefficients for these issue dimensions. The handful of data points, and the paucity of theory on the determinants of issue importance, make the approach a risky one.

than their impact in 1968 or the 1950s. Therefore, this parameter for the North in 1976 is set to the single coefficient that was estimated for those four elections. Since this dimension had the same importance in the South from 1960 to 1972, I assume this level will hold in 1976 as well. I assume that the dimension's effect in 1980 is the same as its effect in 1976.

The importance of racial issues is set in the same way. I assume that racial issues in the North are as important in 1976 as they were in 1948, 1968, and 1972. It seems reasonable to think that race is less important than in 1968 but more important than in 1952, 1956, and 1960. It appears that by 1976, since racial issues in the South had declined in prominence, the dimension would more likely resemble its importance in 1956 and 1960 than in 1964 to 1972. As with the social welfare issues, I assume that in both regions racial issues would be about as important in 1980 as they were in 1976.[4]

PERFECT INFORMATION FORECASTS

To test the theory's predictive validity I assume that the values of the causal variables are known with certainty. Although these "perfect information forecasts" are appropriate for evaluating the theory, they do not reveal how well the model works before an election, when knowledge is imperfect and estimated values for variables must be used. After I discuss the perfect information forecasts, I will relax this assumption and evaluate how the model performs when only data available prior to the election are relied upon.

The full information forecasts generated from the model are reported in tables 6.1 and 6.2. I list for each state the forecasted Democratic percent of the two-party vote, the actual vote, the error (the actual vote minus the forecasted vote), and whether the state popular vote winner was correctly predicted. I provide these same estimates for the national popular and electoral vote as well.

4. The coefficients for the New Deal social welfare and racial dimensions were chosen before the 1976 and 1980 forecasts were made. These assumptions are not based on an a postiori fit to the data, nor were they altered after the forecasts were generated.

The 1976 election was extremely close. Carter won by less than 1 percent of the popular vote; a shift of only a few states would have changed the outcome. The model predicts a national popular vote and electoral college toss-up. The predicted national popular vote for Carter—50.2 percent—underestimates his margin of victory by only .8 percentage points. The model predicts 273 of the 535 electoral votes going to Carter,[5] understating his electoral college victory by only 21 votes. In short, the model forecasts a very narrow Carter victory in 1976, as it should.

Most states are predicted very close to their actual vote. The average state-level error is 3.1 percentage points. More than one-quarter of the states are forecasted within 1 point of their true November vote. Half are missed by less than 2 points; 72 percent by less than 4 points; and 92 percent by less than 8 points. The error is slightly higher in northern states and border states than in the South. Only two states are more than two standard errors away from their actual vote—about what one would predict by chance.

An undesirable characteristic of the misses is that their mean is not zero but .5 percent. In other words, on average, the model overpredicts Ford's vote in each state by about half a percentage point.[6] The practical consequence of this bias is that I underestimate the amount of confidence that should be placed in Carter carrying states forecasted in his column and overstate the probability of Ford carrying states forecasted in his. This causes Carter's electoral college total to be underpredicted.

The 1976 election is a tough test of the model. Many states were won by extremely close margins: one-quarter by 1 percentage point or less; one-third by 2 points or less; more than half by less than 3 points. The paper-thin victories meant that even small popular vote errors could lead to an incorrect prediction of the winner. Eight states predicted in the Carter column ended up

5. There are 535 rather than 538 electoral votes because the District of Columbia is deleted from the analysis.

6. Most of the Ford bias is due to errors in southern states. The mean residual in the South is 1.9 points; it is only .1 in the North. The most likely explanation is the model's overestimate of the incumbency effect or underestimate of the regional appeal of a southern presidential candidate.

Table 6.1 1976 Presidential Election Forecasts (Perfect Information)

State	Forecasted Vote	Actual Vote	Error	Winner Missed
Alabama	57.4	56.7	- .7	
Alaska	48.8	38.1	-10.7	
Arizona	43.0	41.4	- 1.6	
Arkansas	61.1	65.1	4.0	
California	52.3	49.1	- 3.2	×
Colorado	47.5	44.1	- 3.4	
Connecticut	50.4	47.4	- 3.0	×
Delaware	51.2	52.8	1.6	
Florida	49.7	52.7	3.0	×
Georgia	61.9	66.9	5.0	
Hawaii	52.5	51.3	- 1.2	
Idaho	41.8	38.3	- 3.5	
Illinois	48.4	49.0	.6	
Indiana	44.7	46.2	1.5	
Iowa	50.2	49.5	- .7	×
Kansas	40.6	46.1	5.5	
Kentucky	49.0	53.7	4.7	×
Louisiana	54.1	53.0	- 1.1	
Maine	40.6	49.6	9.0	
Maryland	48.9	53.0	4.1	×
Massachusetts	56.2	58.1	1.9	
Michigan	46.7	47.3	.6	
Minnesota	56.4	56.6	.2	
Mississippi	50.4	51.0	.6	
Missouri	50.1	51.8	1.8	
Montana	50.1	46.2	- 3.9	×
Nebraska	47.9	39.4	- 8.5	
Nevada	50.5	47.7	- 2.8	×
New Hampshire	44.4	44.3	- .1	
New Jersey	48.2	48.9	.7	
New Mexico	43.0	48.8	5.8	
New York	51.3	52.2	.9	
North Carolina	53.7	55.6	1.9	
North Dakota	53.9	47.0	- 6.9	×
Ohio	46.2	50.1	3.9	×
Oklahoma	43.4	49.4	6.0	
Oregon	52.1	49.9	- 2.2	×
Pennsylvania	50.2	51.4	1.2	
Rhode Island	56.5	55.7	- .8	
South Carolina	56.8	56.6	- .2	
South Dakota	46.9	49.3	2.4	
Tennessee	50.6	56.6	6.0	
Texas	50.4	51.6	1.2	
Utah	42.3	35.0	- 7.3	
Vermont	38.8	44.2	5.5	
Virginia	50.4	49.3	- 1.1	×
Washington	49.2	48.0	- 1.2	
West Virginia	49.3	58.1	8.8	×
Wisconsin	49.9	50.9	1.0	×
Wyoming	41.2	40.2	- 1.0	
National Vote:				
Popular	50.2	51.0	.8	
Electoral	273	294	21	

going for Ford; 6 states predicted as going for Ford went for Carter. All but 2 of the 14 misses occurred in states carried by less than 53 percent of the vote. Some of these errors were in states that would have gone Democratic had third-party candidate Eugene McCarthy's votes been cast for Carter (Iowa and Oregon); some were in states (Ohio and Connecticut) whose outcomes surprised many analysts. Even though 72 percent of the states are correctly predicted, the magnitude of the state-level misses is one of the model's limitations, particularly in close contests.[7]

The model correctly predicts a Reagan victory in 1980 but underestimates both his popular and electoral vote margins. The national popular vote forecast is 47.8 percent for Carter—3.2 points too high. Reagan's electoral college total is underpredicted by 146 votes. Although the model anticipates Carter's defeat, it misses the decisiveness of the Reagan sweep—as did everyone.

At the state level, 84 percent of the outcomes are correctly forecasted—the model misses only 8 states. Six of these misses occur in states Reagan won by less than 53 percent of the vote; they were all incorrectly forecasted as going for Carter. Despite these accurate state calls, the average state error is 5.8 percentage points—nearly double that in 1976. Only one-fifth of the states are missed by less than 2 percentage points; 42 percent by less than 4 points; and 72 percent by less than 8 points. Eight states are now predicted more than 2 standard errors away from their true vote. The largest errors occur in the West, where Reagan captured over 70 percent of the popular vote. Though the 12 western states were missed by an average of 10.2 points, the error in the rest of the country was 4.4 percent—only a point above the 1976 level. Because Carter's popular vote is overestimated in nearly every state, his electoral college margin was overpredicted. (Later I will speculate on the sources of this error.)

PRE-ELECTION FORECASTS

To evaluate the model as a forecasting tool, rather than as a theory, the perfect-information assumption must be relaxed.

---

7. This same problem appeared in 1948 and 1960 (chap. 5).

Table 6.2 1980 Presidential Election Forecasts (Perfect Information)

State	Forecasted Vote	Actual Vote	Error	Winner Missed
Alabama	56.3	49.3	- 7.0	×
Alaska	45.4	32.7	-12.7	
Arizona	44.2	31.8	-12.4	
Arkansas	53.4	49.7	- 3.7	×
California	46.1	40.5	- 5.5	
Colorado	44.5	36.1	- 8.4	
Connecticut	49.4	44.4	- 4.9	
Delaware	50.9	48.7	- 2.1	×
Florida	46.8	40.9	- 5.9	
Georgia	59.9	57.7	- 2.3	
Hawaii	50.6	51.1	.5	
Idaho	38.6	27.5	-11.2	
Illinois	47.1	45.7	- 1.4	
Indiana	45.3	40.2	- 5.0	
Iowa	45.1	42.9	- 2.2	
Kansas	38.6	36.5	- 2.1	
Kentucky	50.7	49.3	- 1.5	×
Louisiana	51.3	47.2	- 4.1	×
Maine	44.0	48.1	4.1	
Maryland	50.1	51.6	1.5	
Massachusetts	56.4	49.9	- 6.5	×
Michigan	50.1	46.5	- 3.6	×
Minnesota	52.9	52.2	- .7	
Mississippi	47.4	49.3	2.0	
Missouri	52.0	46.4	- 5.6	×
Montana	47.2	36.3	-10.9	
Nebraska	37.5	28.4	- 9.1	
Nevada	46.4	30.1	-16.4	
New Hampshire	44.7	32.9	-11.7	
New Jersey	46.9	42.6	- 4.3	
New Mexico	47.5	40.1	- 7.4	
New York	49.8	48.5	- 1.3	
North Carolina	47.7	48.9	1.2	
North Dakota	40.7	29.0	-11.7	
Ohio	47.5	44.3	- 3.2	
Oklahoma	46.6	36.6	-10.0	
Oregon	48.5	44.4	- 4.1	
Pennsylvania	49.1	46.1	- 3.0	
Rhode Island	54.7	56.2	1.5	
South Carolina	46.9	49.3	2.5	
South Dakota	45.6	34.4	-11.2	
Tennessee	45.7	49.9	4.1	
Texas	37.5	42.8	5.3	
Utah	41.0	22.0	-18.9	
Vermont	32.9	46.4	13.5	
Virginia	46.2	43.2	- 3.1	
Washington	49.2	42.9	- 6.2	
West Virginia	54.8	52.4	- 2.4	
Wisconsin	48.1	47.4	- .7	
Wyoming	42.4	30.9	-11.5	
National Vote:				
Popular	47.8	44.6	- 3.2	
Electoral	192	46	-146	

Prior to the election the forecaster can observe most of the causal variables in the model. He knows how each state has voted traditionally, and who has been nominated; he can estimate the candidates' and the electorate's positions on the issues.[8]

The election year change in real disposable income per capita is one variable that is unobserved. Prior to the election, only first-quarter state income estimates are available. (Five days after the 1980 election, the Carter administration released the second-quarter state data, which showed huge drops in income.) The more the change in real income per capita (based on first-quarter estimates) differs from the state's election year change in real *disposable* income per capita, the greater the error in the pre-election forecast. These data errors will have little impact on the national forecast if they are uncorrelated with the actual vote and have a mean of zero. Unfortunately, this is not the case in 1980: the first-quarter state estimates grossly understate election year economic adversity. The 1980 forecasts suffer accordingly.

To predict the national popular vote the forecaster also must know the voter turnout in each state. As a shortcut, one can estimate the proportion of the total national popular vote contributed by each state. (This proportion multiplied by the percentage of the state's popular vote cast for the Democrats, summed across the states, equals the Democratic percentage of the national popular vote.) To forecast each state's turnout (or even its share of the voters) would require additional equations that I have neither specified nor estimated. Instead, I will assume that each state's share of the national popular vote is the same as its share in the previous presidential election. There are, of course, population changes and shifts in voter turnout that undermine this assumption, but the shifts over a four-year period are relatively small, and most will cancel out unless the forecasted vote is correlated with size of the state or its change in turnout over and above the national trend in participation.

If the model were used prior to November of 1976 to forecast

8. Variables that comprise the New Deal social welfare and racial scales are not all observed prior to the election, but because states move at a glacial pace on these dimensions, this creates few problems.

the presidential election, the predictions would not be much different from those made under perfect information. A toss-up election is still predicted (table 6.3). The model forecasts that Carter would receive 50.1 percent of the national popular vote and 269 of the 535 electoral votes. It predicts only 51 chances out of 100 of a Carter popular vote victory and 52 chances out of 100 that he would carry the electoral college. The national-level errors are only slightly higher than those made under perfect information: the popular vote forecast is off by .9 percentage points; the electoral vote is off by 25 votes.

Although the state errors are slightly higher than those made under perfect information, the state forecasts remain close to the actual outcomes. One state in 5 is forecasted within 1 percent of the actual vote, 42 percent within 2 points, 70 percent within 4 points. The candidate who carried the state is correctly predicted 74 percent of the time.

To a campaign strategist, a state's exact popular vote may not be as crucial a datum as the forecasted probability that his candidate will carry the state. These probabilities are a reliable guide to whether the candidate actually won in November. States predicted with near certainty (probability $> .9$) of going Democratic all went for Carter; Carter also carried 78 percent of the states forecasted as having a 70 to 90 percent chance of going Democratic. States nearly certain to be won by the Republicans (probability $> .9$) all went for Ford; Ford also carried 91 percent of the states forecasted as having a 70 to 90 percent chance of going Republican.

The reason these pre-election forecasts so closely resemble the ones made under perfect information is that the 1976 first-quarter state income estimates were good approximations of the election year change in real disposable income per capita. The imprecise data had an inconsequential effect except in the wheat belt (Kansas, Iowa, Missouri, and South Dakota), where the summer's severe drought, coupled with a drop in grain prices, caused personal income, and support for Ford, to tumble below what it would have been had the first-quarter growth in income been sustained through the year.

When I used the model in October of 1980 to forecast the

Table 6.3 1976 Presidential Pre-election Forecasts (Imperfect Information)

State	Forecasted Probability of Winning	Vote	Actual Vote	Error	Winner Missed
Alabama	.85	56.1	56.7	.6	
Alaska	.27	46.6	38.1	- 8.5	
Arizona	.14	44.2	41.4	- 2.8	
Arkansas	.96	60.1	65.1	- 5.0	
California	.71	52.7	49.1	- 3.6	x
Colorado	.26	46.5	44.1	- 2.4	x
Connecticut	.59	51.2	47.4	- 3.8	x
Delaware	.48	49.7	52.8	3.1	x
Florida	.53	50.4	52.7	2.3	
Georgia	.98	62.3	66.9	4.6	
Hawaii	.69	51.3	52.7	1.4	
Idaho	.09	42.6	38.3	- 4.3	
Illinois	.32	47.5	49.0	1.5	
Indiana	.16	44.5	46.2	1.7	
Iowa	.28	46.8	49.5	2.7	
Kansas	.03	39.4	46.1	6.7	
Kentucky	.50	50.0	53.7	3.7	
Louisiana	.85	56.0	53.0	- 3.0	
Maine	.07	42.1	49.6	7.5	
Maryland	.40	48.5	53.0	4.5	x
Massachusetts	.89	56.2	58.1	1.9	
Michigan	.25	46.1	47.3	1.2	
Minnesota	.86	56.7	56.6	- .1	
Mississippi	.55	50.7	51.0	.3	
Missouri	.39	48.5	51.8	3.3	x
Montana	.22	45.7	46.2	.5	
Nebraska	.10	42.9	39.4	- 3.5	
Nevada	.52	50.4	47.7	- 2.7	x
New Hampshire	.25	45.7	44.3	- 1.4	
New Jersey	.42	48.9	48.9	0	
New Mexico	.23	44.4	48.8	4.4	
New York	.56	50.8	52.2	1.4	
North Carolina	.73	53.6	55.6	2.0	
North Dakota	.83	55.4	47.0	- 8.4	x
Ohio	.27	46.5	50.1	3.6	x
Oklahoma	.10	42.9	49.4	6.5	
Oregon	.63	51.8	49.9	- 1.9	x
Pennsylvania	.52	50.3	51.4	1.1	
Rhode Island	.88	56.5	55.7	- .8	
South Carolina	.86	56.0	56.6	.6	
South Dakota	.06	41.2	49.3	8.1	
Tennessee	.55	50.7	56.6	5.9	
Texas	.59	51.3	51.6	.3	
Utah	.20	45.5	35.0	-10.5	
Vermont	.03	39.1	44.2	5.1	
Virginia	.53	50.5	49.3	- 1.2	x
Washington	.42	48.9	48.0	- .9	
West Virginia	.43	49.0	58.1	9.1	x
Wisconsin	.38	48.3	50.9	2.6	x
Wyoming	.07	41.6	40.2	- 1.4	
National Vote:					
Popular	.51	50.1	51.0	.9	
Electoral	.52	269	294	25	

November presidential election, sizable errors resulted.[9] Instead of forecasting a substantial Reagan popular vote victory, I predicted a toss-up—just a slightly better than even chance that Reagan would win a popular vote majority. The forecast was a 5.2 percent underestimate of Reagan's support. Although the model overstates Carter's standing by 207 electoral votes, I predicted that there were only 14 chances in 100 that Carter would enjoy an electoral college victory.

At the state level the results are even more disheartening. Although the model correctly forecasts the winner in 68 percent of the states, the popular vote was missed, on average, by 6 points; only a third of the states were forecasted within 4 points of the actual vote. The largest errors again occur in the West, where misses average 10.3 points; in the rest of the country the average miss is 4.7 percent.

Despite the sizable state popular vote errors, the forecasted probability of a Carter victory did foretell state outcomes. Carter did not carry a single state that had less than a .5 probability of going for the Democrats. He carried one-third of the states that had a .7 to .9 probability of going Democratic and three-quarters of the states that had at least a .9 probability of being in the Democratic column. (This last figure would have been 100 percent had independent candidate John Anderson's vote in Massachusetts divided 2-to-1 for Carter.) Two-thirds of the misses occur in states Reagan captured by less than 53 percent of the two-party vote.

Nearly all the error in the pre-election forecasts (over and above the perfect-information predictions) can be attributed to my using first-quarter state income data in place of the election year change in real disposable income per capita, which was not available until after the election. Only .1 percent of the additional 2.0 percent national popular vote error stems from the turnout estimate I employed. The 1980 error is due in part to imperfect information, and in part to an imperfect model.

9. These forecasts were made on October 14, 1980, and were mailed to twenty scholars.

Table 6.4 1980 Presidential Pre-election Forecasts (Imperfect Information)

State	Forecasted Probability of Winning	Vote	Actual Vote	Error	Winner Missed
Alabama	.84	58.4	49.3	- 9.1	x
Alaska	.03	41.9	32.7	- 9.2	
Arizona	.20	46.2	31.8	-14.4	
Arkansas	.82	57.7	49.7	- 8.0	x
California	.27	47.3	40.5	- 6.8	
Colorado	.10	44.3	36.1	- 8.2	
Connecticut	.51	50.1	44.4	- 5.7	x
Delaware	.77	52.3	48.7	- 3.6	x
Florida	.60	52.1	40.9	-11.2	x
Georgia	.96	64.7	57.7	- 7.0	
Hawaii	.57	50.8	51.1	.3	
Idaho	<.01	36.7	27.5	- 9.2	
Illinois	.36	48.4	45.7	- 2.7	
Indiana	.16	45.6	40.2	- 5.4	
Iowa	.24	46.9	42.9	- 4.0	
Kansas	.01	39.5	36.5	- 3.0	
Kentucky	.67	51.9	49.3	- 2.6	x
Louisiana	.80	57.0	47.2	- 9.8	x
Maine	.48	49.8	48.1	- 1.7	
Maryland	.73	52.7	51.6	- 1.1	
Massachusetts	.98	59.1	49.9	- 9.2	x
Michigan	.56	50.6	46.5	- 4.1	x
Minnesota	.89	55.5	52.2	- 3.3	
Mississippi	.48	49.6	49.3	- .3	
Missouri	.70	52.4	46.4	- 6.0	x
Montana	.36	48.5	36.3	-12.2	
Nebraska	<.01	36.1	28.4	- 7.7	
Nevada	.33	48.0	30.1	-17.9	
New Hampshire	.19	46.1	32.9	-13.2	
New Jersey	.31	47.9	42.6	- 5.3	
New Mexico	.42	49.1	40.1	- 9.0	
New York	.55	50.6	48.2	- 2.1	x
North Carolina	.59	51.9	48.9	- 3.0	x
North Dakota	.02	40.9	29.0	-11.9	
Ohio	.47	49.7	44.3	- 5.4	
Oklahoma	.40	48.9	36.6	-12.3	
Oregon	.48	49.8	44.4	- 5.4	
Pennsylvania	.54	50.5	46.1	- 4.4	x
Rhode Island	.92	56.1	56.2	.1	
South Carolina	.54	50.9	49.3	- 1.6	x
South Dakota	.32	47.9	34.4	-13.5	
Tennessee	.60	52.1	49.9	- 2.2	x
Texas	.15	41.1	42.8	1.7	
Utah	<.01	36.1	22.0	-14.1	
Vermont	<.01	34.8	46.4	11.6	
Virginia	.49	49.7	43.2	- 6.5	
Washington	.31	47.8	42.9	- 4.9	
West Virginia	.93	56.4	52.4	- 4.0	
Wisconsin	.62	51.4	47.4	- 4.0	x
Wyoming	.01	39.6	30.9	- 8.7	
National Vote:					
Popular	.49	49.8	44.6	- 5.2	
Electoral	.14	253	46	-207	

COMPARISON TO OTHER ELECTION FORECASTS

So far I have evaluated the forecasts in absolute terms—how they differ from the true results. The model's performance can also be assessed by comparing its 1976 and 1980 forecasts to those made by political strategists, pollsters, journalists, and social scientists. Forecasts made under perfect information appear first in table 6.5, followed by those made prior to the election with data available at that time.

At the state level, the model's popular vote forecasts are comparable to the early 1976 public opinion polls (both were off by an average of 3.3 percent), but less accurate than the 1980 state polls. My predictions have larger errors than the state polls conducted in the final weeks before the 1976 and 1980 elections. The model's average pre-election state miss is substantially smaller than Budge and Farlie's 14.2 percent average state error in 1976.

My state-by-state predictions were about as accurate as the forecasts political strategists made in 1976 and 1980. I correctly predicted the winner in 74 percent of the states in 1976, compared to the Carter and Ford teams' average of 71 percent. Only Carter's June 1976 forecasts (82 percent correct) were substantially better than mine. My forecasts were as accurate as the Ford camp's August 1976 predictions (75 percent correct) and made noticeably fewer errors than Carter aide Hamilton Jordan made that August (56 percent correct). My 1980 state errors also were comparable to those made by Carter and Reagan strategists. They correctly called, on average, 72 percent of the states; my pre-election forecasts were 68 percent correct. The Reagan team's October 1980 forecasts were noticeably better than mine.

My state winner predictions were better than those made from early state polls but worse than the final polls. Projections based on the early polls were 69 percent correct in 1976; the final polls were 81 percent correct; my model was 74 percent correct. Poll predictions of state winners were nearly 80 percent correct in 1980—noticeably better than my pre-election forecasts.

At the state level, the model's forecasts are comparable to the journalists'. A month before the 1976 election journalists correctly called an average of 76 percent of the states; they correctly called 80 percent of the states in the final days prior to balloting.

Table 6.5 Accuracy of 1976 and 1980 Presidential Election Forecasts

Forecaster	State Popular Vote (% Point Error)	State Winner (Percent Correct)	National Popular Vote (% Point Error)	National Electoral Vote (Error)
1976				
Perfect information forecasts				
Rosenstone	3.1	72	.8	21
Fair			7.1	
Tufte			2.4	
Pre-election forecasts				
Rosenstone	3.3	74	.9	25
Carter (June)		82		10
Carter (August)		56		22
Ford (August)		75		26
Polls (Early)	3.6	69	6.4	
Polls (Final)	1.9	81	.9	
Journalists (Early)		76		107
Journalists (Final)		80		41
Niskanen			9.0	
Fair			7.1	
Budge and Farlie	14.4	62	14.2	192
1980				
Perfect information forecasts				
Rosenstone	5.8	84	3.2	146
Fair			3.3	
Tufte			3.4	
Pre-election forecasts				
Rosenstone	6.6	68	5.2	207
Carter (June)		76		141
Carter (October)		64		241
Reagan (March)		69		223
Reagan (October)		80		142
Polls (early)	3.5	78	5.9	
Polls (final)	4.6	76	3.9	
Journalists (early)		75		151
Journalists (final)		74		174
Fair (1-year memory)			6.3	
Fair (6-month memory)			3.3	

This compares to my pre-election record of 74 percent. My pre-election forecasts, again like the journalists', were less reliable in 1980. They were correct about 75 percent of the time; I correctly called 68 percent of the states.

Data availability, not theory, was the villain in 1980. If better estimates of state economic conditions had been available prior to the election, I would have correctly forecasted 84 percent of the state winners, outperforming political strategists, pollsters, and journalists.

National popular vote comparisons can also be made. The model's 1976 national popular vote forecast error was smaller than the error from early pre-election polls. Moreover, it performs just about as well as polls conducted the weekend before the election: the model missed the outcome by .8 percent; the election eve polls miss by an average of .9 points. This error is also substantially smaller than Niskanen's (9.0 percent), Fair's (7.1 percent), or Budge and Farlie's (14.2 percent) misses. My 1980 national popular vote forecast was slightly better than predictions made from polls conducted shortly after the conventions and 1.3 points worse than predictions made from the election eve public opinion polls. (Again data, not the model, are to blame. The perfect information predictions outperform election eve polls in 1980.) My pre-election national popular vote forecast was better than Fair's forecast made under the assumption that voters look at annual changes in economic well-being, but less accurate than his forecast that assumed that citizens vote on the basis of their change in income in the previous six months.

My perfect information forecasts are an improvement over those made by other scholars. My 1976 miss is one-third the size of Tufte's error and one-ninth the size of Fair's. My 1980 popular vote error is comparable to Tufte's and Fair's.[10]

Finally, the national electoral vote projections compare favorably to those other forecasters made in 1976 and 1980. Carter and Ford campaign strategists missed, on average, by 20 electoral votes in 1976—only a hair better than my 25-vote error. My 1976 projections are a significant improvement over journalists' early electoral vote predictions (on average 107 votes off the mark) and a shade better than their election eve forecasts. Budge and Farlie's 1976 electoral college prediction is 167 votes worse than mine. My 1980 pre-election electoral college forecast is slightly more in error than the Carter and Reagan strategists' forecasts, but not as accurate as the journalists'. Here again, incomplete information is to blame. If the actual state change in real disposable income per capita had been known prior to the election, the model's electoral vote forecast would have outperformed the journalists and would have been as accurate as the best forecast made by Carter and Reagan strategists.

10. After seeing the election returns, I assume that Fair discards the long-memory model in favor of the short-memory one. Neither Tufte nor I change our specifications after seeing the returns.

EXPLAINING THE 1976 AND 1980 ELECTIONS

Why did the Republicans win in 1972, lose in 1976, and win again in 1980? Their change in fortune is explained by changes in the political and economic conditions that prevailed in these elections. Clearly, although Ford in 1976, and Carter four years later, exploited the advantages of presidential incumbency, this factor did not ensure victory.

Secular political trends, most notably the Watergate scandal, worked to Carter's advantage in 1976. The Democrats won 58.6 percent of the vote cast in the 1974 midterm election. If instead they had captured 54.4 percent (their average vote in the eight previous House elections), the Republican presidential vote would have been approximately 1 to 2 points higher in 1976, a large enough increase to have assured Ford both a popular and electoral vote majority.

The poor economy also helped Carter. Economic problems concerned voters more than any other issue. Ford's 3.0 percent election year increase in real disposable income per capita was slightly lower than the increase enjoyed by 3 of his 4 predecessors who ran as incumbents. If the 1976 election year increase in income had been 1 percentage point higher in every state, Ford's probability of a national popular vote victory would have increased by 8 percent and his probability of victory in the electoral college would have gone up by 40 percent.[11]

Carter's centrist position on both racial and New Deal social welfare issues worked to his advantage in 1976. Carter was the most conservative New Deal social welfare Democrat to run in the elections I considered. (See appendix A, table A.5.) Although Carter's middle-of-the-road position cost him votes in liberal states like Rhode Island and Massachusetts, this loss was more than offset by the votes he gained in the rest of the country. Not only did Carter's moderate stand put him closer to more voters than a more liberal candidate would have been, but his proximity to Ford's position greatly reduced the amount of preference that conservatives had for Ford over Carter. The distance

---

11. The calculations that produce these estimates are described in chap. 7.

between the two candidates on this dimension was about one-third the distance that separated the candidates in 1964 and 1972 and about one-half the distance between the major party candidates in 1968. This helped Carter because it greatly reduced the impact of social welfare issues on the outcome.

Carter's position on racial issues worked to his advantage for similar reasons. Relative to the electorate of the day, Carter was to the right of Johnson, McGovern, and Humphrey—about as liberal as Stevenson and Kennedy. The distance between Ford and Carter on racial issues was about one-half the distance between the major party candidates in 1964, 1968, and 1972. Although Carter's centrist position cost him a few votes among liberals, this loss was again greatly offset by the votes he took from Ford in racially conservative states.

New Deal social welfare and racial issues—which in recent decades have divided Democrats, were also less salient in 1976 than in earlier elections. The close proximity of the candidates on these two sets of issues coupled with a reduction in the importance of these two dimensions meant that New Deal social welfare and racial issues had a much smaller impact on the vote for president in 1976 than they had in 1964, 1968, and 1972. This is a reversal of the trend in increased issue voting, discussed in chapter 4. Only during the 1950s did these issues have a smaller effect on election outcomes than in 1976 (and, as will be seen, in 1980).

Finally, Jimmy Carter's southernness brought in a few votes. Although Carter won 10 of the 11 former Confederate states, only a small proportion of his vote total in the South—2.7 points—can be attributed to a friends-and-neighbors effect. (This small vote advantage, however, was sufficient to bring victory in at least two states.) Carter's place of birth had little to do with the South's return to the Democratic fold in 1976. The 1974 election, which had temporarily derailed the Republican trend in the South, Carter's moderate positions, and the lessening of the importance of issues, particularly racial issues, were all more important than his birthplace.

A similar set of factors explains the 1980 outcome, although then the shoe was on the other foot. Secular trends had swung back to the Republicans. Memories of Watergate had faded; the

Democrats' 1978 midterm vote dropped 4.3 points below its 1974 level. This cost Carter about 1 to 2 percentage points in 1980.

Economic concerns remained the most salient election issue. Carter was saddled with an economy in far worse shape than Gerald Ford's had ever been, and there was widespread dissatisfaction with his management of it. Inflation topped 10 percent; real per capita disposable income *dropped* by .3 percent in 1980—the first presidential election year decline since Hoover lost to Roosevelt in 1932. The poor economy cost Carter about 2.6 percent of the popular vote.

The Democrats were more united than the Republicans in 1976; the situation was reversed in 1980. Reagan was popular within his party, Carter was not. Bitter Democratic disaffection with Carter cost him votes. Had Carter been as popular among Democrats as Reagan was among Republicans, Carter's national popular vote would have been about 1 percentage point higher; his electoral college total would have been boosted by 22 votes.

And, of course, there was the hostage issue, underscored by the one-year anniversary of Iran's taking of the U.S. Embassy, which coincided with the election itself. The last-minute shifts to Reagan, perhaps due to the media's extensive coverage of the situation, certainly contributed to my 3.2 percent underprediction of Reagan's strength. I return to this point in chapter 8.

Carter, who had maintained his centrist positions on New Deal social welfare and racial issues, was now running against Reagan—a conservative who stood substantially to the right of Gerald Ford and two-thirds of the American public. If voters had chosen candidates on these issues, most would have preferred Carter to Reagan. But Carter's problem was that neither set of issues was important in 1980, and he did little to try to increase their salience. Had these issues been as important in 1980 as they had been in 1964 or 1972, Carter's popular vote would have been boosted about 2 points; he would have captured 70 additional electoral votes. Although this strategy would have cost Carter votes in the South, these losses would have been offset by substantial vote gains in other states, particularly in the Northeast. Carter should not have run against Reagan the way he ran against Ford.

7

SIMULATION OF ALTERNATIVE SCENARIOS

My purpose in this chapter is to investigate what the outcome of presidential elections would have been had different political and economic conditions prevailed. If the candidates, the economy, the salient issues, the nominees' positions, or the electorate's preferences change, the election results will change. Through simulation—the modification of model parameters or the values of exogenous causes of the vote to reflect hypothetical conditions (like a better economy or different candidates)—hypothetical election scenarios can be created. A simulation does more than merely satisfy curiosity by answering the "What if . . . ?" question. It helps clarify the impact a variable has on election outcomes. Simulation allows the electoral consequences of conditions that have not occurred naturally to be discovered, and the effectiveness of alternative electoral strategies to be examined.

I will simulate settings that candidates, strategists, or other political elites might try to create because it would be to their electoral advantage to do so. They could manipulate, to some extent, three components of the model: the choice of candidates, the importance of issues, and the state of the economy. Some politicians argue that nominees who would maximize their party's chance of winning should be selected; they think that moderates are better suited to win. How much do outcomes depend on who the candidates are? How sensitive are election results to changes in the nominees and their issue positions? Although a candidate is not free to assume any position he pleases, he can make marginal adjustments in his stance to suit the situation. Would this have much effect on the outcome?

A nominee also can influence which campaign issues will be important, by stressing some issues over others. Although a candidate cannot make extremely salient issues evaporate, he can sidestep those that may work to his disadvantage, resurrect issues that may help him electorally, or ignore dormant issues that may cost him votes. For example, Jimmy Carter could have emphasized traditional New Deal social welfare issues more than he did in 1976 and 1980. The political consequences of this decision will be considered.

The final set of simulations examines how different election year economies would have altered presidential election outcomes. The president has at his disposal "the instruments of economic policy" to affect the election year accelerations he desires (Tufte 1978, chap. 2). Could economic manipulation have altered an election outcome?

An election scenario is simulated in one of two ways. To estimate what would have happened if a different candidate were nominated, the characteristics of the hypothetical candidate (his positions, his state and region of residence, whether he is an incumbent, and so on) are substituted in place of those of the actual candidate. The estimated model is used to generate algebraically the simulated vote for each state. To gauge the effect of this change, the simulated vote is compared to the original predicted vote for the state (estimated from the model using the actual election data).[1] Changes in the national popular and electoral vote and changes in the probability of a national popular and electoral college victory are also estimated.

Alternative economic scenarios are simulated in a similar fashion. A hypothetical election year change in real disposable income per capita is substituted for the actual change that occurred in each state that year; the simulated election outcome is com-

1. The error term in the model appears in the equation for both the simulated vote (V^*) and the vote originally predicted by the model ($\hat{Y}$). Thus, when V^* is compared to $\hat{Y}$, the error terms cancel. If V^* were compared to the actual vote, the error term would appear only in the equation for V^*, and thus the estimated effect would include not only the simulation effect, but the equation error as well.

puted and compared to the predicted vote given the economic conditions that actually prevailed.

Model parameters estimate issue importance, so to simulate changes in their importance the coefficients, rather than the data, must be altered. For example, to simulate in 1960 what would happen if racial issues had been more important, the racial issue's coefficients in that year are increased and the simulated election outcome is algebraically computed.

The simulations are conducted under the assumptions of the model. I assume not only that the estimated coefficients are statistically consistent, but that the causal variables in the vote equation are exogenous. This implies that new, simulated values for one variable in the equation do not cause other election conditions in the model to change as well. For example, when I simulate different economic conditions, I assume that these changes do not affect the values of the other variables, such as the candidates' positions on social welfare or racial issues. Similarly, I also assume that the issue coefficients are not determined by the candidates' positions or the state of the economy.[2]

ALTERNATIVE CANDIDATE SCENARIOS

The first set of simulations examines the extent to which a party's fortunes are determined by the candidate it nominates. Political analysts contend that the Goldwater and McGovern candidacies produced the 1964 and 1972 landslide elections (Converse et al. 1966; Miller et al. 1976; Popkin et al. 1976). How different would the outcomes have been if more "moderate" candidates had been nominated? Conversely, if a noncentrist candidate were to replace centrists, would outcomes change?

Hubert Humphrey sought the Democratic nomination in 1972 and, though he did not actively seek the spot in 1976, sectors of

2. I reflect on this assumption in chap. 8. If a variable manipulated in the simulation appears in the equation for other right-hand-side variables in the model, then the simulated estimates will be biased. The size and direction of the bias depends on which other variables this particular variable causes, the magnitude and direction of its effect on the other variables, and the size and sign of these other right-hand-side variables' coefficients in the vote equation.

the Democratic party supported his candidacy. When some Democrats tried to stop Carter's nomination in late spring, Humphrey's name again came to the fore. Moreover, since other Democrats (Bayh, Shriver, and Udall) who did seek the 1976 nomination held positions similar to Humphrey's, simulating the former vice-president's nomination will also suggest what would have happened if one of these other candidates had been the Democratic standard bearer.

If Humphrey had been the Democratic presidential nominee, Ford probably would have won in 1976. Humphrey would have run behind Carter in 44 states.[3] The drop-off in the Democratic vote would have been greatest in the South, where a Humphrey candidacy would have added about 10.5 percentage points to the Republican total in each state. Nearly 8 of these percentage points would be due to Humphrey's more liberal positions, particularly on race; the remaining effect would have resulted from the loss of a southerner heading the ticket. Humphrey would probably have lost all but one southern and border state in 1976. (He would have had about a fifty-fifty chance of carrying Georgia if the Democratic vice-presidential nominee had come from that state.)

A 1976 Humphrey candidacy would have hurt the Democrats considerably less in the North, where Humphrey would have run only 1 or 2 percentage points behind Carter, although in the liberal states like Massachusetts, Rhode Island, and New York Humphrey would have pulled slightly more support than Carter did.

Nationally, a 1976 Humphrey candidacy would have brought defeat to the Democrats. Ford's popular vote total would have been 2.7 percentage points higher; his electoral college total would have been boosted by 89 votes. There are better than 99 chances in 100 that a Humphrey candidacy would have produced a Ford victory in the electoral college; there are 84 chances out of

3. One potential complication in simulating a Humphrey candidacy in 1972 or 1976 is that the residuals in these years can be autocorrelated with the residuals from 1968 when Humphrey first ran for president. However, because the 1968 Nixon residuals are uncorrelated with the residuals from 1960 when he first ran (r = .04), it seems safe to ignore the autocorrelation problem.

100 that Ford would have been the popular vote victor as well. These national-level forecasts (as well as those from other simulations discussed in this chapter) are summarized in table 7.1.

Humphrey would not have won in 1972 either. Nationally he would have run about 2.2 percent ahead of McGovern in the popular vote, but he would have picked up only an additional 17 electoral votes. Humphrey would have pulled 1 or 2 points more than McGovern in the North and about 5 to 6 points more in the South. However, there would still have been less than 1 chance in 100 of a Democratic victory in 1972.

The Democrats would have been even better off if instead of McGovern in 1972 they had run the "Average Democratic Candidate." A. Dem., as I will call him, is a hypothetical candidate whose positions are assumed to be the average of the positions held by the Democratic nominees between 1948 and 1976. He is more conservative than both Humphrey and McGovern and, as expected, would pull more votes than either of them. A. Dem.'s popular vote in northern states would have been about 2 percent higher than McGovern's vote in 1972. The depths of southern antipathy for McGovern is revealed by this simulation: A. Dem.'s candidacy would have boosted the Democrats' vote in the South by *12* percentage points. Nationally, however, the average Democratic candidate still would have been unable to beat Nixon in 1972. Although A. Dem. would have run 3.8 percent ahead of McGovern, he would have captured only 34 additional electoral votes. The odds would still be better than 99 to 1 that Nixon would have been reelected. The relatively good economy, Nixon's incumbency advantage, the liberalness of the available pool of Democratic candidates, the president's middle-of-the-road positions, and the salience of racial issues, particularly in the South, all contributed to his reelection.

The impact that noncentrist candidates have on election outcomes can be seen from the Republican perspective as well. Here I consider two alternatives to the 1964 Goldwater candidacy: a Rockefeller nomination and an "Average Republican Candidate," A. Rep., whose positions are set to the average of the stands taken by the 1948 to 1976 Republican nominees. Rockefeller would have received about 41 percent of the popu-

Table 7.1 Election Simulations

Simulation	Democratic Popular Vote		Democratic Electoral Vote	
	Change in Percentage	Change in Probability of Victory	Change in Votes	Change in Probability of Victory
1. 1976 Humphrey as Democratic nominee	-2.7	-.36	-89	-.52
2. 1972 Humphrey as Democratic nominee	+2.2	.00	+17	.00
3. 1972 A. Dem. as Democratic nominee	+3.8	.00	+34	.00
4. 1964 Rockefeller as Republican nominee	-3.4	.00	-23	.00
5. 1964 A. Rep. as Republican nominee	-3.3	.00	-45	.00
6. 1980 Kennedy as Democratic nominee	-5.7	.00	-33	.00
7. 1976 Social welfare and racial issues more salient	-.8	-.12	-29	-.49
8. 1960 Racial issues more salient	-1.9	-.41	-70	-.44
9. 1972 Racial issues less salient	+1.5	.00	+9	.00
10. 1980 Social welfare issues more salient	+.4	.00	+43	.00
11. 1976 Income 1 point higher	-.5	-.08	-17	-.40
12. 1960 Income 1 point higher	-.8	-.25	-24	-.44
13. 1960 Normal election year economy	-2.0	-.45	-59	-.44
14. 1964 Normal election year economy	-2.1	.00	-15	.00
15. 1980 Normal election year economy	+2.6	.00	+75	.00

lar vote in 1964, running 3.4 points ahead of Goldwater, but he would have picked up only 23 additional electoral votes. In most states, Rockefeller would have run over 3 points ahead of Goldwater, although in some, like Florida, Rockefeller would have captured an additional 12 percent of the vote for the G.O.P. In the deep South—the most conservative racial and social welfare states in the union—the more liberal Rockefeller would have boosted Johnson's vote by an average of 15 points.[4]

The average Republican candidate would not have done much better than Rockefeller would have in 1964. A. Rep. would have run about 3.3 points ahead of Goldwater in the popular vote, and 45 votes ahead of him in the electoral college. Neither Rockefeller nor A. Rep. would have beaten Johnson in 1964. Under both scenarios, there is less than 1 chance in 100 that Johnson would have lost either his popular vote or electoral college majority.

These simulations suggest that even if Goldwater and McGovern had not been nominated in 1964 and 1972, their parties still would have lost. While these challengers' "extreme" issue positions clearly contributed to the landslide incumbent victories, they added 4 points at most to the incumbent's national popular vote and fewer than 50 votes to his electoral college total.

One cannot help wondering what would have happened in 1980 if Edward Kennedy had captured the Democratic nomination. Had Kennedy been the Democratic standard bearer, the Republican margin of victory would have been even larger—approaching the 1972 Nixon landslide.[5] Nationally, the Democrats' popular vote would have plunged 5.7 points below Carter's total; their electoral college total would have been down 33 votes. The greatest vote disaster would have occurred in the South. Kennedy would have run a whopping 22 points behind Carter in the average southern state. He would have had no more than 5 chances in

4. This assumes that George Wallace, who contemplated a third-party run in 1964 but was discouraged by Goldwater's capture of the nomination, would not have run. (See Rosenstone, Behr, and Lazarus [1984, chap. 4].)

5. I also assume in this simulation that a Kennedy candidacy would have increased the importance of New Deal social welfare issues to their 1972 level and that he would have captured the nomination by winning an additional 15 percent of the convention votes cast by each state.

100 of a popular vote victory in any state south of the Mason-Dixon line. Kennedy's social welfare liberalism, the absence of a southerner at the head of the ticket, and party factionalism, stemming from elite support for Carter, would have produced the southern Democratic debacle.

Kennedy would have run about 1.3 points behind Carter in the average western state, although in the most conservative states in this region—Arizona, Colorado, Idaho, New Mexico, and Wyoming—he would have trailed Carter by 3 points. Only in Oregon would Kennedy have run ahead of Carter. The same result would have unfolded in the Midwest. Kennedy would have trailed Carter on average by 1.6 points, although in Indiana, Kansas, and North Dakota he would have dropped over 3 points. However, in three of the more liberal states in this region—Minnesota, Michigan, and Wisconsin—Kennedy would have polled 1 to 2 points more than Carter did.

The East is the only region where a Kennedy candidacy would have helped the Democrats—but the boost would not have been sufficient to offset losses that would have been incurred in the rest of the country. Kennedy would have run an average of 1.3 points better than Carter in this region, doing worse only in Delaware, New Hampshire, and Vermont. The other states in the region would have given an additional 1 to 3 percent of their vote to the Democrats if Kennedy had headed the ticket. (A Kennedy nomination would have boosted the Democratic vote in his home state of Massachusetts by 8.5 points.)

In sum, Kennedy's nomination in 1980 would have spelled even greater electoral disaster for the Democrats. Only 5 states (Massachusetts, Rhode Island, Hawaii, West Virginia, and Minnesota) would have had more than an 80 percent chance of going Democratic.

CHANGES IN ISSUE IMPORTANCE

The first issue simulation demonstrates how much Carter's 1976 victory depended on the relatively low salience of New Deal social welfare and racial issues. Here, I examine what would have happened had these two dimensions been as important in 1976 as they were in 1968 (their peak year). Although Carter would have run better in 29 states under this scenario, the aggregate shift would not be in his favor. If these two sets of issues had been as important in 1976 as they were in 1968, Carter would have lost .8 percent of his national popular vote, approximately 29 electoral votes, and most likely the election. The probability of a Carter popular vote victory would have been reduced by 12 percent to .41; the probability of a Carter victory in the electoral college would have dropped to 5 chances in 100. The greatest vote loss— 6 to 9 points—would have occurred in the South, costing Carter as many as 8 states in his native region. This loss would not have been offset by his slight vote gain in northern liberal and moderate states, where he would have picked up 2 or 3 more states at most. Clearly, had the fervent issue politics of the sixties prevailed in 1976, the probability is high that Jimmy Carter would not have been elected president.

Had racial issues been as important in 1960 as they were in 1968, John Kennedy would not have been elected either. Although Kennedy's vote total would have been boosted 1 or 2 points in the 15 most racially liberal states, he would have been hurt in the remaining 35. Again, the Democratic loss would have been sharpest in the South, where an increase in racial salience in 1960 would have cost the Democrats between 6 and 9 percent of the popular vote and probably 4 or 5 states' electoral votes. Nationally, if racial issues had been as salient in 1960 as they were by the end of the decade, it would have cost Kennedy 1.9 percent of the popular vote, 70 electoral votes, and would have reduced to near zero the likelihood that he would have attained an electoral college majority. A Nixon victory would have been assured.

On the other hand, if racial issues in 1972 had remained at their 1960 level of importance and the Nixon-McGovern contest were rerun, McGovern's national popular vote would have increased 1.5 points. But only 9 electoral votes would have been added to his column. Thus, unlike 1960, when a change in the importance of race would have reversed the outcome, the mirror image of this change in 1972 would have had little effect: a Nixon popular and electoral vote victory would still have remained a certainty.

Finally, Carter would have done only slightly better in 1980 had New Deal social welfare issues been more important than they were that year. In most northern states his popular vote would have been .5 to 1.5 points higher; in a few states (Massachusetts, New York, Rhode Island, and Oregon) his total would have been boosted by as much as 3.5 percent. However, these gains would have been offset by the greater vote loss—3.6 points—he would have suffered in the South. Nationally, Carter's popular vote would have been only .4 points higher. He would have attained, at most, 43 additional electoral votes, which would still have assured a comfortable Reagan victory.

ALTERNATIVE ECONOMIC SCENARIOS

The final simulations consider the effect that changes in economic conditions have on presidential elections. The election year increase in real disposable personal income per capita in 1976 was 3.0 percent, about average for a presidential election year, but a point lower than the election year increases when Truman, Eisenhower, Johnson, and Nixon ran for election as incumbents. Ford's inability to generate the same election year economic boost enjoyed by his predecessors may have cost him the election. If each state's 1976 change in real disposable income per capita were 1 percentage point higher, Ford's vote in each state would have risen by .3 to .7 percentage points and the probability of his winning each state would have been 1 to 8 percent higher. Nationally, Ford's popular vote would have increased .5 percentage points and 17 electoral votes would have been added to his total. The probability of a Ford popular vote victory would have increased to .55; the probability of a Ford electoral college majority would have increased to .85. This small change alone in the economy, although not guaranteeing a Ford victory, might have generated enough votes, in the right states, to tip the election in his favor.

The effect that small changes in the economy can have on election outcomes can also be seen in 1960. In that year if real disposable income per capita had been only 1 percent higher (1 percent instead of 0 percent), a Nixon victory would have been assured. Kennedy's state-by-state vote would have decreased by .4 to 1.0 percentage points. The aggregate effect of these state shifts would have been a .8 percentage point reduction in Kennedy's national popular vote and his loss of 24 electoral votes. If real disposable income per capita in 1960 had been 1 point higher, the probability of a Kennedy popular vote victory would have been reduced 25 percent (to .2); the probability of a Democratic electoral vote majority would have dropped to 1 chance in 100. Kennedy probably would have lost.

Of course, if 1960 had been a "normal" economic election year—if real disposable income per capita had increased about 3 percent—Nixon would have enjoyed a decisive victory. His national popular vote total would have been 2.0 points higher; he would have received an additional 59 electoral votes, which would have assured him control of the electoral college. Under this scenario, the chances are better than 99 in 100 that Nixon would have defeated Kennedy.

As the 1960 and 1976 simulations demonstrate, in close contests small election year manipulations of the economy can make the difference in the outcome.

Not every election verdict would have changed had different economic conditions prevailed. Although the growth in real disposable personal income per capita in 1964 was higher (5.6 percent) than in any postwar election year, that alone did not generate the Democratic landslide. If 1964 had had a "normal" election year economy (simulated by reducing the change in disposable personal income per capita in each state by 2.6 points), the election outcome would have remained about the same. Though Johnson's national popular vote would have been 2.1 percentage points lower, his margin in the electoral college would have gone down by a mere 15 votes. A Johnson victory would have remained a certainty. To be sure, prosperity contributed to Johnson's popular vote landslide, but it alone did not cause it.

Although the lagging economy contributed substantially to Reagan's 1980 margin of victory, it too was not alone responsible for Carter's defeat. Had 1980 been a normal economic election year,[6] Carter's popular vote would have been 2.6 percent higher;

6. Because the 1980 model was augmented to include variables for both the change in real disposable income per capita and the electorate's evaluation of which party would best manage the economy, in this simulation these two variables were set to their average election value.

he would have captured an additional 75 votes in the electoral college. Even under these circumstances, Reagan's victory would have remained a near certainty.

Could a president's election year manipulation of the economy succeed in keeping an incumbent party in office when it otherwise would have been defeated? Although the incumbent's party was retained in office in 1948, 1956, 1964, and 1972, only in 1948 was his margin of victory sufficiently narrow to have been created by economic manipulation alone. Truman captured only 49.6 percent of the national popular vote in 1948 and won by a slim margin of 37 electoral votes. The Democrats won 6 states by only 52 percent of the two-party vote and won 3 others by less than 53 percent. These 9 marginal Truman states comprised 166 electoral votes (55 percent of his total). It is conceivable that even a small election year manipulation of the economy in 1948 could have been the deciding factor in Truman's victory.[7] This suspicion mounts when one looks at the change in real disposable income per capita (ΔY) for 1948 and the surrounding years:

Year	ΔY
1946	−2.6%
1947	−5.9%
1948	+3.4%
1949	−1.5%

If the 3.4 percent rise in income in 1948 resulted, in part, from Truman's creating an election year boom, the strategy payed off. Without it, he would have probably been denied a majority of the electoral vote, if not swinging the election to Dewey, certainly tossing it into the House of Representatives.

In summary, an electoral-economic cycle may have generated a victory for Truman in 1948. Election year economic booms did not reelect Eisenhower in 1956, Johnson in 1964, or Nixon in 1972, nor did they provide victories for Stevenson in 1952, Nixon in 1960, Humphrey in 1968, Ford in 1976, or Carter in 1980. Certainly, as the 1960 and 1976 simulations make clear, it is easy

7. Because Wallace and Thurmond votes were scored as Democratic votes to simplify model estimation, I cannot accurately simulate how much the 1948 outcome would have changed had real disposable income per capita been lower.

to envision scenarios under which relatively minor economic manipulations could produce different outcomes.

IMPLICATIONS

Several generalizations about the impact of the economy, issues, and candidates on election outcomes can be drawn from these simulations. The findings have implications for optimal candidate strategies, the electoral college system, and the Democratic party's future prospects.

1. Although the election year economy has a considerable effect on the presidential vote, it is only one of many factors that determine election outcomes. Who the candidates are, what their positions are on the issues, and whether an incumbent president runs all have a greater impact on the outcome than the incumbent party's management of the economy. This is not to say that changes in the economy cannot alter the result: better economies alone would have elected Nixon in 1960 and Ford in 1976. Although manipulation of the election year economy by incumbents may take place, it is unlikely that this manipulation has changed an outcome, except perhaps in 1948.

2. An issue's importance has an independent and significant effect on presidential election results. The more salient an issue, the larger a candidate's vote will be in those states where his position is preferred to his opponent's. Relatively minor tinkerings with racial and social welfare issue importance can change the national popular vote by as much as 2 percentage points.

3. The simulations point out the frailties of the Democratic party coalition. If the Democrats continue to nominate presidential candidates who are as liberal on New Deal social welfare and racial issues as the party nominees traditionally have been, then it will be difficult for them to win an electoral majority, if these issues are important to voters. This point is particularly clear in 1976 when Carter, the most conservative Democratic candidate in recent history, barely won election. If Carter had been as liberal as his Democratic predecessors, he would surely have lost. If social welfare or racial issues had been as important as they were in the 1960s, he would have lost. Similarly, it is also clear

that if a liberal, like Kennedy, had been nominated, it would have meant an even more decisive Reagan victory in 1980.

Southern allegiance to the Democratic party in presidential elections is extremely tenuous. Even if racial and social welfare issues remain less prominent than they were in the 1960s, liberal Democrats will have a difficult time capturing the South. If the Democratic candidate is to the left of Carter and racial or social welfare issues are important, the Republicans are assured a southern sweep. The only way the South's 138 electoral votes will remain in the Democratic fold is if Democrats nominate moderates or conservatives, the underlying issue cleavage changes, or three decades of secular trends are reversed.

4. The widely held belief that the best candidate position on issues is the middle of the road does not hold if the goal is to maximize electoral rather than popular votes. A candidate who moves toward the center of the distribution of voter preferences may end up pursuing a suboptimal electoral vote strategy. For example, the average Republican candidate (A. Rep.) would have run 3.3 percent ahead of Goldwater's 1964 popular vote. Rockefeller, slightly closer to the center than A. Rep., would have run 3.4 percent ahead of Goldwater and thus .1 percent ahead of A. Rep. However, the more centrist candidate (Rockefeller) would have received 22 *fewer* electoral votes than A. Rep., who was farther off center. This is because a Rockefeller candidacy would have pushed southern states—states that a more conservative Republican probably would have carried—into the Democratic column. Thus, if candidates or issue positions are chosen to maximize the national popular vote, in some cases a party will actually do worse in the electoral college than if a less rational popular vote strategy were pursued.

The implication, of course, for those who model electoral college strategies (Colantoni, Levesque, and Ordeshook, 1975; Brams and Davis 1974), is that a rational strategy depends on both the distribution of voter preferences in each state and on the probability that each state will be won in the election. This probability of victory (the expected vote) varies across states and across time. It is inappropriate to assume that in every election a candidate has an equal probability of winning each state (Brams and Davis 1974; Brams 1978, chap. 3). He does not. A rational electoral college strategy in 1980 may be irrational in 1984.[8]

5. The rate at which changes in the national popular vote are converted into electoral votes varies considerably. As the simulations show, in close elections a 1 percent change in the national popular vote will generate a change of over 30 electoral votes. The conversion rate is less than half that size in landslide elections. Virtually anything, of course—the economy, the candidates, the saliency of issues—can tip the electoral college scale in close contests. But in landslides, where the margin of victory in most states is wide, comparable popular vote changes will produce fewer changes in the winner-take-all state electoral vote allocation.[9]

Popular vote shifts yield fewer electoral votes if the popular votes are produced by a change in the candidates than if the equivalent popular vote swing is generated by a change in the economy. The 15 simulations discussed in this chapter show that a 3 percent change in the popular vote owing to a uniform shift in the economy across states produces 36 more electoral votes than a comparable popular vote change that stems from either different candidates or changes in importance of issues.[10] In general, a

8. In a similar vein, strategies designed to gain votes in a majority of the states can also reduce the candidate's national popular and/or electoral vote total. For example, if New Deal social welfare and racial issues were more important in 1976, Carter would have run better in 29 of the 50 states, but would have lost .8 percent of the popular vote, 29 electoral votes, and perhaps the election.

9. The 1964, 1972, and 1980 simulations also clearly show that it is inappropriate to try to explain landslide elections by a single variable like extreme candidates or a poor economy. A change in one factor alone would not have reversed these verdicts.

10. The estimated equation is as follows:

$$\text{Elvote} = -20.2 + 7.8 \text{ Dempop} + 15.0 \text{ Reppop} + 32.6 \text{ Y72} + 44.6 \text{ Y76}$$
$$(5.6) \qquad (2.9) \qquad (17.9) \qquad (10.0)$$
$$+ 77.3 \text{ Y80} - 12.0 \text{ Candiss}$$
$$(11.2) \qquad (8.7)$$

$N = 15$
$R^2 = .95$

where Elvote is the change in the electoral vote;

      Dempop is the Democratic increase in the popular vote (0 otherwise);

      Reppop is the Republican increase in the popular vote (0 otherwise);

popular vote swing will more efficiently convert to electoral votes
if it results from a uniform shift across states than if it is the net
result of the gain of popular votes in some states but the loss in
others. Hence, how much a particular strategy will pay off in the
electoral college is not revealed solely by the number of popular
votes a party gains. Its electoral impact depends on the geographic distribution of the voters whose preferences shift. To see
this point, recall that a Rockefeller candidacy in 1964 would have
increased the Republicans' popular vote by 3.4 percent and their
electoral college total by 23 votes. On the other hand, a normal
economy in the same year would have boosted their popular vote
by only 2.0 percent, but their electoral college total would have
increased by 59 votes.

6. The electoral college system currently disadvantages the
Democratic party. Simulations that increased the Republican
popular vote generated nearly twice as many electoral votes as
were produced by comparable popular vote gains for the
Democrats.[11]

This bias also can be seen from the estimate of the percentage
of the popular vote the Democrats would need, on average, to
obtain an electoral college majority. The figures for sets of elections since 1932, reported in table 7.2, reveal that the slight pro-
Democratic bias in the electoral college that existed during the
1936 to 1960 period has been reversed. The Republican bias is
now substantial. While the Democrats on average needed only
49.38 percent of the two-party popular vote to capture 50 percent
of the two-party electoral college vote between 1940 and 1960, in
an average election between 1964 and 1980 the Democrats
needed 51.91 percent of the popular vote to win 50 percent of the
electoral college. (They needed 51.98 percent of the popular vote
to capture 270 electoral votes [a majority].) In short, given the

---

Y72, Y76, and Y80 are dummy variables for the 1972, 1976, and 1980
simulations respectively; and

Candiss is 1 if a candidate or issue simulation, and 0 if an economic
simulation.

11. The estimated coefficients are reported in n. 10. There are 83 chances out
of 100 that pro-Republican popular vote shifts have a larger electoral vote impact
than equivalent shifts in the Democratic direction.

Table 7.2 Popular Vote and Electoral Vote, 1932–80

Years	Democratic Percentage of Two-Party Popular Vote Required for 50.0 Percent of Electoral Vote*
1932-48	50.10
1936-52	49.81
1940-56	49.43
1944-60	49.38
1948-64	50.43
1952-68	50.73
1956-72	50.89
1960-76	50.92
1964-80	51.91**

* Estimated from $Log (EV/(1-EV)) = a + b(Pop)$; where EV = Democratic proportion of the two-party electoral vote; and Pop = Democratic proportion of the two-party popular vote.
** To obtain 270 electoral votes (50.47 percent) the Democrats need 51.98 percent of the two-party popular vote.

current match between electoral votes and state patterns of presidential voting, the Democrats need nearly 2 points over and above a majority of the popular vote to be assured an electoral college victory. Moreover, this bias will be increased when the electoral vote reallocations (as a result of the 1980 census) take effect in 1984. The states that will gain in the electoral college are more Republican (6 percent more so in 1980) than the rest of the country.

8
FINAL CONSIDERATIONS

The political conditions that prevail on election day determine which party will win the presidency. Change the setting, and the results will change. When we can explain differences among outcomes—develop rules to account for why the Democrats win one year but lose another—we can forecast elections. Presidential elections are not idiosyncratic events; future outcomes are not terra incognita.

Elections have always been forecasted and no doubt always will be. The only question is how future forecasts will be made. As we approach the next presidential election, and concern mounts over who will win, the rules developed in the preceding chapters can be used to guide a prediction. First, consider how each state has traditionally voted. If an incumbent runs, his party will do better than otherwise would be expected. The vote boost will be largest in states least supportive of the president's party in the last midterm election. If a vice-president is a presidential nominee, expect a small vote boost for him as well. If the administration has mismanaged the economy or foreign affairs, voters will punish that party. If one of the candidates is out of step with the electorate on an issue, he will suffer at the polls. The more important the issue, and the greater the distance between the candidate and the voters, the more votes that candidate will lose. Consider where the candidates are from: presidential and vice-presidential nominees enjoy a small home-state advantage, and southern presidential candidates will pull in additional votes from their home region as well. Secular political trends reflected in the midterm vote will affect the presidential result, but bear in mind that Democratic trends will not yield as many votes for the Democrats as Republican trends will produce for the G.O.P.

Remember, count electoral votes—they win presidential elections.

EXTENSION OF THE THEORY

To be sure, this book is just a first step toward a general theory of elections. The explanation is incomplete. Issues that are salient only in the short run (such as civil unrest in 1968 and 1972 or the Iranian hostages in 1980) and aspects of the incumbent administration's performance, beyond its management of the economy and foreign affairs, may also affect who wins. Outcomes also may hinge on voters' evaluations of the incumbent party's ability to enhance personal security, happiness, social services, or national prestige. The electorate's assessment of the candidates themselves—their competence, trustworthiness, and other personal attributes—probably matter as well (Popkin et al. 1976; Kinder and Abelson 1981).

The theory can also be refined to take into account the political consequences of shifts in turnout. Long-term changes in the composition of the electorate caused by the re-enfranchisement of blacks in the 1960s or increased white participation in the South, as well as short-term changes due to economic fluctuations, disaffection with candidates, or mobilization of voters by issues or the campaign, may all affect the final tally (Clymer 1980, p. 1; Rosenstone 1982).

Support for third parties, which contributed to some of the 1948, 1976, and 1980 errors, might also be examined. Although the model's misses are not associated in any simple way with the votes cast for minor-party candidates, it may be that a third party does not damage the same major party to the same degree in every state. (Anderson may have cut deeper into Carter's strength in Massachusetts than in Connecticut.) The theory could be extended to predict support for third-party candidates as well as the political consequences of that support for major party fortunes. (See Rosenstone, Behr, and Lazarus 1984.)

The model could also be expanded to account better for political differences among the states. The candidates' campaign efforts in each state (their level of spending, media expenditures, organization, and activity), social, ethnic, or political cleavages within the state, as well as other contests that might affect the presidential vote, could all be considered. Particular issues or candidates may affect voters in some states differently than in others.

The theory has been tested over a relatively short span of U.S. presidential elections. Whether its basic structure will generalize to other contests, time periods, or polities is still undetermined. Because scholars have been alert to the effect that changes in the electoral context have on voting for members of Congress, and district-level data are readily available, models are easily imagined that will both explain and predict district-by-district election outcomes.

Although the theory captures secular realignments that have occurred over the past three decades—the decay of the Democratic coalition in particular—it is not clear whether it will anticipate a critical election. If the realignment first surfaces in the previous midterm election, results from economic debacle, or is a reinstatement of an existing political cleavage, the model should catch it. However, if the new coalition appears for the first time in the presidential contest, establishes new political cleavages, or is not tied to economic concerns, it may well be missed. The model will work best during periods of "normal politics," less well during periods of political upheaval.

This raises a more general concern. The most challenging problem is to develop theories that will predict the weight that should be given to each of the model's components. When will issues matter most? How much should the hostage issue in 1980 or Carter's perceived incompetence count? Of course, this can always be learned after the fact. But the accuracy of many forecasts may hinge on whether shifts in the importance voters give to an issue, their usual vote, candidate attributes, or secular trends can be anticipated before the election.

The model should be expanded so that each cause of the election outcome is explained. We need to account for changes in the electorate's positions on issues, their evaluation of the incumbent party's performance, and secular political trends. We need to understand better the forces that generate the candidates. Under what conditions are liberals, or incumbents, likely to capture the nomination? These additional equations will not only make the theory more complete, they will allow one to forecast elections much earlier—perhaps even before the identity of candidates is known with certainty. In principle, election outcomes could be forecasted one, two, or more years in advance.

Further disaggregation of the model to the county or city level may also prove profitable. Although data limitations make this path unpromising at present, it would offer several advantages. The model and the effect of variables could vary within states (e.g., New York City versus upstate New York; southern versus northern California, etc.). This would allow potentially important local conditions to be taken into account. State forecasts produced from combining county or town forecasts would most likely have smaller errors than do my state forecasts. This in turn would also make electoral college forecasts more accurate.

The model might also be disaggregated down to the individual level. The chief drawback, at least at present, is that the state popular vote and the electoral college result could not be forecasted because self-representing state surveys are not readily available. If survey data were employed to explain elections, the surveys would have to be pooled across years to capture the impact on the outcome of changes in the electoral context. A variable's impact could vary across different types of voter. If comparable survey questions were available over time and across states, some of the measurement problems encountered at the state level would be eased. The assumptions I made about voters' perceptions of the candidates could be relaxed: each voter could be assumed to have his own view of where the candidates stand. The complication, of course, is that simultaneity in the data would make it difficult to unravel the effect of some variables to get consistent and efficient estimates of their impact on the outcome.

The lack of data—particularly state-level data—is the chief hurdle to overcome if many of these ideas are to be integrated into the model. Our ability to forecast elections accurately is constrained not only by our limited capacity to understand the complexities of human behavior, but by our lack of data as well.

Finally, the model might also be modified to allow information gathered during the course of the campaign to be incorporated to update initial forecasts. Intracampaign shifts in issue importance, candidate positions, or campaign strategies might be taken into account. The model could be dynamic both within the campaign and across elections. Revised forecasts could be generated whenever new information becomes available.

IMPLICATIONS

It is important to reflect on the probable impact of election forecasting on the conduct of elections and on democratic political systems. When accurate election forecasting models become as commonplace as polls or direct mail solicitations are today, presidential campaign strategy will change dramatically. Months before an election, strategists will be able to estimate the likelihood of each state being won. Before a candidate decides which issues to stress, which positions to take, which groups to attract, or in which states to invest his scarce resources, alternative strategies will be simulated, and the one that maximizes the probability of victory will be chosen.

It is unlikely that both parties will have the same capabilities. One will inevitably be able to buy better forecasts than the other. Inequalities in economic resources will produce political inequalities. Obviously, this is not much different from the current situation: well-financed candidates and causes can more easily hire experts (pollsters, media consultants, and the like) who provide information and skills necessary for a successful campaign. The inequality will continue. Money and information, not people, will be the important political resources.

Citizens will be less able to influence government through elections. As candidates depend less on state and local politicians for political intelligence, presidential campaigns will become further isolated from political parties. As candidates' certainty about the political consequences of specific campaign strategies increases, voters will be even less able than today to learn much from the campaign about the candidates' true positions or capabilities. When strategists can predict with greater certainty which groups of citizens they can afford to ignore, they will feel less compelled to attend to these constituencies. In general, the ability of citizens to constrain politicians through the ballot box rests, in part, on politicians' uncertainty about their electoral futures. As politicians are better able to predict electoral outcomes, this uncertainty will be reduced—and so will the power of some voters.

As presidential candidates become more certain about which states will be won and which lost, their campaigns will focus even more than today on states close to the 50 percent mark. Incumbents will be more likely to woo these states with particularized benefits. Geographic politics will flourish. As campaigns become more local, the trend toward national issues and a national campaign will be reversed: candidates will take stands that address the concerns of voters in particular states, and local rather than network media campaigns will be the norm. As the number of states candidates write off increases, more states will be won by wide margins. The outcome will increasingly depend on the extent to which a campaign can mobilize its supporters in the few competitive states. Small fluctuations in the popular vote will produce large electoral vote swings. The likelihood that the electoral college result will be at variance with the popular vote will rise, renewing efforts to reform the electoral college system. As it is unlikely that the same states will be written off every year, it is difficult to say which social groups will be most hurt.

When congressional elections can be accurately forecasted, well-financed groups will have an even greater influence over their outcome. Those with economic resources will be greatly advantaged because they will be better able to identify districts where their contributions will make the difference. When sure losers can be identified, money will also be invested in the more promising candidates. Interest groups, of course, currently forecast elections and follow this kind of spending strategy. But uncertainty means that mistakes are made, money wasted, and influence diluted. When an interest group can accurately forecast congressional elections, this uncertainty will be reduced; its influence over outcomes and members of Congress will increase.

The question "Who will win the next election?" should not only motivate us to formulate better theories of human behavior—it should prompt us to consider the repercussions that this knowledge will be likely to have on our representative system of government. As election forecasts are refined and forecasting models become an integral part of candidates' and interest groups' political arsenals, the costs to democracy may far outweigh any benefits. Our ultimate challenge will be to put these discoveries to work in ways that will better enable citizens to select leaders who will represent their interests.

APPENDIX A

MEASURING PREFERENCES
FOR CANDIDATES ON ISSUES

Two variables in the model—the aggregate state preference for the Democratic candidate on New Deal social welfare and racial issues—are unobserved. Their component parts (the positions of the state and the candidates) are also unobserved.[1] Before the effect of issue preferences on the vote can be estimated, the position of the candidates and the states on the two dimensions must be measured in a consistent way across time and states. This appendix discusses these measurement procedures.

ALTERNATIVE WAYS TO MEASURE STATE ISSUE POSITIONS

Survey Data

One way to assess a state's liberalness is to tally its citizens' responses to relevant survey questions. The more liberal the answers, the more liberal the state. The practical problem with this approach is that the typical national survey does not include people in every state, and the people who are interviewed generally are not a representative sample of the state's population. Obviously if there were reliable state-level surveys

---

1. Recall from chap. 3 that

$(P_{D>R})_{ijt} = |X_{ijt} - R_{jt}| - |X_{ijt} - D_{jt}|$

where $(P_{D>R})_{ijt}$ is state$_i$'s preference for the Democrat over the Republican on issue$_j$ in election$_t$;

X_{ijt} is state$_i$'s position on issue$_j$ in election$_t$;

R_{jt} is the Republican's position on issue$_j$ in election$_t$; and

D_{jt} is the Democrat's position on issue$_j$ in election$_t$.

that asked the same questions across time and states, the measurement problem would be solved.

Pool, Abelson, and Popkin (1965) cleverly try to sidestep this sampling problem by simulating state electorates with national poll data. This approach, discussed in chapter 2, has been extended by Ronald E. Weber (1971).[2] Weber, like Pool and his associates, classifies a person in a particular "voter-type" on the basis of his or her occupation, race, sex, age, religion, region, and dwelling place. A professional, white, male Catholic under the age of 35 who lives in a city in the Northeast would be one voter-type. There are 960 different voter-types in all—one for each combination of demographic variables. For a particular issue the "simulated" state electorate is estimated by weighting each voter-type by the proportion of the state population that has those characteristics (estimated from aggregate data).

This method does not produce reliable estimates of state preferences. For example, the actual state presidential vote in 1956, 1960, and 1964 explains less than 60 percent of the variance in the simulated vote in those years; the average state error is 9.3 percentage points (Weber 1971, chap. 4).[3]

Even if this method could be refined, its underlying assumptions would still be troublesome (Seidman 1975). The scheme assumes that, with the exception of region, political context does not influence a person's positions on the issues. The only difference between one state and another is demographics: the frequency of each voter-type in the state. Once these variables are accounted for, it is alleged, there are no other political differences between people who live in Massachusetts and those who live in New Hampshire, Iowa, or California. Other dubious assumptions (Seidman 1975) also undermine the estimates.

2. See Weber et al. 1973; Uslaner and Weber 1975; Sullivan and Minns 1976; and Uslaner and Weber 1979 for further applications. Because Weber uses a region code different from that used by the Simulmatics group, adds age, changes the place of residence code, and drops party identification, 960 voter-types emerge rather than 480.

3. Other coding schemes and data sets perform even more poorly. The fit between the simulated and actual vote is about the same whether one uses Gallup data, Center for Political Studies National Election data, or different voter-types. Weber also tries to pool several Gallup surveys conducted within a few months of the election, but this does not produce a significant improvement over the single survey estimates (1971, pp. 51–53).

Aggregate Election Returns

Aggregate election returns are commonly used to assess a state's liberalness. Massachusetts, which voted for McGovern in 1972, is regarded as a liberal state on social welfare issues; states that went for Wallace in 1968 are viewed as racially conservative.

William Schneider (1978; 1981) has popularized an approach first employed by MacRae and Meldrum (1969). "Voting behavior in the United States," he says, "responds to two distinct issue dimensions: a *partisan* dimension related primarily to economic issues, and an *ideological* dimension reflecting social and cultural conflict." He describes this ideological dimension as including "social and cultural issues [that] tap such values as tolerance, authoritarianism, and support for social change" (1978, pp. 183, 203–04). Schneider analyzes state presidential and congressional election returns since 1896 to extract two dimensions—an "ideological" factor, with Wallace's 1968 vote at one end, Humphrey's at the other, and Nixon's in the middle, and a "partisan" factor, which differentiates Humphrey from Nixon.

Schneider's implicit statistical model is represented in equation A.1.

$$\text{Vote}_{it} = \lambda_1 I + \lambda_2 P + e_i \tag{A.1}$$

where Vote_{it} is the aggregate presidential vote in state_i at time_t;

    I is the unobserved "ideology" dimension;

    P is the unobserved "partisanship" dimension;

    e_i is an error term;

    λ_1 and λ_2 are weights applied to the ideology and partisanship dimensions respectively; and

    $E(I,P) = 0$.

Schneider assumes that each state is as Democratic and liberal today as it was in 1896. This, of course, is silly in light of political changes that have occurred over this period, say in the South (Key 1949; Wolfinger and Arseneau 1979) and in the Northeast (Key 1956; Ladd and Hadley 1975; Phillips 1970). He further assumes that partisanship and ideology have had the same effect on the vote in every presidential and congressional election since the turn of the century (i.e., that λ_1 and λ_2 are constant across states and years). It is unreasonable to assert that ideology was as important a cause of the vote in 1944 or 1960 as it was in 1964 or 1972. It is equally unrealistic to assume that ideology and partisanship affect congressional voting as much as presidential. Moreover, it is doubtful whether ideology, as Schneider defines it, has *any* effect on how people vote in congressional elections. Finally, despite evidence to the contrary (p. 262), Schneider assumes, by his Varimax rotational scheme, that Democratic states are no more liberal than Republican ones (i.e., $E[I,P] = 0$).[4]

There is no theoretical justification for why the first dimension from a Varimax factor analysis of congressional and presidential votes magically produces a scale that measures such values as "tolerance, authoritarianism and support for social change," and the second dimension reveals state partisanship. (See Armstrong 1967.)

MEASURING NEW DEAL SOCIAL WELFARE LIBERALISM

The Measurement Model

The New Deal social welfare dimension, defined in chapter 3, is concerned with the extent to which the federal government should manage the economy, police business, solve social problems, and provide for human needs. Liberals favor an interventionist government that legislates, reforms, regulates, and litigates; conservatives want less government, less regulation, less interference, fewer social programs, and more reliance on the free market and local communities.

There are large differences in the degree to which states have embraced New Deal social welfare liberalism. Some, like Massachusetts, Rhode Island, and New York, provide a wide range of social services and devote a large proportion of their budgets to them. Other states, such as Mississippi, Montana, Arizona, and Arkansas, provide fewer programs to meet human needs. The more liberal its citizens, the more a state's policies will embrace the precepts of New Deal social welfare liberalism. States with few services and programs are assumed to be peopled by citizens who are, on the whole, conservative on this dimension.

It can be argued that a state's policies indicate nothing about its citizens, but only reflect the preferences of its political elites. However, legislators who have social backgrounds similar to their constituents', or are concerned with reelection, are likely to share many of their preferences—which means that policies will reflect more than just the whims

---

4. Schneider's unique weighting scheme for the South produces further problems. He finds in his preliminary analysis that "the inclusion of all eleven Southern states, with their immoderate behavior, tends to distort the results" (1971, p. 261). Rather than modify the model to account for this, Schneider suppresses their effect by weighting "all eleven Southern states equal to *one state*" (p. 261, his emphasis).

of elected officials. I contend that one reason Massachusetts and New York have more liberal social welfare policies than Arizona or New Hampshire is that their citizens are more liberal. I will demonstrate the validity of this assumption later.

One model for measuring how liberal a state's population is on the New Deal social welfare dimension can be represented as:

$$x_i = \lambda_1 d^* + e_i \qquad (A.2)$$

where x_i is an indicator of New Deal social welfare liberalism;
d^* is the underlying unobserved New Deal social welfare dimension to be estimated;
λ_1 is a weight applied to the dimension; and
e_i is an error term.

In words: each indicator of social welfare liberalism x_i (called a *variate*) is determined by the underlying dimension ($\lambda_1 d^*$) plus a random disturbance (e_i). It is further assumed that $E(e) = 0$; $E(e,d^*) = 0$; and $E(e_i)^2 = \sigma^2$ which is constant across cases. Equation A.2 is a simple one-dimension factor analysis model (Lawley and Maxwell, 1971).

Clearly this is an incomplete representation of the process that generates social welfare programs. There are obviously additional variables. If the other causes of state commitment to these policies are correlated with New Deal social welfare liberalism, then the assumption that the error term (e_i) is uncorrelated with the dimension (d^*) would not hold and the analysis would fail.

A state institutes services not only because its population is liberal but because of exogenous *demand* or *need*. Likewise, a state may choose not to adopt a particular program because it is not needed, rather than because the citizenry is conservative. The proportion of a state's expenditures devoted to public welfare assistance, for example, is determined not only by how liberal the state is, but by its rate of unemployment or poverty. Thus, exogenous conditions clearly place demands on a state to devote a higher proportion of its resources to public welfare than citizens otherwise would call for. If these differences in demand are ignored, the liberalness of states with high unemployment or many poor people will be overestimated; the liberalness of states that do not have these problems will be underestimated.

A state's *capacity* to provide these services must also be considered. Rich states obviously can afford to fund more programs at higher levels than poor states can (Anton 1967). How rich a state is determines in part its expenditures per pupil on primary and secondary education, for instance. Wealthy states can pay teachers more, build more schools, set up special educational programs, and the like; poor states cannot.[5]

Thus, three causes of a state's level of commitment to New Deal social welfare programs will be considered: the liberalness of its citizens, exogenous demand for services, and the state's capacity to provide programs.

The first indicator of social welfare liberalism is the size of a state's bureaucracy. Liberal states, because of their higher level of government activity, ought to have a larger number of state employees per capita (excluding teachers and other school personnel) than states with a narrower range of social programs. Rhode Island had 145 noneducation state employees per ten thousand residents in 1972, New York had 275, New Hampshire had only 117 and Arkansas 85. A large public payroll indicates not only a state's liberalness, but its prosperity. Economies of scale must also be considered: large states need to hire fewer state employees per capita than small ones.

These causes of the size of the state's bureaucracy can be represented as follows:

$$x_1 = \lambda_{11}\text{NDSW} + \lambda_{12}\text{Income} + \lambda_{13}\text{Population} + e_i \qquad \text{(A.3a)}$$

where x_1 is the number of noneducation state employees per capita in state$_i$;

NDSW is the unobserved New Deal Social Welfare dimension;
Income is the log of the state's total personal income per capita;
Population is the log of the state's population;
λ_{11}, λ_{12}, and λ_{13} are weights to be applied to the NDSW dimension, income, and population respectively; and
e_i is a random error term.

The employer contribution rate to unemployment insurance is a second indicator of New Deal social welfare liberalism. Unemployment insurance was established by the Social Security Act of 1935 and, except those for railroad workers and veterans, compensation programs have been run by the states.[6] The proportion of workers' salaries that em-

5. Income is generally found to be the best predictor of a state's spending on social welfare programs (Dawson and Robinson 1963; Dye 1967).

6. "It [is] not a unitary national system with uniform benefits and tax which Congress could amend as it saw fit. Each state retain[s] final authority to determine coverage, eligibility, levels and duration of benefits and tax rates for its own programs" (*Congressional Quarterly* 1965, p. 1293).

ployers contribute to unemployment insurance is small in some states (in 1972 less than 1 percent in Mississippi, Nebraska, and New Hampshire); in other states (like New Jersey, Oregon, New York, and California), employers contribute more than 2 percent. The argument here is: the higher the unemployment compensation contribution rate, the more liberal the state. States with extensive unemployment insurance programs, paid for by high employer taxes, though, are also states where the need for these programs is likely to be greatest. Where few people are out of work, the demand for unemployment insurance programs presumably is less, so employers' taxes are lower. Because there is a lag between unemployment and legislative remedy, the previous year's unemployment rate in the state is used as the control variable.

These claims are represented as follows:

$$x_2 = \lambda_{21}\text{NDSW} + \lambda_{24}\text{Unemployment}_{t-1} + e_2 \qquad\qquad \text{(A.3b)}$$

The rate at which employers contribute to unemployment insurance programs (x_2) is determined by how liberal the state is on the NDSW dimension and the level of unemployment in the state in the previous year.

State primary and secondary education expenditures per pupil in average daily attendance is a third indicator of social welfare liberalism. There is tremendous variation in how much states spend on educating children. Rhode Island, Massachusetts, Pennsylvania, and Minnesota all spent over $1,000 per pupil in 1972; Maine, Arkansas, Idaho, and Utah spent under $760. State educational expenditures also obviously reflect a state's wealth: rich states can simply afford to spend more on public education than poor states can. Accordingly, the equation for state primary and secondary education expenditures per pupil in average daily attendance (logged) is written as:

$$x_3 = \lambda_{31}\text{NDSW} + \lambda_{32}\text{Income} + e_3 \qquad\qquad \text{(A.3c)}$$

Government assistance to the poor, the disabled, and the needy is also part of the New Deal ideology. Two indicators reflect a state's commitment to these social programs: the average monthly Aid to Families with Dependent Children (AFDC) payments per recipient family, and the proportion of a state's expenditures devoted to public welfare programs. Liberal states provide higher AFDC payments and spend a greater proportion of their resources on welfare programs than conservative states. Massachusetts, New York, Wisconsin, and Hawaii led the nation in 1972 in AFDC assistance, providing, on average, over $270 a month per recipient family—Maine, Indiana, Mississippi, and Nevada provided less than half that amount.

Other factors influence a state's welfare and AFDC spending. The demand for welfare programs in populous states is higher because of their urban centers, disproportionately composed of the poor. Furthermore, the level of AFDC payments also reflects the wealth of a state. Short-term economic fluctuations such as unemployment will also affect the proportion of a state's resources devoted to public assistance programs.[7]

The equations for these two variates can be written as follows:

$$x_4 = \lambda_{41}\text{NDSW} + \lambda_{42}\text{Income} + \lambda_{43}\text{Population} + e_4 \qquad \text{(A.3d)}$$

$$x_5 = \lambda_{51}\text{NDSW} + \lambda_{53}\text{Population} + \lambda_{54}\text{Unemployment} + e_5 \qquad \text{(A.3e)}$$

where x_4 is average AFDC assistance per recipient family; and

x_5 is the log of the proportion of state expenditures devoted to public welfare (federal assistance excluded).

Finally, in addition to these five equations (one for each indicator), there is an identity for each control variable:

$$x_6 = \lambda_{62}\text{Income per capita (logged)} \qquad \text{(A.3f)}$$

$$x_7 = \lambda_{73}\text{Population (logged)} \qquad \text{(A.3g)}$$

$$x_8 = \lambda_{84}\text{Unemployment rate}_{t-1} \qquad \text{(A.3h)}$$

where x_6, x_7, and x_8 are income per capita (logged), population (logged), and the unemployment in the previous year, respectively.

Thus, $\lambda_{62} = \lambda_{73} = \lambda_{84} = 1.0$. Unlike the indicators of New Deal social welfare liberalism, these variates are observed without error.

To summarize, each indicator of New Deal social welfare liberalism is represented by an equation. A state's liberalness is one cause of each variate; the other causes are its ability to supply the social service and the demand for the program. There are also three identities—one for each control variable. The eight equations, A.3a through A.3h, can be represented in matrix notation as follows:

$$X = \Lambda D^* + \epsilon \qquad \text{(A.4)}$$

where X is an $8 \times n$ matrix of observed variates (8 variates, n cases);

D^* is a $4 \times n$ matrix, the first row is the unobserved NDSW dimension, rows 2 through 4 are the other causes of the variates: income, population, and unemployment;

---

7. Because part of a state's welfare bill is paid by the federal government, this assistance is deleted from the analysis.

Λ is an 8×4 matrix of weights applied to D^* to produce each variate; and

ϵ is an $8 \times n$ vector of random disturbances.

In addition, let $E(\epsilon\epsilon')$ be an 8×8 matrix of covariances between the random disturbances. It is assumed that ϵ is diagonal (when $i \neq j$, $E[\epsilon\epsilon'] = 0$), that is, the random disturbances in each equation are uncorrelated. For example, the other causes of monthly AFDC assistance per recipient family (that are not right-hand-side variables in the model, but in the error term) are uncorrelated with the other causes of the employers' contribution rate to unemployment insurance programs.

Each variate is standardized within each year to a mean of 0 and a variance of 1. Finally, if $\Sigma = E(XX')$, (where Σ is the 8×8 correlation matrix between the variates), equation A.4 can be rewritten as:

$$\Sigma = \Lambda\Phi\Lambda' + \Psi \qquad (A.5)$$

where Φ is $E(D^*D^{*\prime})$, the correlation matrix between the four dimensions that comprise the rows of D^*.

The general model described by equation A.5 has an infinite number of solutions because a nonsingular transformation of D^* will change Λ and usually Φ but will leave Σ unaffected (Jöreskog 1969, p. 184; 1970, p. 243). The usual solution to this indeterminacy is to estimate Λ and Ψ subject to the constraints that $\Phi = I$ and $\Lambda'\Psi^{-1}\Lambda$ is diagonal. In other words, force the dimensions to be uncorrelated. The result is an arbitrary set of factors that are usually rotated until the analyst finds some "meaningful" interpretation (Lawley and Maxwell 1971; Jöreskog 1970, p. 243).

An alternative is to impose restrictions on k^2 elements of Λ and/or Φ (where k = the number of columns in Λ—in this case 4), so that equation A.5 will have a unique solution.[8] To proceed in this manner requires theory about the underlying causes of each variate. My earlier discussion of equations A.3a to A.3d provides the justification for the constraints. Recall that in equation A.3a, for instance, λ_{14} is assumed to be zero, (i.e., unemployment is not a cause of the number of government employees per capita). In equation A.3b λ_{22} is assumed to be zero (i.e., income does not affect the employer contribution rate to unemployment insurance). Λ is appropriately restricted to produce a unique set of estimates. The validity of these assumptions, and the others imposed on Λ, will be discussed in a moment.

An iterative minimization procedure is used to estimate the parame-

8. See Jöreskog (1969, p. 186) for discussion of the identification conditions.

ters and their variances (Jöreskog 1970, p. 231). The variates are pooled across 1948 to 1972 to yield 344 cases.[9] I report the maximum likelihood estimates for Λ and Ψ and their standard errors in table A.1. A blank cell indicates that the coefficient has been constrained to zero. In the income, population, and unemployment equations the zeros appear because these are identities. In the remaining equations coefficients are constrained to zero because the dimension is either insignificantly correlated with the variate or the estimated loading is equivalent to zero.

A state's position on the New Deal social welfare dimension in year$_t$ is the weighted sum of its variates in that year.[10] Within each year, the scale is again standardized to a mean of 0 and a variance of 1: conservative states have negative numbers, liberal states have positive ones.[11] The weights, estimated over the 1948–72 period, are applied in a similar fashion to construct the 1976 and 1980 scales.

The New Deal Social Welfare Scale

The scale is both reliable[12] and valid.[13] The face validity of the indicators has already been established: each measures a specific program or ser-

9. I assume that the coefficients are constant across years and that the errors are uncorrelated over time and across states.

10. The weights are the factor scores (S*), defined as
$$S^* = \Gamma^{-1}\Lambda\Psi^{-1}$$
where $\Gamma = \Lambda^{-1}\Psi^{-1}\Lambda$.

11. The difference between the model employed here and simple factor analysis should be noted. One-dimension analysis would assume that only New Deal social welfare liberalism produces each variate. Instead, I take into account state capacity to provide services and exogenous demand placed upon it to do so. The estimated factor scores reflect this: the scale is corrected for wealth, size of population, and unemployment. The scale that results is different from one produced by the simpler model. A single variate—primary and secondary education expenditures per pupil in average daily attendance—would dominate the one dimensional scale. Texas, Florida, Ohio, and Arizona, for example, because of their relative wealth, would all appear to be significantly more liberal than they are on the scale computed here. Rhode Island would be inappropriately listed as more conservative than Connecticut.

12. The greater the proportion of total variation due to true variation on the dimension, as opposed to measurement error, the more reliable a scale. The estimated reliability is .6. Reliability = $\Lambda'\Psi^{-1}\Lambda$ (Lawley and Maxwell 1971, pp. 110; Fuller and Hidiroglow 1978, p. 99). A correction for this measurement error is discussed in appendix B.

13. The scale is valid if the positions of the states on the *scale* reflect the true differences between the states on the underlying *dimension*.

Table A.1 New Deal Social Welfare Dimension: Factor Loadings and Error Variances, 1948–72

Variate	Dimensions				
	New Deal Social Welfare	Income	Population	Unemployment	Error Variance
State employees per capita (excluding teachers and other school personnel)	.28* (.09)	.33 (.08)	-.18 (.06)	**	.80 (.03)
Employer contribution rate to unemployment insurance	.40 (.05)			.51 (.06)	.78 (.03)
Primary and secondary education expenditures per pupil in average daily attendance (logged)	.38 (.06)	.57 (.07)		.48 (.03)	
Average AFDC assistance per recipient family	.66 (.12)	.20 (.12)	.23 (.07)		.59 (.05)
Proportion of total state expenditures on public welfare (federal assistance excluded) (logged)	.44 (.06)		.21 (.06)	.08 (.06)	.89 (.04)
Income per capita (logged)		1.00 (.04)			
Population (logged)			1.00 (.04)		
Proportion of the work force unemployed(t-1)				1.00 (.04)	

* Maximum likelihood estimate. Standard error of estimate appears in parentheses.
** A blank cell indicates the loading was constrained to zero.

vice that has been advocated by social welfare liberals for half a century. The New Deal social welfare scales for two years, 1948 and 1972, are displayed in figure A.1. The South as well as states like Indiana, Missouri, Arizona, Oklahoma, and Ohio are grouped at the conservative end in 1972; Oregon, Pennsylvania, New Jersey, Wisconsin, Rhode Island, Hawaii, Vermont, and Massachusetts appear at the liberal end. In the South, Arkansas, Louisiana, Georgia, Tennessee, Virginia, and Florida are slightly more liberal than North Carolina, Mississippi, South Carolina, Texas, and Alabama. The midwestern states of Minnesota, Michigan, and Illinois are more liberal than Ohio, Missouri, and Indiana. In the West, Oregon is the most liberal state, followed by California, Washington, New Mexico, and Colorado, and then Utah and Arizona. Finally, Massachusetts, New York, Vermont, Rhode Island, New Jersey, and Pennsylvania are the most liberal states in the East, while New Hampshire, Connecticut, Maine, and Delaware show up as more conservative.

The ordering of the states on the social welfare scale makes sense given other things we know about states' politics. Barone and associates (1977, p. 372) label Massachusetts, the only state carried by McGovern in 1972, as the "premier" liberal state. Oregon and Hawaii are viewed as left of center (pp. 207, 704); Arizona, Iowa, and Nevada are identified as bastions of conservatism (pp. 22, 285, 505). Mississippi's social welfare conservatism has been noted as well (Peirce 1974, pp. 164, 173, 191, 200).

Movements on the scale over time also parallel changes political observers have noted. Over the past two decades the Northeast has grown more liberal (Phillips 1970; Ladd and Hadley 1975); New Jersey, Pennsylvania, Rhode Island, and Vermont moved to the left on the scale. Wisconsin has gone from a middle-of-the-road state on this dimension to a liberal one; Hawaii too has become more liberal since it first entered the Union (Barone, Ujifusa, and Matthews 1977, p. 207). The slight increase in liberalism in the South that many have observed (Bartley and Graham 1975) is also evident in figure A.1. Eight former Confederate states were more than one standard deviation to the right of the average state in 1948; by 1972 only 5 were this far right of center. Washington moved from being one of the most liberal states in 1948 to its moderate position in 1972; Arizona shifted from slightly left of center to the right (Barone, Ujifusa, and Matthews 1977, p. 22); and Utah moved to the right between 1948 and 1964, then moved slightly to the left in subsequent years (Barone, Ujifusa, and Matthews 1977, p. 854; Peirce 1972, pp. 199–211; Jonas 1969, pp. 375–77).

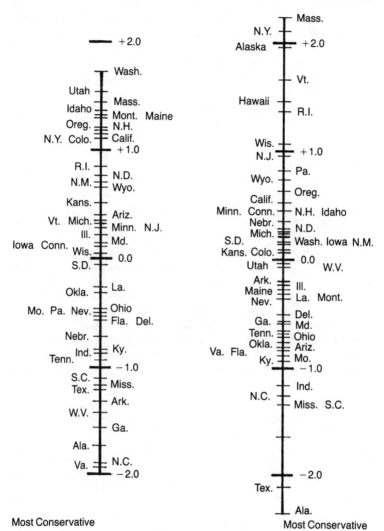

Figure A.1 State Positions on New Deal Social Welfare Dimension

The New Deal social welfare scale can be further validated by comparing states' positions to their citizens' responses to survey questions. Survey estimates of state liberalism from the 1968 Comparative State Elections Project's 13 state samples (Black, Kovenock, and Reynolds 1974) correlate positively with the New Deal social welfare scale. Survey responses to whether government spending should be cut correlate .83 with the NDSW scale; responses to whether Social Security benefits should be increased correlate .32. The Democratic proportion of the state's population is positively correlated (r = .41) with scale positions, as one would expect given the New Deal political alignment.[14] This convergence between the 1968 survey responses and state positions on the New Deal social welfare scale should alleviate concern over using policies to indicate the liberalness of the state's citizens.[15]

One more way to establish the scale's validity is to show that it can predict future political behavior. The 1972 scale discriminates among states that in 1976 (1) had right-to-work laws, (2) had not ratified the Equal Rights Amendment, and in 1978 (3) had called either for a constitutional convention or constitutional amendment to require a balanced budget. As one would expect, liberal states are less likely to have right-to-work laws, more likely to have ratified the ERA, and less likely to have called for a balanced budget (table A.2).

To summarize, the scale is a valid measure of New Deal social welfare liberalism. The items have face validity. The ordering of the states on the scale at specific periods, and the movement of states on the scale over time, correspond to observers' assessments about the relative liberalism of the states on these issues. The scale correlates with party identification, people's responses to social welfare survey questions, and the demographic causes of social welfare liberalism. The measure has predictive validity.

14. In all three calculations region is held constant and the correlation coefficient is corrected for attenuation.

15. The demographic correlates of social welfare liberalism are also associated with the scale. States with large Baptist, Methodist, or Presbyterian populations are more conservative; states with large proportions of Jews and Catholics are more liberal. Urban states are generally more liberal than rural ones. Wealthy states are more conservative than poor states between 1948 and 1956; in subsequent years wealthy states are the more liberal ones (Ladd and Hadley 1975).

As one would expect given the dominant party alignment of the past fifty years, once region has been held constant, the scale is positively correlated with the Democratic presidential and congressional vote. In addition, liberal states were more likely to vote for Henry Wallace in 1948 than conservative states; in 1968 liberal states were less likely than conservative states to vote for George Wallace.

Table A.2 Predictive Validity of the 1972 New Deal Social Welfare Scale

	Position of State on the 1972 NDSW Scale		
	15 Most Conservative States	20 Middle-of-the-Road States	15 Most Liberal States
Percentage with "right to work" laws	73	40	7
Percentage not passing the ERA	60	30	0
Percentage calling for balanced federal budget	60	50	20

Source: Figure A.1; *Christian Science Monitor*, 28 September 1976, p. 10; *The Book of States, 1978-1979*, p. 226, n. 1; *Congressional Quarterly Weekly Report*, 8 July 1978, pp. 1729-30.

MEASURING RACIAL LIBERALISM

The extent to which state electorates support racial equality must also be measured. Few would question the observation that, at least prior to the civil rights movement of the 1960s, blacks were subjected to greater inequality in the South than anywhere else in the country. Blacks were disenfranchised, received separate and unequal educations, were denied access to many southern universities, and rarely were considered for professional or managerial positions. Southern blacks' median education in 1960 was under 70 percent that of whites; it was over 80 percent of whites' in the North. Southern black craftsmen earned less than 60 percent of white craftsmen's salaries, compared to about 75 percent in the North. The median black family income in the South was about 60 percent that of whites; northern blacks' median income was over 80 percent that of whites.

I will use this last measure—the differences between black and white median family incomes—to indicate the amount of racial inequality in a state:

$$\text{Racial Liberalism} = \frac{\text{Log (Median Family Income of Blacks)}}{\text{Log (Median Family Income of Whites)}} \quad \text{(A.6)}$$

The more racially conservative a state's population, the lower the ratio of black income to white.[16] This difference in income results from dis-

16. Logging both variables yields a measure that is more nearly normally distributed.

crimination in formal education, hiring, promotion, and salaries. Inequality results both from government policies and decisions made in the private sector. Whites in Mississippi in 1970, for instance, had a median family income of $7,578; black income was only $3,202, about 42 percent that of white. Black family income in Vermont was 91 percent that of white ($8,094 versus $8,928).[17] As before, the scale is standardized within each year. Conservative states have large negative scores; liberal states have large positive ones. The positions of the states on the racial dimension for 1948 and 1968 are reported in figure A.2.

The most conspicuous point to note about the racial liberalism scale is that the 11 southern states are clustered at the conservative end of the continuum. The 5 most conservative states in 1948 were all from the former Confederacy, and all the southern states are among the 15 most racially conservative. In addition, as one would expect, the deep South is generally more conservative than the rim South. Mississippi, unsurprisingly, emerges as the most racially conservative state in the Union. At the liberal end of the scale are states that have been devoid of a slave heritage and have had few incentives for racial discrimination because blacks comprise a tiny share of their population (Vermont, New Hampshire, North Dakota, Washington, Indiana, and Minnesota).

A state's scale position reflects its citizens' positions on racial issues. Here again I rely on interviews conducted by the 1968 Comparative State Elections Project. Citizens' responses to questions about school integration and open housing are positively correlated with states' positions on the racial dimension ($r = .78$ and $.66$ respectively).[18]

The racial liberalism scale also predicts political behavior when race is the predominant issue. There is a strong negative relationship between how liberal a state is on the racial scale and the proportion of its vote cast for Strom Thurmond in 1948 ($r = -.70$). Thurmond's votes come almost exclusively from states on the conservative end of the dimension (fig. A.3); no state on the liberal side of the continuum cast as much as 1 percent of its vote for the Dixiecrat. A similar pattern emerges in 1968

17. Since additional state-level indicators of racial liberalism are not readily available for every election year since 1948, I am unable to use the statistical model developed for the social welfare dimension.

18. These estimates are corrected for attenuation. Demographic variables also are associated with the scale in expected ways. Liberalism on the racial scale is positively correlated with aggregate education and with the religious composition of the state: the higher the proportion of the state population that is Baptist, Methodist, or Presbyterian, the more conservative the state; the higher the proportion of Catholics or Jews, the more liberal the state.

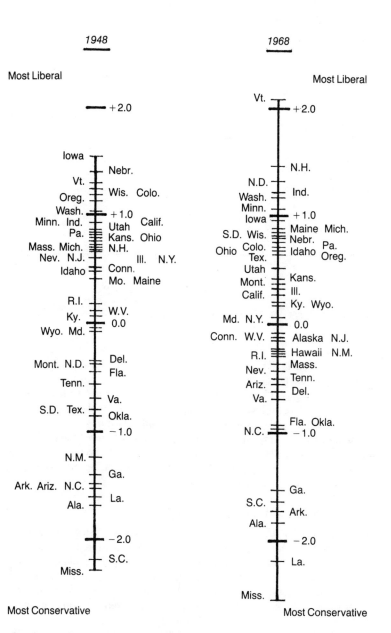

Figure A.2 State Positions on Racial Dimension

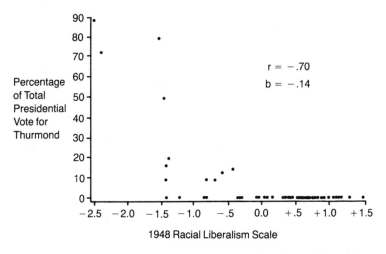

Figure A.3 Relationship between Racial Scale and 1948 Presidential Vote for Thurmond

(fig. A.4). The racial scale is negatively related to the proportion of the state's vote cast for George Wallace ($r = -.83$).[19] The most liberal states all cast less than 10 percent of their ballots for Wallace, while the most conservative states (such as Mississippi, Louisiana, and Alabama) gave the third-party challenger between half and two-thirds of their votes.

Summarizing, then, the racial liberalism scale has face validity; it correlates with citizens' positions on racial issues as recorded by state surveys; it accurately predicts the votes cast for third-party candidates who ran on racial issues.

PRESIDENTIAL CANDIDATES' POSITIONS

An estimate of a state's preference for the Democrat stance on a given issue over the Republican requires not only information about the electorate's position but also knowledge of where the candidates stand. There is general consensus, of course, on such assertions as: Goldwater was a social welfare conservative; George Wallace was conservative on racial issues. The point is to establish *how* conservative (or liberal) these

19. The racial scale has a higher correlation with the vote for George Wallace in 1968 than the New Deal social welfare scale does ($r = -.83$ versus $-.65$). This establishes the divergent validity of both scales. The same pattern holds for Thurmond's vote in 1948.

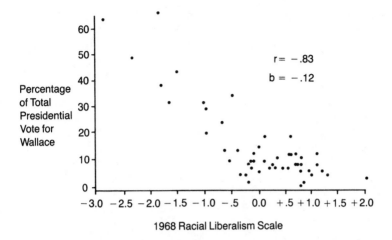

Figure A.4 Relationship between Racial Scale and 1968 Presidential Vote for Wallace

and the other candidates were. And these estimates must be comparable both across time and with the state scales already developed.

One approach, taken by Pomper (1970, chaps. 7–8), is to estimate candidate positions from the party platforms. The problem with this is that the nominee rarely writes the platform and often it even contains planks that are at odds with the candidate's own positions. Platforms are frequently compromises between warring factions (Ford and Reagan; Carter and Kennedy) (Agar 1966, pp. 346–47). They, of course, also contain pledges explicitly designed to placate a segment of the party or to attract outside groups (Ostrogorski 1926, p. 216). Party platforms do not faithfully represent the nominee's positions.

An alternative method is to analyze a candidate's addresses, statements, interview responses, and position papers. Benjamin Page (1978) examined more than 276 texts and transcripts from the 1968 election. Replicating this analysis for the nine elections I consider would clearly be impractical. Moreover, because this approach does not allow a candidate's positions to be estimated at the beginning of the campaign, it could not be used to make forecasts. A more crucial problem, however, is that campaign statements, like party platforms, are tactical devices for attracting votes. They may reveal little about a candidate's positions.[20]

20. Yet another approach would be to estimate a candidate's positions by examining his record: his actions in previous offices, his votes on key issues, and

I will use assessments made by scholars of American political parties and elections to estimate candidates' positions on the New Deal social welfare and racial dimensions. I asked historians and political scientists to gauge each candidate's position on the two dimensions relative to the electorate's position in the corresponding year.[21] They were instructed not to judge how the public perceived the candidates, or to recall the results of public opinion polls. Rather, I asked the scholars to score the candidates' actual positions on these dimensions "the way an insightful political observer of the day would have evaluated the actions and positions of the candidate prior to the election."

My preliminary analysis of the 43 sets of evaluations[22] showed that some scholars scored the average presidential candidate slightly to the right of center (a mean of 55); others placed him slightly to the left of center (a mean of 45). (The responses to the questionnaires are coded 0 to 100; 0 is the liberal end, 100 the conservative end.) Some experts, seeing little difference among the candidates, scored them very close to

---

the like. The chief drawback is that many candidates have incomplete pre-nomination records. For example, what record would be used to estimate Eisenhower's positions on social welfare or racial issues in 1952? To estimate Nixon's position in 1960 or 1968 would be equally difficult, since (excluding the few votes cast as vice-president) he had not voted on legislation since his membership in the 83rd Congress in 1952.

21. The scholars were: Christopher Achen, Robert Arseneau, F. Christopher Arterton, Richard Brody, Walter Dean Burnham, James MacGregor Burns, Beth Capell, William Cavala, Jack Citrin, Thomas Cronin, Eric Davis, Richard Fenno, William Flanigan, Fred Greenstein, Tom Hammond, Gary Jacobson, Richard Jenson, Samuel Kernell, John H. Kessel, Everett Carll Ladd, Martin Landau, James Lengle, Seymour Martin Lipset, John McCarthy, David Magleby, Thomas Mann, Ernest May, David R. Mayhew, Warren E. Miller, William K. Muir, Frank Munger, Benjamin Page, Michael Parish, Gerald M. Pomper, Austin Ranney, Michael Rogin, Robert Salisbury, Byron Shafer, Merrill Shanks, Frank J. Sorouf, Stephen Van Evera, Raymond E. Wolfinger, and John Zaller. I am grateful for their assistance.

22. Sixty-four questionnaires were mailed during the first week of December 1977. Three scholars disqualified themselves; two were prevented from replying by illness. Of the remaining 59 questionnaires, 45 (76 percent) were completed and returned by the end of January of 1978. (One follow-up letter was sent three weeks after the original mailing.) Political scientists were more likely to respond than historians (87 percent versus 47 percent). Two questionnaires were only partially completed, so 43 sets of evaluations were available for the initial analysis. The 1980 candidate evaluations were solicited from a subset of these scholars in June of that year.

each other (a standard deviation of 10); others, seeing greater ideological diversity among the nominees, scored them farther apart (a standard deviation of 20 or more). To correct for the idiosyncratic frame of reference, each person's responses were standardized by his own mean and standard deviation, so all the evaluations would be in comparable units.

There is a remarkable consensus among the scholars' assessments of where the presidential candidates have stood on the two dimensions. Over half of the interscholar correlations were above .89; 95 percent were greater than .82 in magnitude (p < .001).[23] The scholars' judgments were averaged to produce the estimated candidate positions.[24] The presidential candidates' positions, relative to the electorate of their day, are displayed in figure A.5.

The estimates are both reliable and valid. The strong agreement among the experts yields a very small standard error for each estimate: the largest is .3; the average is .2. The scales' reliability strongly suggests that scholars responded with more than their personal reactions to the candidates, and probably carefully evaluated the candidates' stand on the issues.

The candidate positions have face validity. On the New Deal social welfare dimension John Schmitz, a member of the John Birch Society and American Independent Party nominee in 1972, shows up as the most conservative presidential candidate. Nine out of 10 Americans were more liberal on social welfare issues than Schmitz was in 1972. Thurmond, Goldwater, and George Wallace stand to the left of Schmitz, with better than 7 citizens out of 10 more liberal on this dimension than these candidates were when they ran. It is no surprise that Goldwater is scored the most conservative major party candidate, followed by Reagan. Goldwater attacked key social welfare programs, such as social security and welfare relief for the poor. "On domestic questions, Goldwater resolutely opposed most forms of federal government action" (Page 1978, p. 53).

The other Republican candidates stand together to the right of center. Ford is the most conservative of the group, the 1972 Nixon the most liberal. Nixon moved slightly closer to center each time he ran, but he was still to the right of 58 percent of the electorate in 1972. Eisenhower

23. When a scholar indicated uncertainty about an evaluation, his response was removed from the analysis. Also at this point, 6 respondents were deleted because their responses correlated poorly with those of the other 37. (The only personal characteristic these deleted cases share is that 5 of the 6 did not have electoral politics as their primary area of research.)

24. The original scale metric is recaptured by multiplying this average by the pooled standard deviation and adding the pooled mean to the result.

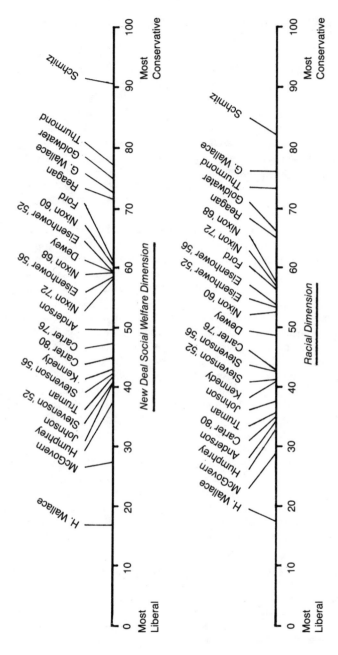

Figure A.5 Position of Presidential Candidates, 1948–80, Relative to the Electorate in Each Year

likewise moved about a point closer to the center in his 1956 reelection bid. With the exception of Goldwater and Reagan, there is considerable homogeneity among the Republican nominees' social welfare positions.

All the Democratic presidential candidates are on the liberal side of the New Deal social welfare dimension. Carter in 1976 is the most conservative Democratic candidate; he was about 3 points more liberal in 1980. Directly to his left are Kennedy, Stevenson, and Truman. Like Eisenhower, Stevenson moved a point closer to center in the 1956 election. Humphrey, a supporter of the War on Poverty, increases in federal aid to citizens, social security and unemployment benefits, the expansion of the welfare system, and the establishment of income maintenance programs, is more liberal than Kennedy, Stevenson, and Truman in their day; only about 3 citizens in 8 were to his left in 1968. McGovern's income redistribution plan, which included new taxes, particularly on the rich, and a guaranteed annual income for all citizens, put him substantially to the left of the average citizen: not 1 citizen in 3 was more liberal than McGovern on social welfare issues.

The distribution of candidate positions on the New Deal social welfare dimension does not correspond to the pattern predicted by rational actor theories of candidate behavior (Downs 1957). Rather than converging to the median voter's position, the Democratic candidates have clustered, on average, 11.0 points to the left of center, and the Republican nominees an equal distance (10.9 points) to the right. It appears that candidates assume positions closer to their party's mean than to the mean of the entire electorate (Page 1978).

Convergence also does not occur on racial issues, though the pattern is slightly different. Republican presidential candidates generally have taken much more centrist positions than Democrats. On average, Republicans are only 6.4 points from the center of the electorate, while the Democrats have been 11.9 points left of center. (The electoral repercussions of noncentrist positions are examined in chapter 7.)

The ordering of the candidates on the racial dimension also makes sense. The most conservative candidates are Schmitz, George Wallace, and Thurmond. Goldwater, who voted against the Civil Rights Act of 1964 and opposed other civil rights legislation, was the most conservative major party candidate. Except for Reagan, who is a bit more liberal than Goldwater, the other Republican candidates are grouped between 49 and 56 on the scale. Nixon moved 4 points to the right between 1960 and 1968; Eisenhower assumed about the same position in 1956 that he held the first time he ran. On racial issues, Dewey was the most liberal postwar Republican candidate.

All the Democratic candidates are on the liberal side of the racial scale. Kennedy, Stevenson, and Carter are more conservative than Johnson, Truman, Humphrey, or McGovern. In 1976, Carter opposed school busing and active federal efforts to integrate housing (Page 1978, p. 75). Truman, in his day, was more liberal on race. He proposed a permanent Fair Employment Procedures Committee, a Justice Department Civil Rights Division, and statutes to provide federal protection against lynching and to protect the right to vote. By executive order Truman desegregated the armed forces and instituted fair employment boards in government departments (Berman 1970). Humphrey, in 1968, stands just slightly to the left of Truman in 1948. Over Truman's opposition, Humphrey fought for strengthened civil rights planks in the 1948 Democratic party platform. Twenty years later Humphrey remained a staunch civil rights advocate, favoring school desegregation and the vigorous enforcement of fair housing laws (Page 1978, pp. 70, 82). The salient racial issue in 1972 was school busing. Although two-thirds of the public opposed mandatory busing, McGovern supported it. Fewer than 30 percent of the public were as liberal as McGovern in 1972.[25]

ESTIMATING STATE PREFERENCES FOR THE DEMOCRATIC CANDIDATE

To estimate a state's preference for the Democratic candidate on an issue, one final problem must be solved. For each election year, I now have a measure of the positions of both the states and the candidates on the New Deal social welfare and racial dimensions. However, the state positions are measured relative to the average *state;* the candidate positions are measured relative to the average *citizen*. The average state does not necessarily correspond to the average citizen, and a unit on the state scale, as it now stands, does not match a unit on the candidate scale. The state's position on the *state* scale must be converted to a position on the *candidate* scale. The conversion for each dimension$_j$ at time$_t$ is written as:

25. Aldrich and McKelvey (1977) gauge candidates' positions from citizens' evaluations of their stands. Based upon responses to the question of whether the federal government should see to it that every person has a job and a good standard of living, they score Nixon at 62 and McGovern at 25 in my units. My estimates are 58 and 28, respectively. Aldrich and McKelvey's analysis of a school busing and aid to minorities question produces estimates of Nixon standing at 61 and McGovern at 27. My estimates of their positions on the racial scale are 56 and 29.

$$X^*_{ijt} = m_{jt} + w_j X_{ijt} \qquad (A.7)$$

where X^*_{ijt} is the position of state$_i$ on the *candidate* scale;

X_{ijt} is the position of state$_i$ on the *state* scale;

m_{jt} is the mean of the population on the *state* scale (not the mean of the states, but the mean of the population); and

w_j is a weight to convert state scale units to candidate scale units.

I assume that the conversion weight w_j is constant across time, although it can vary by dimension. The adjustment of the mean of the state scale for each dimension (m_{jt}) can vary across dimensions and time. Substituting A.7 into 3.2 allows the preference for the Democratic party candidate in state$_i$ at time$_t$ on dimension$_j$ to now be written as:

$$(P_{D>R})_{ij} = |(m_{jt} + w_j X_{ijt}) - R_{jt}| - |(m_{jt} + w_j X_{ijt}) - D_{jt}| \qquad (A.8)$$

where R_{jt} is the position of the Republican candidate on dimension$_j$ in election$_t$; and

D_{jt} = the position of the Democratic candidate on dimension$_j$ in election$_t$.

The parameters m_{jt} and w_j are unknown and must be estimated. m_{jt} can be computed directly from the data. It is merely:

$$m_{jt} = \sum_{i=1}^{n} [(X_{ijt} \times \text{Population}_{it})/\text{Population}_t]$$

where n is the number of states at time$_t$ (48 in 1948 to 1956; 50 otherwise).

The population mean on dimension$_j$ is the weighted mean of the state positions.

I employed an iterative maximum likelihood procedure to estimate w_j (the conversion factor) for each dimension. The full vote equation (equation 3.8) was estimated for alternative values of w_j. For each dimension the value of w_j that best fit the data was chosen as the estimate of the conversion weight for that dimension.[26]

26. For each dimension, values of w_j were selected at 1.0 intervals between 2.0 and 18.0. On the basis of these first-round estimates, a more refined grid was selected and w_j was estimated to one decimal place. Since the dependent variable and the degrees of freedom are the same for each equation estimated, the maximum likelihood estimate of w_j is the value that maximizes the regression sum of squares. The maximum likelihood estimate of w_j for the New Deal social welfare

For both the New Deal social welfare and racial dimensions, the candidates' and states' positions in each year are now in equivalent units. Equation 3.2 can be used to calculate, for each state, its preference for the Democratic candidate on each issue dimension.

---

dimension is 9.0; it is 9.2 for the racial dimension. There is little doubt that the estimated values of w_j are global maximums. A wide range of search values were examined and the derivative of the curve at the endpoints of each grid was negative. Furthermore, the maximum for each w_j was stable regardless of the value imposed on w_j for the other dimension.

APPENDIX B
ESTIMATION OF THE VOTE EQUATION

Ordinary least squares (OLS) regression does not yield unbiased and efficient estimates when data are "pooled"—that is, when there is a time-series of cross-sections (Chetty 1968; Nerlove 1971; Maddala 1971). One solution is to include a unique intercept for each unit observed over time. This approach, commonly referred to as a "fixed effects model" or as "dummy variable least squares" (DVLS) (Balestra and Nerlove 1966; Maddala 1977, chap. 14), removes from the error term the other causes of the vote that are unique to each state and constant over time, and treats them as explicit right-hand-side variables in the model. In essence, each state's vote is allowed to fluctuate around its own mean (its usual presidential vote in my case).

To insure that the coefficients are efficient, three potential problems with the residuals were examined. If the residuals are temporally auto-correlated ($E[U'_{it}U_{is}] \neq 0$ for $t \neq s$), the DVLS standard errors would be underestimated and forecasts would be inefficient (Johnston 1972, p. 246). Serially autocorrelated residuals appear in only two pairs of years—1952 and 1956, and 1968 and 1972. When incumbent presidents run a second time, the other causes of their vote in the first election are correlated with the other causes of the vote in the second. Generalized least squares (GLS) resolves this problem. Rho (the estimate of autocorrelation) was constrained to zero in 1948, 1952, 1960, 1964, and 1968 and was estimated to be .22 in 1956 and 1972.

The errors are not spatially autocorrelated ($E[U'_{it}U_{jt}] = 0$ for $i \neq j$). The misses in one state are independent of the misses in adjacent states. This was determined by examining the correlation matrix between the state residuals. Although the matrix is not perfectly diagonal (off-diagonal elements are not all equal to zero), most of the correlations are insignificant: only 22 percent of the 1,225 nonredundant coefficients

have more than 90 chances in 100 of being different from zero. Moreover, the substantive pattern of the coefficients does not suggest spatial
autocorrelation. Illinois's residuals, for example, are positively correlated with residuals from Kansas, Minnesota, Nebraska, and Tennessee,
negatively correlated with residuals for Ohio and Wisconsin, and uncorrelated with residuals for Indiana, Iowa, Kentucky, and Michigan.

The errors also are homoskedastic ($E[U'_{it}]^2$ is constant across cases).
By the Goldfeld-Quandt test (1965), the hypothesis that the residuals are
heteroskedastic can be rejected ($p > .18$).

One final problem—measurement error in the estimate of state preference for the candidates on the New Deal social welfare and racial
dimensions—was considered. Measurement error would attenuate the
coefficients for the issue variables and would bias the estimates for the
other parameters in the model as well (Warren, White, and Fuller 1974;
Hanushek and Jackson 1977, chap. 10; Greene 1978). To correct for this
measurement error I employ a method suggested by Warren, White, and
Fuller (1974). Their estimator can be written as:

$$\beta = (X'X - [(1 - \alpha/n)S])^{-1}X'y \tag{B.1}$$

where X is an $n \times k$ matrix of observations on the independent variables;

y is an $n \times 1$ vector of observations on the dependent variable;

k is the number of independent variables;

α is $k + 1$;

n is the number of observations;

S is a $k \times k$ diagonal matrix ($S_{ij} = 0$ when $i \neq j$). If variable$_i$ is
not measured with error, then S_{ij} (where $i = j$) is equal to zero.
If variable$_i$ is measured with error, then S_{ij} ($i = j$) is the variance of the variable's measurement error.

In other words, for each variable measured with error, a proportion $(1 - \alpha/n)$ of its measurement error variance is subtracted from its total variance. This procedure produces consistent estimates (Warren, White, and
Fuller 1974; Fuller and Hidiroglou 1978).

The effect of the preference for the Democratic candidate on an
issue dimension was estimated separately for each region and election.
When coefficients within a region were the same across years, a single
parameter was estimated for that set of elections. For each set of elections within the region the variance of the measurement error in the
preference for the candidates was calculated and equation B.1 was used
to estimate the parameters correcting for the measurement error. However, because the coefficients from equation B.1 were indistinguishable

from the DVLS estimates that ignored the correction (differences appeared in the third and often fourth decimal place), this correction was abandoned.

Although there is measurement error in the preference for candidates on the issues, there are two reasons why it does not bias the coefficients. First, because there are a large number of variables in the model (the unique state intercepts plus the other right-hand-side variables), α in equation B.1 is quite large, which means that the proportion of the measurement error variance subtracted from the $X'X$ matrix is relatively small. In addition, because separate coefficients were estimated for sets of elections in each region, only a small proportion of the cases for each variable were measured with error. For example, one coefficient was estimated for the New Deal social welfare issues in the North in 1948, 1960, 1964, and 1972, so only in these years, in northern states, was there measurement error. The remaining 55 percent of the cases (the southern states in each year and the northern states in 1952, 1956, and 1968) were set to zero and thus were not measured with error.

APPENDIX C
DESCRIPTION AND CODING OF VARIABLES

Variables in the Vote Equation

Presidential vote: In 1952, 1956, 1960, 1964, 1972, 1976, and 1980 the proportion of the two-party vote cast for the Democrats; in 1948 the proportion of the total votes cast for Truman, Wallace, and Thurmond; in 1968 the proportion of the total votes cast for Humphrey. The Democrats did not appear on the Alabama ballot in 1964, so this case was deleted from the analysis. *Source:* Walter Dean Burnham, Jerome M. Clubb, and William Flanigan, "State-Level Presidential Election Data for the United States, 1824–1972." Ann Arbor, Mich.: Inter-University Consortium for Political and Social Research. *Congressional Quarterly, Guide to 1976 Elections.* Washington, D.C.: Congressional Quarterly, Inc., 1977. *Congressional Quarterly Weekly Report,* 17 January 1981.

South: Alabama, Arkansas, Florida, Georgia, Louisiana, Mississippi, North Carolina, South Carolina, Tennessee, Texas, and Virginia = 1; 0 otherwise.

Change in real disposable income per capita (ΔY): Proportion change in real disposable income per capita times 1 if the Democrats are the incumbent party; times -1 if the Republicans are. *Source:* U.S. Department of Commerce, Bureau of Economic Analysis (personal communication), and *Survey of Current Business,* various issues.

Change in real disposable income per capita squared: If $\Delta Y > 0 = \Delta Y^2$; if $\Delta Y < 0 = -(\Delta Y^2)$.

Incumbent president: Incumbent president running = 1; 0 otherwise.

Incumbent president $\times$ the congressional vote$_{t-2}$ for opposition party: Incumbent president running = the proportion of the congressional vote cast in the previous midterm election for the opposition party; 0 otherwise.

Incumbent vice-president: Incumbent vice-president running for president = 1; 0 otherwise.

Home state presidential candidate: Democratic presidential candidate from the state = 1; Republican presidential candidate from the state = -1; 0 otherwise.

Home state vice-presidential candidate: Democratic vice-presidential candidate from the state = 1; Republican presidential candidate from the state = -1; 0 otherwise.

Home state third-party presidential candidate: Third-party presidential candidate from the state = 1 (except in 1948 = -1); 0 otherwise.

Southern presidential candidate: Southern states = 1 in 1948, 1976, and 1980; -1 in 1968; 0 otherwise. Preliminary analysis failed to turn up a southern regional effect for Texas and Florida, so they were deleted from the South on this variable.

Catholic population (1960 only): In 1960 the proportion of the state population who are Catholic; 0 otherwise. *Source: The Official Catholic Directory, 1961.* New York: P. J. Kenedy and Sons, 1961.

Mismanagement of war: In 1952 and 1968 the proportion of the population who oppose the incumbent's handling of the war; 0 otherwise. *Source:* John E. Mueller, *Wars, Presidents and Public Opinion.* New York: Wiley, 1973.

Congressional vote$_{t-2}$: Democratic proportion of the two-party vote cast for the House of Representatives in the previous midterm election. *Source:* Walter Dean Burnham, Jerome M. Clubb, and William Flanigan, "State-Level Congressional, Gubernatorial and Senatorial Election Data for the United States, 1924–1972," Ann Arbor, Mich.: Inter-University Consortium for Political and Social Research. *Congressional Quarterly, Guide to U.S. Elections.* Washington, D.C.: Congressional Quarterly, Inc., 1975. *Statistical Abstract of the United States,* 1976, 1980.

Uncontested congressional seats$_{t-2}$: Proportion of congressional seats$_{t-2}$ where a Democrat ran unopposed minus the proportion of seats where a Republican ran unopposed. *Source: Congressional Quarterly, Guide to U.S. Elections.* Washington, D.C.: Congressional Quarterly, Inc., 1975. *Congressional Quarterly Weekly Reports,* various issues.

Incumbent congressional seats$_{t-2}$: Proportion of congressional seats$_{t-2}$ where a Democrat is the incumbent minus the proportion of the seats where a Republican is the incumbent. *Source: Congressional Quar-*

terly, Guide to U.S. Elections. Washington, D.C.: Congressional Quarterly, Inc., 1975. *Congressional Directory,* 1945–79.

Incumbent congressional seats$_{t-2}$ × time: Proportion of congressional seats$_{t-2}$ where a Democrat is the incumbent minus the proportion where a Republican is the incumbent multiplied by time where 1946 = 1, 1950 = 2 . . . 1978 = 9.

Variables Added for 1980 Forecasts

Party best for prosperity: Percentage of people who think the Democrats will do a better job keeping the country prosperous divided by the percentage who think the Republicans will do a better job. *Source: Gallup Opinion Index,* September 1976; *Gallup Poll Release,* 28 September 1980.

Party best for peace: Percentage of people who think the Democrats will better provide peace divided by the percentage who think the Republicans will better provide peace. *Source: Gallup Opinion Index,* September 1976; *Gallup Poll Release,* 28 September 1980.

Party factionalism: Proportion of the state's Democratic National Convention delegation who voted for the Democratic nominee on the last ballot (before shifts) minus the proportion of the state's Republican National Convention delegation who voted for the Republican nominee on the last ballot (before shifts). *Source: Congressional Quarterly, Guide to U.S. Elections.* Washington, D.C.: Congressional Quarterly, Inc., 1975. *Congressional Quarterly, Guide to 1976 Elections.* Washington, D.C.: Congressional Quarterly, Inc., 1977. *Congressional Quarterly Weekly Reports,* various issues.

Variables Used to Measure New Deal Social Welfare and Racial Liberalism

State employees per capita (excluding teachers and other school personnel). *Source:* U.S. Department of Commerce, "State Distribution of Public Employment in 1952," *Statistical Abstract of the United States,* 1957, 1961, 1965, 1969; "Public Employment in 1972"; "Public Employment in 1976."

Employer contribution rate to unemployment insurance. *Source:* Department of Labor, Bureau of Employment Security, "Handbook on Unemployment Insurance Financial Data," 1948–64; *Statistical Abstract of the United States,* 1969–81.

Primary and secondary education expenditures per pupil in average daily attendance. *Source: Statistical Abstract of the United States,* 1951–81.

Average AFDC assistance per recipient family. *Source:* "Annual Report of the Federal Security Agency," 1948, 1952; *Statistical Abstract of the United States,* 1957–81.

Proportion of total state expenditures on public welfare (federal assistance excluded). *Source:* U.S. Department of Commerce, Bureau of the Census, Governments Division, "Compendium of State Government Finances," 1948–64; "State Government Finances in 1968," 1972, 1976, 1980.

Population. *Source: Statistical Abstract of the United States,* 1948–81.

Proportion of the work force unemployed. *Source: Manpower Report of the President,* 1957–79. The unemployment rate for each state had to be estimated for years prior to 1957. Over the 1957–75 period, the log of the unemployment in the state was regressed onto the log of the national unemployment rate, the log of the insured unemployment rate, and the log of the insured unemployment rate multiplied by the year. For each state, I used the coefficients from this equation to estimate the unemployment rate for years prior to 1957. Each equation explained between 96 and 98 percent of the variance in the actual unemployment rate; the average error was .17 percentage point.

Median family income for whites; median family income for blacks: These estimates are based on U.S. Census data from 1960 and 1970. In 1960 data are for whites and nonwhites; in 1970 data are for whites and blacks. For years prior to 1960, the 1960 data were used; between 1960 and 1970 the data were linearly interpolated; 1970 data were used for years subsequent to 1970.

REFERENCES

Achen, Christopher H. (1977) "Measuring Representation: Perils of the Correlation Coefficient." *American Journal of Political Science* 21 (November 1977), pp. 805–15.

———. (1979a) "Some Thoughts on Adding Demographic Variables to an Ecological Regression." Unpublished manuscript, University of California, Berkeley.

———. (1979b) "The Bias in Normal Vote Estimates." *Political Methodology* 6 (May 1979), pp. 343–56.

———. (1983) *The Statistical Analysis of Quasi-Experiments.* Berkeley: University of California Press.

Agar, Herbert. (1966) *The Price of Union.* Boston: Houghton Mifflin.

Aldrich, John H., and McKelvey, Richard D. (1977) "A Method of Scaling with Applications to the 1968 and 1972 Presidential Elections." *The American Political Science Review* 71 (March 1977), pp. 111–30.

Alexander, Herbert E. (1979) *Financing the 1976 Election.* Washington, D.C.: Congressional Quarterly, Inc.

Anton, Thomas J. (1967) "Roles and Symbols in the Determination of State Expenditures." *Midwest Journal of Politics* 11 (February 1967), pp. 27–43.

Apple, R. W., Jr. (1976a) "Now the Candidates Must Go in Search of the Electoral Votes," *New York Times,* August 22, 1976, sect. 4, p. 1.

———. (1976b) "Presidential Rivals in a Very Tight Race, Final Surveys Find," *New York Times,* October 31, 1976, p. 1.

———. (1979) "Mrs. Thatcher's Lead Slipping in 'Barometer District,' " *New York Times,* April 29, 1979, p. 3.

Arcelus, F., and Meltzer, A. H. (1975) "The Effect of Aggregate Economic Variables on Congressional Elections." *American Political Science Review* 61 (December 1975), pp. 1222–39.

Armstrong, J. Scott. (1967) "Derivation of Theory by Means of Factor

Analysis or Tom Swift and His Electric Factor Analysis Machine." *American Statistician* 21 (December 1967), pp. 17–21.

———. (1978) *Long-Range Forecasting from Crystal Ball to Computer.* New York: Wiley.

Arseneau, Robert B., and Wolfinger, Raymond E. (1973). "Voting Behavior in Congressional Elections." Paper read at the Annual Meeting of the American Political Science Association, New Orleans, September 4–8, 1973.

Ascher, William. (1978) *Forecasting an Appraisal for Policy-Makers and Planners.* Baltimore: Johns Hopkins University Press.

Attneave, Fred. (1950) "Dimensions of Similarity." *American Journal of Psychology* 63 (October 1950), pp. 516–56.

Balestra, Pietro, and Nerlove, Marc. (1966) "Pooling Cross Section and Time Series Data in the Estimation of a Dynamic Model: The Demand for Natural Gas." *Econometrica* 34 (July 1966), pp. 585–612.

Barber, James David. (1980) *The Pulse of Politics Electing Presidents in the Media Age.* New York: Norton.

Barone, Michael, Ujifusa, Grant, and Matthews, Douglas. (1977) *The Almanac of American Politics 1978.* New York: Dutton.

Bartley, N. V., and Graham, H. D. (1975) *Southern Politics and the Second Reconstruction.* Baltimore: Johns Hopkins University Press.

Bean, Louis H. (1948) *How to Predict Elections.* New York: Knopf.

———. (1969) *The Art of Forecasting.* New York: Random House.

———. (1972) *How to Predict the 1972 Elections.* New York: Quadrangle Books.

Behr, Roy L. (1982) "Convention Conflict and Presidential Elections." Unpublished manuscript, Yale University, May 1982.

Benhan, Thomas W. (1965) "Polling for a Presidential Candidate." *Public Opinion Quarterly* 29 (Summer 1965), pp. 185–99.

Berman, William C. (1970) *The Politics of Civil Rights in the Truman Administration.* Columbus: Ohio State University Press.

Black, Merle, Kovenock, David M., and Reynolds, William C. (1974) *Political Attitudes in the Nation and the States.* Chapel Hill: Institute for Research in Social Sciences.

Bloom, H. S., and Price, H. D. (1975) "Voter Response to Short-Run Economic Conditions: The Asymmetric Effect of Prosperity and Recession." *American Political Science Review* 69 (December 1975), pp. 1240–54.

Boyd, Richard W. (1972) "Popular Control of Public Policy: A Normal Vote Analysis of the 1968 Election." *American Political Science Review* 66 (June 1972), pp. 429–49.

Brams, Steven J. (1978) *The Presidential Election Game.* New Haven: Yale University Press.

———— and Davis, Morton D. (1974) "The 3/2's Rule in Presidential Campaigning." *American Political Science Review* 68 (March 1974), pp. 113–34.

Brody, Richard A. (1977) "Stability and Change in Party Identification: Presidential to Off-Years." Paper read at the 1977 Annual Meeting of the American Political Science Association.

———— and Page, Benjamin I. (1972) "Comment: The Assessment of Policy Voting." *American Political Science Review* 68 (June 1972), pp. 450–58.

Broh, C. Anthony. (1980) "Whether Bellwethers or Weather-Jars Indicate Election Outcomes." *Western Political Quarterly* 33 (December 1980), pp. 564–70.

Brunn, Stanley S. (1974) *Geography and Politics in America.* New York: Harper & Row.

Budge, Ian, and Farlie, Dennis. (1977) *Voting and Party Competition.* New York: Wiley.

Burke, Robert E. (1971) "Election of 1940." In *History of American Presidential Elections 1789–1968,* ed. Arthur M. Schlesinger, Jr., and Fred L. Israel, pp. 2917–46. New York: Chelsea.

Burnham, Walter Dean. (1970) *Critical Elections and the Mainsprings of American Politics.* New York: Norton.

Bryson, Maurice C. (1976) "The Literary Digest Poll: Making of a Statistical Myth." *American Statistician* 30 (November 1976), pp. 184–85.

Caddell, Patrick H. (1976) "Initial Working Paper on Political Strategy." Cambridge Survey Research, December 10, 1976.

————. (1980) "Playboy Interview," *Playboy* (February 1980), pp. 63–84.

————. (1981) "Memorandum I: General Election Strategy June 25, 1980." In *Portrait of an Election,* ed. Elizabeth Drew, pp. 388–407. New York: Simon & Schuster.

Cain, Glen G., and Watts, Harold W. (1970) "Problems in Making Inferences from the Coleman Report." *American Sociological Review* 35 (April 1970), pp. 228–42.

Campbell, Angus, Converse, Philip E., Miller, Warren E., and Stokes, Donald E. (1960) *The American Voter.* New York: Wiley.

Carmody, Deirdre. (1976) "Poll-Takers Voice Some Reservations in Analysis of Coverage by Newspapers of Campaign Polls," *New York Times,* November 13, 1976, p. 21.

Chester, Lewis, Hodgson, Godfrey, and Page, Bruce. (1969) *An American Melodrama.* New York: Penguin.

Chetty, V. K. (1968) "Pooling of Time Series and Cross Section Data." *Econometrica* 36 (April 1968), pp. 279–89.

Church, George J. (1980) "Battling down the Stretch," *Time,* November 3, 1980, pp. 18–21.

Clark, Timothy B. (1980) "As Long as Carter's Up He'll Get You a Grant," *New York Times,* April 21, 1980, p. A19.

Clymer, Adam. (1978) "For Once, Some Polls Were Off, Way Off," *The New York Times,* November 19, 1978, p. E4.

———. (1980) "Poll Shows Economy and Iran Hurt Carter among Late-Shifting Voters," *New York Times,* November 16, 1980, p. 1.

Colantoni, Claude S., Levesque, Terrence J., and Ordeshook, Peter C. (1975) "Campaign Resource Allocation under the Electoral College." *American Political Science Review* 69 (March 1975), pp. 141–61.

Congressional Quarterly. (1965) *Congress and the Nation, 1945–1964.* Washington, D.C.: Congressional Quarterly, Inc.

Converse, Philip E. (1966a) "The Concept of the Normal Vote." *Elections and the Political Order,* ed. Angus Campbell, Philip E. Converse, Warren E. Miller, and Donald E. Stokes, pp. 9–39. New York: Wiley.

———. (1966b). "Religion and Politics: The 1960 Election." In *Elections and the Political Order,* ed. Angus Campbell, Philip E. Converse, Warren E. Miller, and Donald E. Stokes, pp. 96–124. New York: Wiley.

———, Miller, Warren E., Rusk, Jerrold G., and Wolfe, Arthur G. (1969) "Continuity and Change in American Politics: Parties and Issues in the 1968 Election." *American Political Science Review* 63 (December 1969), pp. 1083–1105.

Cook, Rhodes. (1979) "History Is Working in Carter's Favor," *Congressional Quarterly Weekly Report,* May 5, 1979, pp. 825–27, 871.

Coombs, Clyde H., Daves, Robyn M., and Tversky, Amos. (1970) *Mathematical Psychology.* Englewood Cliffs, N.J.: Prentice-Hall.

Cover, Albert D. (1977) "One Good Term Deserves Another: The Advantages of Incumbency in Congressional Elections." *American Political Science Review* 21 (June 1977), pp. 523–42.

——— and Mayhew, David R. (1981) "Congressional Dynamics and the Decline of Competitive Congressional Elections," in *Congress Reconsidered,* 2nd ed., ed. Lawrence C. Dodd and Bruce I. Oppenheimer. Washington, D.C.: Congressional Quarterly, Inc.

Crossley, Archibald M., and Crossley, Helen M. (1979) "Polling in 1968." *Public Opinion Quarterly* 33 (Spring 1969), pp. 1–16.

Davis, Otto A., Hinich, Melvin J., and Ordeshook, Peter C. (1970) "An Expository Development of a Mathematical Model of the Electoral

Process." *American Political Science Review* 64 (June 1970), pp. 426–48.

Dawson, Richard E. (1973) *Public Opinion and Contemporary Disarray.* New York: Harper & Row.

——— and Robinson, James. (1963) "Interparty Competition, Economic Variables and Welfare Politics in the American States." *Journal of Politics* 25 (May 1963), pp. 265–89.

Dennis, Jack, and Webster, Carol. (1975) "Children's Images of the President and of Government in 1962 and 1974." *American Politics Quarterly* 3 (October 1975), pp. 386–405.

Dionne, E. J. (1980) "1980 Brings More Pollsters Than Ever," *New York Times,* February 16, 1980, p. 10.

Downs, Anthony. (1957) *An Economic Theory of Democracy.* New York: Harper & Row.

Drew, Elizabeth. (1977) *American Journal.* New York: Random House.

Drummond, Roscoe. (1976) "Is the Election Over?" *The Christian Science Monitor,* August 25, 1976, p. 27.

Dye, Thomas R. (1967) *Politics, Economics and the Outcomes in the American States.* Chicago: Rand McNally.

Easton, David, and Dennis, Jack. (1969) *Children in the Political System.* New York: McGraw-Hill.

Erickson, Robert S. (1972) "Malapportionment, Gerrymandering, and Party Fortunes in Congressional Elections." *American Political Science Review* 66 (December 1972), pp. 1234–45.

Fair, Ray C. (1978) "The Effect of Economic Events on Votes for President." *The Review of Economics and Statistics* 60 (May 1978), pp. 159–73.

Farley, James A. (1938) *Behind the Ballots.* New York: Harcourt, Brace.

Farlie, Dennis J., and Budge, Ian. (1981) "Explaining and Forecasting Elections: Issue Effects and Party Strategies in 23 Democracies." Unpublished manuscript.

Felson, Marcus, and Sudman, Seymour. (1975) "The Accuracy of Presidential-Preference Primary Polls." *Journal of Politics* 39 (Summer 1975), pp. 232–36.

Fenno, Richard F. (1978) *Home Style.* Boston: Little, Brown.

Fenton, John. (1960) source unknown.

Fiorina, Morris P. (1981a) *Retrospective Voting in American National Elections.* New Haven: Yale University Press.

———. (1981b) "Some Problems in Studying the Effects of Resource Allocation in Congressional Elections." *American Journal of Political Science* 25 (August 1981), pp. 543–67.

Friedman, Leon. (1971) "Election of 1944." In *History of American Presidential Elections 1789–1968*, ed. Arthur M. Schlesinger, Jr., and Fred L. Israel, pp. 3009–38. New York: Chelsea.

Fuller, Wayne A., and Hidiroglou, Michael A. (1978) "Regression Estimation after Correction for Attenuation." *Journal of the American Statistical Association* 73 (March 1978), pp. 99–104.

Gallup, George. (1972a) *The Sophisticated Poll Watcher's Guide*. Princeton: Princeton Opinion Press.

————. (1972b) *The Gallup Poll: Public Opinion 1935–1971*. New York: Random House.

Gans, Herbert J. (1979) *Deciding What's News*. New York: Pantheon.

Goldberg, Arthur S. (1966) "Discerning a Causal Pattern among Data on Voting Behavior." *American Political Science Review* 60 (December 1966), pp. 913–22.

Goldfeld, S. M., and Quandt, R. E. (1965) "Some Tests for Heteroskedasticity." *Journal of the American Statistical Association* 60 (1965), pp. 539–47.

Greene, Vernon L. (1978) "Aggregate Bias Effects of Random Error in Multivariate OLS Regression." *Political Methodology* 4 (November 1978), pp. 461–68.

Greenstein, Fred I. (1960) "The Benevolent Leader: Children's Images of Political Authority." *American Political Science Review* 54 (December 1960), pp. 934–43.

————. (1969) *Children and Politics*. New Haven: Yale University Press.

————. (1974) "What the President Means to Americans: Presidential 'Choice' Between Elections." In *Choosing the President*, ed. James David Barber, pp. 121–48. Englewood Cliffs, N.J.: Prentice-Hall.

Grossman, Michael B., and Kumar, Martha J. (1981) *Portraying The President*. Baltimore: Johns Hopkins University Press.

Hanushek, Eric A., and Jackson, John E. (1977) *Statistical Methods for Social Scientists*. New York: Academic Press.

Hempel, Carl G. (1965) *Aspects of Scientific Explanation and Other Essays in the Philosophy of Science*. New York: Free Press.

Hofstadter, Richard. (1948) *The American Political Tradition*. New York: Vintage Books.

Hudson, Richard L. (1980) "Carter, Worried about Farm Vote, Slates $1 Billion Boost in Grain Price Supports," *Wall Street Journal,* July 29, 1980, p. 3.

Jacobson, Gary C. (1979) "On Adding Contextual Variables to National Election Surveys." Paper read at the Annual Meeting of the Midwest Political Science Association, Chicago, April 19–21, 1979.

———— and Kernell, Samuel. (1981) *Strategy and Choice in Congressional Elections.* New Haven: Yale University Press.

Johannes, John R., and McAdams, John C. (1981) "The Congressional Incumbency Effect: Is It Casework, Policy Compatibility, or Something Else?" *American Journal of Political Science* 25 (August 1981), pp. 512–42.

Johnston, J. (1972) *Econometric Methods,* 2nd ed. New York: McGraw-Hill.

Jonas, Frank H. (1969) *Politics in the American West.* Salt Lake City: University of Utah Press.

Jöreskog, Karl G. (1969) "A General Approach to Confirmatory Maximum Likelihood Factor Analysis." *Psychometrika* 34 (June 1969), pp. 183–202.

————. (1970) "A General Method for Analysis of Covariance Structures." *Biometrika* 57 (June 1970), pp. 239–51.

Kagay, Michael R. (1981) "Trends in Partisan Advantage: Attitudinal Components of the Presidential Vote 1952–1980." Unpublished manuscript, Princeton University.

———— and Caldeira, G. A. (1975) "I Like the Looks of His Face: Elements of Electoral Choice, 1952–1972." Paper read at the 1975 Annual Meeting of the American Political Science Association, San Francisco, September 2–5, 1975.

Kayden, Xandra. (1978) *Campaign Organization.* Lexington, Mass.: D. C. Heath.

Keith, Bruce E., Magleby, David B., Nelson, Candice J., Orr, Elizabeth, Westlye, Mark, and Wolfinger, Raymond E. (1977) "The Myth of the Independent Voter." Paper read at the 1977 Annual Meeting of the American Political Science Association.

Kelley, Stanley, Jr. (1961) "The Presidential Campaign." In *The Presidential Election and Transition, 1960–1961,* ed. Paul T. David. Washington, D.C.: Brookings Institution.

————. (1966) "The Presidential Campaign." In *The National Election of 1964,* ed. Milton C. Cummings, Jr. Washington, D.C.: Brookings Institution.

Kessel, John H. (1968) *The Goldwater Coalition.* New York: Bobbs-Merrill.

————. (1980) *Presidential Campaign Politics.* Homewood, Ill.: Dorsey.

Key, V. O., Jr. (1949) *Southern Politics in State and Nation.* New York: Random House.

————. (1956) *American State Politics: An Introduction.* New York: Knopf.

———. (1959) "Secular Realignment and the Party System." *Journal of Politics* 21 (May 1959), pp. 198–210.

———. (1960) "The Politically Relevant in Surveys." *Public Opinion Quarterly* 24 (Spring 1960), pp. 54–61.

———. (1964) *Politics, Parties and Pressure Groups,* 5th ed. New York: Crowell.

———. (1966) *The Responsible Electorate.* New York: Vintage Books.

Kiewiet, D. Roderick. (1982) *Macroeconomics and Micropolitics.* Chicago: University of Chicago Press.

Kinder, Donald R., and Abelson, Robert P. (1981) "Appraising Presidential Candidates: Personality and Affect in the 1980 Campaign." Paper read at the Annual Meeting of the American Political Science Association, New York, September 3–6, 1981.

Kinder, Donald R., and Kiewiet, D. Roderick. (1981) "Sociotropic Politics: The American Case." *British Journal of Politics* 11 (February 1981), pp. 129–61.

King, Anthony. (1978) "The American Polity in the Late 1970s: Building Coalitions in the Sand." In *The New Political System,* ed. Anthony King, pp. 371–96. Washington, D.C.: American Enterprise Institute.

Kirkpatrick, Jeane J. (1976) *The New Presidential Elite.* New York: Russell Sage.

———. (1978) "Changing Patterns of Electoral Competition." In *The New American System,* ed. Anthony King, pp. 249–86. Washington, D.C.: American Enterprise Institute.

Kissinger, Henry. (1979) *The White House Years.* Boston: Little, Brown.

Kostroski, Warren. (1973) "Party and Incumbency in Postwar Senate Elections: Trends, Patterns and Models." *American Political Science Review* 67 (December 1973), pp. 1213–34.

Kramer, Gerald H. (1971) "Short-Term Fluctuations in U.S. Voting Behavior, 1896–1964." *American Political Science Review* 65 (March 1971), pp. 131–43.

———. (1981) "Ecological Fallacy Revisited: Aggregate- Versus Individual-Level Findings on Economics and Elections, and Sociotropic Voting." Unpublished manuscript, California Institute of Technology, December 1981.

Ladd, Everett Carll. (1970) *American Political Parties.* New York: Norton.

——— and Hadley, Charles D. (1975) *Transformations of the American Party System.* New York: Norton.

Lawley, D. N., and Maxwell, A. E. (1971) *Factor Analysis as a Statistical Method.* New York: American Elsevier.

Leiser, Ernest. (1980) On *MacNeil/Lehrer Report,* Public Broadcasting Service, September 10, 1980.

Lepper, Susan J. (1974) "Voting Behavior and Aggregate Policy Targets." *Public Choice* 18 (Summer 1974), pp. 68–81.

Leuchtenburg, William E. (1963) *Franklin D. Roosevelt and The New Deal.* New York: Harper & Row.

———. (1971) "Election of 1936." In *History of American Presidential Elections 1789–1968,* ed. Arthur M. Schlesinger, Jr., and Fred L. Israel, pp. 2809–49. New York: Chelsea.

Levin, Murray B. (1962) *The Compleat Politician.* New York: Bobbs-Merrill.

Lewis, Flora. (1980) "Europe's Presidential Worries," *New York Times,* June 10, 1980, p. A19.

Lichtman, A. J., and Keilis-Borok, V. I. (1981) "Pattern Recognition Applied to Presidential Elections in the United States, 1860–1980: Role of Integral Social, Economic and Political Traits." *Proceedings of the National Academy of Science* 78 (November 1981), pp. 7230–34.

Longley, Lawrence D., and Braun, Alan G. (1975) *Politics of Electoral College Reform.* New Haven: Yale University Press.

MacRae, Duncan, and Meldrum, James A. (1969) "Factor Analysis of Aggregate Voting Statistics." In *Quantitative Ecological Analysis in the Social Sciences,* ed. Mattei Dogan and Stein Rokkan, pp. 485–506. Cambridge, Mass.: M.I.T Press.

Maddala, G. S. (1971) "The Use of Variance Components Models in Pooling Cross Section and Time Series Data." *Econometrica* 39 (March 1971), pp. 341–58.

———. (1977) *Econometrics.* New York: McGraw-Hill.

Mann, Thomas E., and Wolfinger, Raymond E. (1980) "Candidates and Parties in Congressional Elections." *American Political Science Review* 74 (September 1980), pp. 617–32.

Markus, Gregory B., and Converse, Philip E. (1979) "A Dynamic Simultaneous Equation Model of Electoral Choice." *American Political Science Review* 73 (December 1979), pp. 1055–70.

Martin, John B. (1971) "Election of 1964." In *History of American Presidential Elections 1789–1968,* ed. Arthur M. Schlesinger, Jr., and Fred L. Israel, pp. 3565–94. New York: Chelsea.

May, Ernest, and Fraser, Janet. (1973) *Campaign '72: The Managers Speak.* Cambridge, Mass.: Harvard University Press.

Mayhew, David R. (1974a) "Congressional Elections: The Case of the Vanishing Marginals." *Polity* 6 (Spring 1974), pp. 295–317.

————. (1974b) *Congress, The Electoral Connection.* New Haven: Yale University Press.

McCloskey, Herbert, Hoffman, Paul J., and O'Hara, Rosemary. (1960) "Issue Conflict and Consensus among Party Leaders and Followers." *American Political Science Review* 54 (June 1960), pp. 406–27.

Meltzer, Allan H., and Vellrath, Marc. (1975) "The Effects of Economic Polities on Votes for the Presidency: Some Evidence from Recent Elections." *Journal of Law and Economics* 18 (December 1975), pp. 781–805.

Miller, Arthur H., Miller, Warren E., Raine, Alden S. and Brown, Thad A. (1976) "A Majority Party in Disarray: Policy Polarization in the 1972 Election." *American Political Science Review* 70 (September 1976), pp. 753–78.

Miller, Warren E. (1967) "Voting and Foreign Policy." In *Domestic Sources of Foreign Policy,* ed. James N. Roseneau, pp. 213–30. New York: Free Press.

————, Miller, Arthur H., and Schneider, Edward J. (1980) *American National Election Studies Data Sourcebook 1952–1978.* Cambridge: Harvard University Press.

Moore, Jonathan. (1981) *The Campaign for President 1980 in Retrospect.* Cambridge: Ballinger.

———— and Fraser, Janet. (1977) *Campaign for President: The Managers Look at '76.* Cambridge: Ballinger.

Mosteller, Frederick, Hyman, Herbert, McCarthy, P. J., Marks, E. S., and Truman, David R. (1949) *The Pre-Election Polls of 1948.* New York: Social Science Research Council.

Mueller, John E. (1973) *War, Presidents and Public Opinion.* New York: Wiley.

Napolitan, Joseph. (1972) *The Election Game and How to Win It.* New York: Doubleday.

Nelson, Candice J. (1978) "The Effect of Incumbency in Congressional Elections, 1964–1974." *Political Science Quarterly* 93 (December 1978), pp. 665–78.

Nerlove, Marc. (1971) "Further Evidence on the Estimation of Dynamic Economic Relations from a Time Series of Cross Sections." *Econometrica* 39 (March 1971), pp. 359–82.

Nie, Norman H., Verba, Sidney, and Petrocik, John R. (1976) *The Changing American Voter.* Cambridge: Harvard University Press.

Niskanen, William A. (1975) "Economic and Fiscal Effects on the Popular Vote for President." Working Paper no. 25, Graduate School of Public Policy, University of California, Berkeley.

Ostrogorski, Moisei. (1926) *Democracy and the Party System in the United States*. New York: Macmillan.

Page, Benjamin I. (1978) *Choices and Echoes in Presidential Elections*. Chicago: University of Chicago Press.

———— and Brody, Richard A. (1972) "Policy Voting and the Electoral Process: The Vietnam War Issue." *American Political Science Review* 66 (September 1972), pp. 979–95.

———— and Jones, Calvin G. (1979) "Reciprocal Effects of Policy Preferences, Party Loyalties and the Vote." *American Political Science Review* 73 (December 1979), pp. 1071–89.

Patterson, Thomas E., and McClure, Robert D. (1976) *The Unseeing Eye*. New York: Putnam.

Peirce, Neal R. (1972) *The Mountain States of America*. New York: Norton.

————. (1974) *The Deep South States of America*. New York: Norton.

————. (1968) *The People's President: The Electoral College in American History and the Direct-Vote Alternative*. New York: Simon and Schuster.

———— and Longley, Lawrence D. (1981) *The People's President: The Electoral College in American History and the Direct Vote Alternative*, rev. ed. New Haven: Yale University Press.

Perry, Paul. (1972) "Election Survey Procedures of the Gallup Poll." In *The Gallup Poll: Public Opinion 1935–1971*, ed. George Gallup, pp. xi–xliv. New York: Random House.

————. (1979) "Certain Problems in Election Survey Methodology." *Public Opinion Quarterly* 43 (Fall 1979), pp. 312–25.

Phillips, Kevin P. (1970) *The Emerging Republican Majority*. New York: Doubleday.

Pine, Art. (1980) "Pre-Election Rise Expected in Milk Price Supports," *Washington Post,* September 16, 1980, p. E1.

Plissner, Martin. (1979) "Battered Polls: Round Two," *Columbia Journalism Review* (May/June l979), pp. 85–88.

Polsby, Nelson W. (1981) "The Democratic Nomination." In *The American Elections of 1980,* ed. Austin Ranney, pp. 37–60. Washington, D.C.: American Enterprise Institute.

———— and Wildavsky, Aaron. (1976) *Presidential Elections,* 4th ed. New York: Scribner.

Pomper, Gerald. (1966) *Nominating the President.* New York: Norton.

————.(1967) "Classification of Presidential Elections." *Journal of Politics* 29 (August 1967), pp. 535–66.

————. (1970) *Elections in America.* New York: Dodd, Mead.

————. (1972) "From Confusion to Clarity: Issues and American Voters 1956–1968." *American Political Science Review* 66 (June 1972), pp. 415–28.

————. (1981) *The Election of 1980.* Chatham, N.J.: Chatham.

Pool, Ithiel de Sola, Abelson, Robert P., and Popkin, Samuel. (1965) *Candidates, Issues, and Strategies.* Cambridge: M.I.T. Press.

Popkin, Samuel, Gorman, John W., Phillips, Charles, and Smith, Jeffrey A. (1976) "Comment: What Have You Done for Me Lately? Toward an Investment Theory of Voting." *American Political Science Review* 70 (September 1976), pp. 779–805.

Rabinowitz, George, and Zechman, Martin. (1978) "Aggregate Models of Presidential Voting: 1896–1972." Paper presented at the 1978 Annual Meeting of the American Political Science Association, New York, August 31–September 3, 1978.

Rae, Douglas, and Taylor, Michael. (1973) "Decision Rules and Policy Outcomes." *British Journal of Political Science* 1 (April 1973), pp. 71–90.

Reich, Kenneth. (1980) "Pollsters Spat Over Why They Erred So Badly," *Los Angeles Times,* November 6, 1960, pp. 1, 24.

Riker, William H., and Ordeshook, Peter C. (1973) *An Introduction to Positive Political Theory.* Englewood Cliffs, N.J.: Prentice-Hall.

Roberts, Steven V. (1980) "County That Votes with Winners Seems a Tossup," *New York Times,* November 2, 1980, p. 36.

Robinson, Claude E. (1932) *Straw Votes: A Study of Political Prediction.* New York: Columbia University Press.

Roll, Charles W., Jr. (1966) "Straws in the Wind: The Record of the *Daily News* Poll." *Public Opinion Quarterly* 32 (Summer 1966), pp. 251–60.

———— and Cantril, Albert H. (1972) *Polls: Their Use and Misuse in Politics.* New York: Basic.

Rosenbaum, David E. (1980) "Carter Playing Trump Cards of Incumbency," *New York Times,* October 18, 1980, pp. 1, 32.

Rosenstone, Steven J. (1982) "Economic Adversity and Voter Turnout." *American Journal of Political Science* 26 (February 1982), pp. 25–46.

————, Behr, Roy L., and Lazarus, Edward H. (1984) *Third Parties in America.* Princeton: Princeton University Press.

Ross, Irwin. (1968) *The Loneliest Campaign, The Truman Victory of 1948.* New York: Signet Books.

Schneider, William. (1978) "Democrats and Republicans, Liberals and Conservatives." In *Emerging Coalitions in American Politics,* ed. Seymour Martin Lipset, pp. 183–265. San Francisco: Institute for Contemporary Studies.

———. (1981) "November 4 Vote for President: What Did It Mean?" In *The American Elections of 1980,* ed. Austin Ranney, pp. 212–62. Washington, D.C.: American Enterprise Institute.

Schram, Martin. (1977) *Running for President, 1976, The Carter Campaign.* New York: Stein & Day.

Sears, John. (1980) "What Polls Can't Tell You," *Washington Post,* November 18, 1980, p. A19.

Seidman, David. (1975) "Simulation of Public Opinion: A Caveat." *Public Opinion Quarterly* 39 (Fall 1975), pp. 331–42.

Shafer, William R. (1975) "Simple and Inexpensive Election Prediction: A Practical Alternative." *Western Political Quarterly* 28 (September 1975), pp. 506–15.

Shephard, R. N. (1964) "On Subjectively Optimum Selections among Multiattribute Alternatives." In *Human Judgments and Optimality,* ed. M. W. Shelley and G. L. Bryan, pp. 257–81. New York: Wiley.

Sindler, Allan P. (1976) *Unchosen Presidents.* Berkeley: University of California Press.

Slovic, Paul, Fischhoff, Baruch, and Lichtenstein, Sarah. (1977) "Behavioral Decision Theory." *Annual Review of Psychology* 28 (1977), pp. 1–39.

Smith, Hedrick. (1980a) "Reagan Aims at Northeast and Midwest in Fall Race," *New York Times,* May 12, 1980, p. D14.

———. (1980b) "With a Month to Go, Reagan Is Given Lead in the Electoral Vote," *New York Times,* October 5, 1980, p. 1.

———. (1980c) "Survey Indicates Reagan Is Holding Lead in Battle for Electoral Votes," *New York Times,* November 2, 1980, p. 1.

Sorensen, Theodore C. (1965) *Kennedy.* New York: Harper & Row.

Steinberg, Arnold. (1976) *Political Campaign Management.* Lexington, Mass.: D. C. Heath.

Stigler, George J. (1973) "Micropolitics and Macroeconomics: General Economic Conditions and National Elections." *American Economic Review* 63 (May 1973), pp. 160–80.

Stokes, Donald E. (1966) "Spatial Models of Party Competition." In *Elections and the Political Order,* ed. Angus Campbell, Philip E. Converse, Warren E. Miller, and Donald E. Stokes, pp. 161–79. New York: Wiley.

———. (1967) "Parties and the Nationalization of Electoral Forces." In *The American Party Systems,* ed. William Nisbet Chambers and Walter Dean Burnham, pp. 182–202. New York: Oxford University Press.

Stroud, Kardy. (1977) *How Jimmy Won.* New York: Morrow.

Sullivan, John L., and Minns, Daniel Richard. (1976) "Ideological Distance between Candidates: An Empirical Examination." *American Journal of Political Science* 20 (August 1976), pp. 439–60.

Sundquist, James L. (1973) *Dynamics of the Party System.* Washington, D.C.: Brookings Institution.

Teer, Frank, and Spence, James D. (1973) *Political Opinion Polls.* London: Hutchinson.

Theil, Henri. (1954) *Linear Aggregation of Economic Relations.* Amsterdam: North-Holland.

———.(1971) *Principles of Econometrics.* New York: Wiley.

Tolchin, Martin. (1980) "Congress Leaders Split with Carter on Revising Budget," *New York Times,* May 29, 1980, pp. A1, B7.

Tufte, Edward R. (1978) *Political Control of the Economy.* Princeton: Princeton University Press.

——— and Sun, Richard A. (1975) "Are There Bellwether Electoral Districts?" *Public Opinion Quarterly* 39 (Spring 1975), pp. 1–18.

Tversky, Amos, and Kahneman, Daniel. (1974) "Judgment under Uncertainty: Heuristics and Biases." *Science* 185 (September 1974), pp. 1124–31.

Uslaner, Eric M., and Weber, Ronald E. (1975) "The 'Politics' of Redistribution." *American Politics Quarterly* 3 (April 1975), pp. 130–70.

———. (1979) "U.S. State Legislators' Opinions and Perceptions of Consistency Attitudes." *Legislative Studies Quarterly* 4 (November 1979), pp. 563–85.

Warren, Richard D., White, Joan Keller, and Fuller, Wayne A. (1974) "An Errors-In-Variables Analysis of Managerial Role Performance." *Journal of the American Statistical Association* 69 (December 1974), pp. 886–93.

Weber, Ronald E. (1971) *Public Policy Preferences in the States.* Bloomington, Ind.: Institute of Public Administration.

———, Hopkins, Anne H., Mezey, Michael L., and Munger, Frank J. (1973) "Computer Simulation of State Electorates." *Public Opinion Quarterly* 36 (Winter 1973), pp. 459–65.

White, Theodore. (1961) *The Making of the President, 1960.* New York: Signet.

———. (1973) *The Making of the President, 1972.* New York: Atheneum.

Whiteley, Paul. (1976) "Self-Perceived Economic Change and Political Orientations: A Preliminary Exploration." *British Journal of Political Science* 9 (April 1979), pp. 219–36.

Wirthlin, Richard. (1981). "Memorandum I: Some Initial Strategic and Tactical Considerations for the 1980 Presidential Campaign," March 28, 1980. In *Portrait of an Election,* ed. Elizabeth Drew, pp. 351–62. New York: Simon & Schuster.

Witcover, Jules. (1977) *Marathon, The Pursuit of the Presidency, 1972–1976.* New York: Viking.

Wolfinger, Raymond E., and Arseneau, Robert A. (1979) "Partisan Change in the South, 1952–1976." In *Political Parties: Development and Decay,* ed. Louis Maisel and Joseph Cooper, pp. 179–210. Beverly Hills: Sage.

Yarnell, Allen. (1974) *Democrats and Progressives.* Berkeley: University of California Press.

INDEX

ABC News: coverage of presidential candidates, 62

ABC News/Harris Poll: *1980* forecast, 28n; nonresponse error, 31

Abelson, Robert A., 3, 37, 38, 39, 98, 148, 156

Achen, Christopher H., 72n, 77n, 87n

Afghanistan: Soviet invasion of, 59–60

Aid to Families with Dependent Children (AFDC): measure of New Deal social welfare liberalism, 161–62

Anderson, John: network news coverage of, 62; positions, 176

Armstrong, J. Scott, 3n, 6, 72n, 158

Arseneau, Robert B., 67, 157

Ascher, William, 3n, 6

Associated Press: *1976* forecast, 34; *1980* forecast, 36. *See also* NBC News/Associated Press Poll

Average Democratic Candidate (A. Dem.): defined, 134; simulated *1972* vote, 136

Average Republican Candidate (A. Rep.): defined, 134; simulated *1964* vote, 136

Balanced budget: relationship to New Deal social welfare liberalism, 168, 169

Balanced ticket, 64–65

Baptists: issue positions, 168n, 170n

Bean, Louis H., 22, 42

Behr, Roy L., 95, 113n, 136n, 148

Bellwether districts: as election forecasts, 21–24; used in Great Britain, 21n; *1976* forecasts, 23; *1980* forecasts, 23; evaluation of forecasts, 23–24

Benefits from voting, 53

Black income: as measure of racial liberalism, 169–70

Brody, Richard A., 57, 71n, 77n, 85n

Broh, C. Anthony, 22

Brown v. *Board of Education,* 48

Brunn, Stanley D., 22

Budge, Ian, 39–40, 43, 44, 124, 125, 126

Busing: candidate positions on, 178. *See also* Racial issues

Caddell, Patrick H., 2n, 15, 27, 28n, 59

Campaigns: future of, 152

Campaign strategists. *See* Political strategists

Campbell, Angus, 3, 46, 56, 64n, 73, 85

Candidates: electoral impact of, 73, 77–82, 134, 141, 147, 148; relationship between positions and level of issue voting, 81–82; simulation of alternative scenarios, 132–34, 136–37; forecasts of, 150; measurement of positions, 172–78; positions, 172–80. *See also specific candidate names, e.g.* Carter, Jimmy

Canvass: method explained, 18; forecasts, 18, 20–21; evaluation of method, 20–21